Dickens
and
Phiz

Hablot Knight Browne, head of Charles Dickens, pencil drawing
c. 1839 (BM). Anon., head of Hablot Knight Browne, wood engraving.

Dickens
AND
Phiz

BY

MICHAEL STEIG

INDIANA UNIVERSITY PRESS

Bloomington and London

Manufactured in the United States of America

Library of Congress Cataloging in Publication Data
Steig, Michael, 1936-
Dickens and Phiz.
Includes bibliographical references and index.
1. Dickens, Charles, 1812-1870—Friends and
associates. 2. Dickens, Charles, 1812-1870—Illustra-
tions. 3. Browne, Hablot Knight, 1815-1882. I. Ti-
tle.
PR4583.S8   823'.8   77-23645
ISBN 0-253-31705-3   1 2 3 4 5 82 81 80 79 78

To the Memory of My Father,
Henry Steig (1906–1973)
And to His Brothers,
Arthur Steig
Irwin Steig
William Steig

CONTENTS

ACKNOWLEDGMENTS

Of all those who have given me encouragement and aid at various stages in the progress of my work, I must single out three for special thanks: John R. Harvey and Robert L. Patten, who generously supplied advice and information, and Michael Slater, who has been helpful and encouraging in many ways before, during, and after my research year in England. Miss Marjorie Pillers, Curator of Dickens House Museum, was generous of time and attention. Others to whom I am grateful for assistance and encouragement include Anthony Burton, Leonard F. Manheim, J. Hillis Miller, Robert B. Partlow Jr., and John R. Reed.

Special thanks are due to the American Council of Learned Societies for the fellowship which made my year in England possible. The President's Research Grant Fund of Simon Fraser University helped with photographic expenses, and the Administration of Simon Fraser University was especially generous in guaranteeing financial aid toward publication.

To Howell J. Heaney, Rare Book Librarian at the Free Library of Philadelphia; John Podeschi, formerly of Yale University Library; and P. A. H. Smith of the Department of Printed Books of the British Library, I am grateful for the opportunity to examine materials in the Elkins, Gimbel, and Dexter collections, and I wish to thank the staff of the Huntington Library and Art Gallery for helpful attention by mail. I am grateful to the Trustees of the British Museum and Library, Free Library of Philadelphia, Yale University Library, Huntington Library and Art Gallery, and the Dickens House for permission to reproduce material in their collections.

Some portions of this book appeared, in very different form, in *Criticism, Dickens Studies Annual, Dickens Studies Newsletter, English Language Notes, Hartford Studies in Literature,* and the *Huntington Library Quarterly.* I thank the editors and publishers of these journals for permission to make use of this material.

Finally, I wish to thank my wife, Katharine, and my sons, Joseph and Eric, for their patience and encouragement over a period of years of incessant typing, scattered books and papers, and intermittent anxieties. Without their help, this book might never have been completed.

The book has been published with the help of a grant from the Humanities Research Council of Canada, using funds provided by the Canada Council.

PREFACE

It is not what Dickens might have called a "bran-new" idea that certain nineteenth-century books have been reprinted incompletely if they do not include their original illustrations in their original positions. The drift of scholarly work in the past fifteen years has been toward the view that the illustrated novel is a kind of nineteenth-century subgenre of the novel proper. Yet it is also a subgenre of which the only two major practitioners who are also major literary artists are Dickens and Thackeray. Thackeray's first illustrated novel in monthly shilling parts, *Vanity Fair*, probably took this form because Thackeray and his publishers were consciously emulating and competing with Dickens, whose success in the format dated back to the *Pickwick Papers*, ten years earlier.

There is, however, a fundamental difference in that *Vanity Fair* was illustrated by Thackeray himself, who, however poor a draftsman and etcher, graphically articulated thematic motifs in initial letters, headpieces, tailpieces, and full page etchings. Dickens, by contrast, relied upon the graphic work of freelance artists, primarily that of Hablot Knight Browne ("Phiz"). Dickens' illustrated novels have been assumed by many critics to fall into essentially the same mode as *Vanity Fair* because it has been, at least until recently, an article of faith that Dickens ruled his illustrators with a heavy hand, using them merely as vehicles to translate his own visual conceptions into graphic images. Part of the purpose of this book is to demonstrate how much more complex the situation really was, and in what respects Hablot Browne can be considered a collaborator rather than a mere employee or drudge.

Not only is Browne important as a collaborator, but as the very first interpreter of each of the novels he illustrated; an artist who was, on the one hand, operating within certain traditions upon which Dickens also drew, and thus complementing the novelist's highly visual style; and who, on the other hand, was a contemporary required by his vocation and inspired by his own intelligence to understand and interpret Dickens' art. If Dickens' close friend and associate John Forster appreciated Dickens' genius with greater intellectual depth and championed him with disinterested fervor, we must not let the fact that Browne was by contrast a mercenary stand in the way of our recognizing the special talents he brought to his task as an interpreter.

The present book is an attempt to go further than any previously published scholarship in comprehensiveness, depth of analysis, and attention to the technical and historical details of Dickens' and Browne's association. I have tried to give full acknowledgment to the work of Joan Stevens, Robert L. Patten, John R. Harvey, and Q. D. Leavis throughout, recognizing when we share similar views of Dickens and Browne; yet this study is not derivative from theirs. A commentary which included every illustration Browne did for Dickens would be not only exhaustive but, for the reader, exhausting, and thus although it has caused me some pain to resist commenting on certain illustrations, I have tried to keep my selection representative, including all those etchings which demand explication owing to emblematic complexity, thematic emphasis, or visual brilliance. The wood engravings for *The Old Curiosity Shop* and *Barnaby Rudge* function in an essentially different way, and require less individual comment. None of my disputes with earlier scholarship should be taken as rancorous; I am well aware of the danger of errors in work that is virtually pioneering, and I have published my own share of such errors in the past.

Finally, I should like to say a word about the illustrations in the present volume. There are numerous etchings by Phiz for Dickens which I discuss in some detail, but which are not reproduced in this book. Because of the sheer number of illustrations Phiz did, some priorities had to be established. In making my selection, I have tried to include many of those etchings on which my commentary is extensive; but since the original Dickens illustrations are readily accessible in libraries or in the New Oxford Illustrated Dickens, it seemed most valuable to include unpublished or inaccessible material, such as drawings and sources for Browne's illustrations.

Dickens
and
Phiz

CHAPTER ONE

Dickens and Browne: Illustration, Collaboration, and Iconography

I t would be misleading to suggest that the illustrated novel dominated Victorian fiction, since throughout the era many writers, major and minor, published their books without pictures, and without any apparent sense that something was lacking. The Brontës come immediately to mind among the major Victorian novelists, and with a few exceptions both George Eliot and George Meredith published their novels unillustrated, while Anthony Trollope's novels contained illustrations during only a limited segment of his long career. Nonetheless, the illustration of novels in their first appearance *was* widespread; for certain authors it was a significant factor in the process of creation and in the total form of their books. Generalizations about so large a field are inevitably treacherous, but if we are to understand the role of illustrations in Dickens' novels, and in particular those of his main illustrator, Hablot Knight Browne, we must hazard some theories about the historical, aesthetic, and interpretative implications of this mixture of artistic media.

To account historically for the pervasiveness of illustrations in Victorian fiction we must look back to the *Posthumous Papers of the Pickwick Club,* whose publication began in 1836. Dickens' financial success with *Pickwick*'s mode of publication—monthly, one-shilling parts, with two full-page illustrations in each—encouraged other authors and publishers to try something similar. Among the many novelists operating at least sporadically in

1

this mode we may mention Charles Lever, W. Harrison Ainsworth, William Makepeace Thackeray, and Anthony Trollope. It can be argued that the non-intellectual, largely middle-class audiences to whom the publishers hoped to sell the novels of Dickens, Lever, Ainsworth, Thackeray, and Trollope found the illustrations especially attractive as a supplementary form of visualization, whereas more intellectual novelists such as Eliot and Meredith did not require illustrations for their particular audiences.

Even if these generalizations are valid, further distinctions must be made among the five illustrated novelists mentioned. Lever and Ainsworth were both something more than hacks and something less than artists. Dependent to some degree upon their illustrators to attract sales, they made no particularly complex or original use of illustrations. Trollope (though he was gratified to have so famous an artist as Millais to illustrate several novels) was not very interested in the illustrations, and the fact that he would always complete his novel before the publication of Part 1—in contrast to the other four novelists, who published the installments while the novels were in progress—would tend to diminish if not eliminate meaningful collaboration between author and illustrator. On the other hand, even though their work in the dual medium originated in a series of historical accidents, Thackeray and Dickens found it a congenial mode and made it into a distinct subgenre of the novel.

Despite their very great differences as men and as novelists, Dickens and Thackeray shared common influences, such as the emblem book and the satirical engraving, which made available to them a range of visual and verbal techniques including metaphor, allusion, and analogy. Thackeray, as his own illustrator, used these techniques most frequently in the wood-engraved initial letters and tailpieces to chapters, illustrations additional to the two etchings per monthly part. Thus in *Vanity Fair* the fool in cap and bells recurs as a visual motif, while Becky Sharp appears as a mermaid, a female Napoleon, and, in a full-page etching, as Clytemnestra. But *Vanity Fair* is also conceived verbally in similar terms from its title onward: the puppet motif is carried through the novel, and the clock bearing the sacrifice of Iphigenia as an emblem (which represents the sacrifice of an Osborne daughter's fulfillment in life to her father's selfish needs) occurs first in the text, and only later in an illustration. In Dickens' novels, such a detail appears in one of Browne's illustrations (to *Dombey and Son*—published concurrently with *Vanity Fair*).

By the time *Vanity Fair* began publication, Dickens and Browne had already established their relationship in five novels, three of which were in what became the commonest format for their collaboration: monthly parts with two etched illustrations in each, usually a total of nineteen parts in all, the final one of double length with four etchings. (Because of the haphazard nature of its origins, *Pickwick* was a few parts longer, and *A Tale of Two Cities*, the last Dickens novel to be illustrated by Browne, appeared in only eight installments.) Dickens' comfort with the format is suggested by the fact that he used it twice more after dropping Browne as illustrator, in *Our Mutual Friend* and the unfinished *Edwin Drood*. From the very beginning, as I hope to demonstrate, Browne seems to have taken it upon himself to introduce his own emblematic details, thereby commenting upon or pointing up some aspect of the text, and by the time of *Martin Chuzzlewit*, the third collaboration with Dickens in monthly installments, a complex relationship had developed between text and illustration.

Victorian illustrated novels, and in particular those of Dickens and Thackeray, present certain aesthetic and interpretative problems. In many of Thackeray's novels we have a self-illustrated writer, whose artistic intention may be thought of as unified even though he works in two media. But with Dickens and his illustrators we cannot, despite Dickens' practice of giving detailed instructions, assume such a single intention. Because the illustrations include elements which are specified by the author, but are not the author's own creations, and further because the artist introduces details of his own, we find that the illustrator is at once collaborator, attempting to express the author's intention visually; interpreter, offering his own comments on the meaning of the work; and perhaps even an *artist*, sometimes creating independently valuable works of art. The paramount problem for readers of Dickens, a problem at once both aesthetic and interpretative, is how to "read" the text and illustrations in conjunction with one another. In the renowned etching for *Vanity Fair*, in which Becky Sharp appears in both the caption and a small allusive detail as Clytemnestra (i.e., a murderess), Thackeray's intention can hardly be doubted. The critic may feel that to make Becky a murderess is incompatible with her character as presented in the novel, but Thackeray surely intended this illustration as a hint (a rather heavy-handed one) about something never directly confirmed in the text.

In Browne's illustrations for Dickens we cannot always be certain of such a unity of intention. There are many examples, indeed, of discrepancies, as when the author—both in his text and his instructions to Browne—specifies ten young gentlemen at Doctor Blimber's academy (*Dombey and Son*) and the illustrator depicts seventeen.[1] Such instances do not, however, pose the main theoretical problem. In some cases they are the result of inadequate direction from the author, in others, of the illustrator's carelessness. At any rate, such discrepancies may be seen as artistic slips which do not affect the meaning of the novel— although they may disrupt the full enjoyment of the reader determined to read the work as an integration of words and pictures.

But emblematic detail, seemingly introduced by the artist without the author's direction or overt approval, raises more serious problems. There seems to be no alternative but to recognize Hablot Browne as both collaborator and interpreter; however, the problem is complicated by the fact that we often lack adequate evidence to distinguish with certainty between Dickens' intention and Browne's, between collaboration and interpretation. For the reader of Dickens the problem is made less formidable, even if it is not resolved, by the consideration that Dickens and Browne, though widely different in temperament and talent, like Dickens and Thackeray shared certain artistic traditions. Dickens' use of imagery is often analogous to Browne's use of emblematic details, whereby perceptions of the sometimes daunting and sometimes comical circumstances of human existence may be expressed in condensed allusions—not reduced to them, but signposted, as it were, in a form reminiscent of the poem-plus-picture of the emblem book.

The degree of insight and originality of these images varies in both author and illustrator, and in Browne's illustrations they can at times seem almost crude. Thus the book titles, *Paradise Lost* and *Tartuffe*, in the illustration depicting Mr. Pecksniff's defeat in *Martin Chuzzlewit*, may seem merely facile comments on the fawning hypocrite's fall from grace with the wealthy. But upon further reflection the analogy with Satan implies a much broader significance: Blake's observation that Milton was on the devil's side without knowing it still has force for many readers of *Paradise Lost*, and equally, many readers see Mr. Pecksniff's linguistic brilliance and personal resiliency as qualities which make him perhaps the most interesting character in the novel (and which are not dissimilar to the author's own qualities).

Such a flight into implicit meanings raises the further question of the extent of Browne's awareness of such complexities, and also of the Victorian reader's ability to notice and interpret such details and integrate them into his reading of the text. I have uncovered no evidence of how subtly contemporary readers "read" Browne's illustrations, nor do we have access to Browne's or Dickens' thoughts on the matter. What we do know is that Dickens was capable of an astonishing range of insight and expression, and that Browne was a literate man, widely read and fully conscious of his predecessors in English graphic art, from Hogarth through John Doyle ("HB") and the Cruikshanks. Even if not a single Victorian reader recognized the complexities of the illustrations they are there, like the complexities of the texts; they are at once an expression of Dickens' intentions and Browne's interpretations, at once a visual accompaniment to the text and a commentary upon it. They were important to Dickens, and they can be important to any reader who makes the effort to recapture a mode of "reading" graphic art which may have already been dying out in the mid-nineteenth century.

Hablot Knight Browne (with no circumflex over the *o*, a journalistic addition unaccountably followed by some modern scholars) was born on 11 June 1815, the ninth son in a middle-class family which would ultimately number ten sons and five daughters. His father having died in 1824, the main influence upon the early course of Browne's life seems to have been his brother-in-law, Mr. Elnahan Bicknell, a wealthy, self-made businessman and self-taught collector of modern English art (Turner in particular), who was in later years a neighbor and friend of

Ruskin. It was Bicknell who encouraged Browne's artistic talent and arranged for his apprenticeship to the prominent steel engravers, Finden's, as a way of acquiring a trade which would provide a means of self-support for this ninth son in a family of fifteen children.[2] The biographical sources agree that Hablot was not very happy with the tedious labor of engraving, and although he always described his profession as that of "engraver,"[3] he did not use this technique during his long career and the few steel engravings he designed were executed by others. He did certainly become proficient in etching, for in 1833 he was awarded a medal from the Society of Arts for "John Gilpin's Ride," a rather crude performance which nevertheless shows considerable skill in the drawing of horses and the use of light and shadow to indicate modeling of forms.[4] There are stories of Hablot's truancy (visits to the British Museum) and his penchant for fanciful drawing rather than tedious engraving. Whatever the immediate cause, his indentures were canceled in 1834, two years early by mutual consent, and he set up shop sometime during the next two years with Robert Young, a fellow apprentice at Finden's, as etcher, engraver, and illustrator.[5]

Finden's was engaged in the production of many of the popular engravings of the time, including picturesque views and plates for the annuals, which were intended largely as gift books for young ladies. The subjects of such plates were usually portraits of titled ladies and scenes from Byron or Moore, with the occasional comic scene thrown in. Browne must have been influenced to a degree by his tenure at Finden's, but the only known work tying him even indirectly to his unloved masters is Winkles's *Cathedrals* (1835–42),[6] the first two volumes of which contained designs by Browne. Winkles had been an apprentice at Finden's, and a number of the line-engraved plates of English and Welsh cathedrals are signed "HKB"; we can perhaps see Browne's characteristic touch in the incidental figures that populate some of the views, but there is really no hint at all of the illustrator about to emerge into public favor, briefly as "N.E.M.O.," and then permanently as "Phiz."

The early life of Charles Dickens, three years Browne's senior, is too familiar to recount here; but a few points about his early writings should be recalled. Dickens' first book-length work, *Sketches by Boz*, is perhaps more dependent upon its illustrations for appeal than anything else he subsequently wrote; in fact, its illustrator, George Cruikshank, was the famous member of the duo, the pseudonymous "Boz" a complete unknown. The original intention of Chapman and Hall for *The Posthumous Papers of the Pickwick Club* was that the author "write up to" a series of comic illustrations on sporting subjects, after the fashion of the Combe–Rowlandson collaboration in the Doctor Syntax books (1817–22), or the Egan–Cruikshank brothers' collaboration on *Life in London* (1821), with four etchings per monthly part forming the basis for the text. Dickens was evidently not even the first choice as an author, but once hired he took over the reins with great assurance and immediately reversed the intended relationship between himself and his artist, Robert Seymour. It is useless to conjecture whether this relegation to secondary status somehow led to Seymour's suicide: the important point is that Dickens, almost accidentally, as it were, created a new art form in his simultaneous composition of the texts for the novel's parts and supervision of its illustrators. But new as the form was, both he and his most frequent illustrator, Hablot Browne, drew upon a rich set of iconographical traditions.

Iconography is a term used more than a bit loosely by modern literary scholars, possibly because the word *icon* (understood as equivalent to *image*) can when translated from the pictorial to the verbal mode encompass such a wide range of literary elements. But however wide this range may be, the word must refer specifically to a system or set of systems for communicating meaning: in literature, a consistent use of elements to convey some set of emotions or ideas. These elements (usually metaphoric or symbolic) may be objects, characters, colors, or landscapes.

Thus, one can without difficulty speak of the iconography of the text of *Bleak House*, though one may have in mind the use of images of fog and mud, the parallels between Chancery, Parliament, and Tom-All-Alone's, or the structure of the plot centering on Esther Summerson's lost and recovered identity. These are distinct systems of meaning in that novel, though they overlap and intersect at various points: in the connection between Esther's identity, the family of the Dedlocks, the place of the

Dedlocks in the social system (including the iconographical significance of their name), and so on. The relation among systems of iconography in Dickens can be taken as parallel to systems of meaning in graphic art, and particularly in reference to the moral art of William Hogarth—for as soon as one turns to a title such as *Oliver Twist; or, the parish boy's progress*, the conscious connection to Hogarth (though possibly to Bunyan as well) becomes apparent.

Indeed, each of Dickens' novels presents some kind of progress—whether Pickwick's or Copperfield's or Pip's—and while to say this may be little more than to say that they are each some variety of *Bildungsroman*, most of them are specifically linked to Hogarth via their illustrations, which from the beginning function in a number of ways. First, they offer fixed visual images of the characters, something some modern readers may feel constricting to their reading experience,[7] but which may have served a necessary function in the original serial versions by maintaining continuity over the many months of publication. Further, through inscription and emblem, the illustrations frequently emphasize moral meanings which are understated or even unstated in the text; at times they provide crucial information absent from the text; and, finally, they offer interpretations of certain aspects of the novel, revealing implications of which the novelist himself may not be fully conscious. In the latter respect, the illustrators are Dickens' first critics.

Only Hablot Knight Browne, more familiarly known as Phiz, illustrated the whole of more than one of Dickens' novels in its original form; thus only he can be seen developing as an artist during Dickens' career in ways parallel to the novelist's development. My subsequent chapters dealing with individual novels will trace such parallels; but first three general topics require examination: Browne's iconographical methods and their relation to tradition; his methods of work; and the nature of his collaboration with Dickens. Perhaps the most controversial issue is the degree of his independence as an interpreter of the novelist's works.

Browne's and Dickens' most obvious mutual influence is the satiric work of William Hogarth, in particular his "progresses"—

series of plates telling a story. According to Ronald Paulson, Hogarth's visual–narrative art develops in its modes of expression from a predominant use of "learned and popular" iconography and of "meaning based primarily on explicit readable structures to meaning based on spatial and formal structures."[8] Plate I of *A Harlot's Progress* (1732) reads like a printed text from left to right—the elements representing the young girl's past (her country clergyman father), present (her own countrified and innocent appearance in the plate's center), and future (the bawd, and to her right the girl's first customer as a prostitute.)[9] It also implies to the astute "reader" a parody of the Choice of Hercules between vice and virtue. On a less classical level, the goose in the basket alludes to the girl as a "silly goose."[10] Typically, these early engravings are full of such objects as clocks, suggesting the passage of time, and paintings, such as those in *A Harlot's Progress*, II, which "imply the stern Old Testament justice that Moll can expect from the Jew."[11]

The later series, *Industry and Idleness* (1742), Paulson shows, is virtually devoid of emblem or allusion, and seems to put forth a very simple industry–idleness, good–evil opposition. But Hogarth now uses the more subtle means of arranging figures and paralleling the positions of the Industrious and Idle apprentices in the last two plates, undercutting the apparent opposition and implying an ambiguous analogy, a moral uncertainty about the "good" apprentice.[12] Without claiming that I can prove a direct influence of this development in Hogarth upon Browne, I think it is interesting that it is in some ways paralleled by Browne's career as Dickens' illustrator: having begun with an emphasis upon emblematic details and progressing through a more ingenious and involved use of such techniques in his middle career, Browne also developed the technique of visual parallelism of structures and gradually reduced the use of emblems in Dickens' later novels, finally relying upon the inventive use of striking tonalities (through the innovative use of what was called the "dark plate," a specially prepared etching resembling the mezzotint).

As Paulson tells us, eighteenth-century painting tended to move from an appeal from *difficultas*, the pleasure of reading complex visual structures, to a preference for *claritas*, "a totally and immediately graspable impression."[13] Similarly, the development of nineteenth-century British book illustration would move in such a direction: from complex emblematic structures to simple pictorial design. By the 1860s Browne's art as an illustrator would be noticeably out of step with this development.

In the early Victorian period, however, the illustrative work of Cruikshank, Thackeray, and Browne still drew extensively on the techniques of Hogarth and his followers in "lower" graphic art—the multitude of graphic satirists from Gillray to Cruikshank himself. The mode of the "progress" was already familiar to early Victorian readers not only through Hogarth (whose works were frequently reprinted, often in very portable book form, as in Trusler's *Hogarth Moralized*) but also through many subsequent series of comic or satiric aquatints and etchings, published with or without letterpress, right up through the 1830s.[14] Furthermore, the use of emblems with traditional, more or less fixed meanings would be familiar from numerous sources in addition to that mass of comic graphic art: from reprinted and original emblem poetry such as that of Quarles; translated versions of such continental emblematists as Alciati and Ripa; and perhaps most widely, moral and instructive emblem books for children, of which Bunyan's *Divine Emblems* (1686—first printed with illustrations in 1724 and frequently reprinted), Wynne's *Choice Emblems, Natural, Historical, Fabulous, Moral and Divine; For the Improvement and Pastime of Youth* (1772), and W. Pinnock's *Iconology: Or Emblematic Figures Explained* (1830) may serve as representative titles.

But by the early 1840s the coming change in illustration was already heralded by the work of at least one popular illustrator, John Leech, whose work superficially resembles Browne's and Cruikshank's but who abandoned the old emblematic modes for a simpler and clearer style (Illus. 1).* Leech was never really comfortable in Browne's and Cruikshank's favorite technique, etching. He became known primarily as the designer of straightforward, humorous, wood-engraved cartoons—in our modern sense—for *Punch*. In turn, Leech's art influenced *Punch* artists and illustrators including Tenniel, Du Maurier, and

---

*Citations in the form "Illus. 1" refer to illustrations following Chapter Six of this volume.

Keene, while simultaneously the dominant mode of book illustration by these artists and such others as Marcus Stone, Fred Walker, and John Everett Millais became by the 1860s almost totally divorced from Browne's mode. Thus, wood engraving replaced etching, a quasi-caricatural way of drawing characters became a blander, rather idealized style, and emblem and allusion disappeared almost totally. It is not insignificant that some of these younger artists had pretensions to high art, nor that Millais in particular may have been slumming (though for very good pay) when he did illustrations for Trollope and others.

Cruikshank was already having difficulty finding employment by the late 1840s, but Browne worked steadily into the 1850s, to some extent varying his style (as distinct from his iconographic techniques) to suit the new tastes. It is important to stress here that serious interest in Browne's emblematic and somewhat caricatural art has been revived only in the 1960s, and that for many decades it was fashionable to champion the more austere "Sixties" illustration as the great maturation of the English illustrated book—Cruikshank and Browne being seen as rather vulgar, inartistic craftsmen. Browne's failure to make the transition to the new kind of illustration is epitomized in his etchings for the first ten parts of Trollope's *Can You Forgive Her?* in 1864 (Illus. 2). These wholly nonemblematic depictions of Trollope's rather mundane characters simply lack the life of Browne's best work; and although they displeased Trollope because of their inaccuracy, one may speculate that in addition they still looked too much like the famous illustrations for Dickens. That the second half of the novel was given instead to a woman who drew for the woodblock (Illus. 3) was a real slap in the face to Browne, and when Dickens (who had not employed Browne since 1859) hired Marcus Stone to illustrate *Our Mutual Friend* with wood engravings at around the same time, the rejection was complete.[15] Although we may feel that Browne at his best would have been a more suitable illustrator than Stone for Dickens' last completed novel, it is clear that Browne, like Uncle Sol Gills, was behind the times. Yet the inference one draws from such critics as Gleeson White and Forrest Reid[16] that Victorian popular book illustration can be taken seriously only from the 1860s onwards, must be thoroughly resisted—unless, that is, one is willing to reject Thackeray's writing along with his illustration, and Dickens along with Browne. For a nonallusive, nonsymbolic writer like Trollope the rather static, totally nonemblematic, and ostensibly realistic art of a Millais may be fully adequate, though it is hardly essential. But Dickens' literary art is of a different kind. Allusive, symbolic, and yet in some ways more overtly didactic than the work of Trollope, Dickens' novels are also strongly visual, and his influences are as much those of the graphic as of the verbal artist. In fact, in many ways it can be argued that Dickens inherited Hogarth's mantle as the great English comic and satiric artist, developing his own artistic vision of the realities of his society without becoming a simple portrayer of "hard times," and penetrating below the human surfaces without adopting psychological realism as his primary method. And it is Dickens who, after being thrown into authorship of an illustrated novel in monthly parts by Chapman and Hall's failure to obtain William Clarke,[17] developed his own kind of novel, the illustrations to which were to be his continuing concern over a period of twenty-three years.

The first collaboration between Dickens and Browne was on something considerably less than a novel, but it clearly shows their joint debt to the Hogarthian tradition.[18] The first two of the three small wood engravings for the anti-Sabbatarian pamphlet *Sunday Under Three Heads* demonstrate the complementary nature of Browne's and Dickens' art, for they make explicit a quality which is only latent in the text. Dickens conceived his tendentious pamphlet in the mode of Hogarth's *Beer Street* and *Gin Lane* (1751), posing alternative consequences which will result from two opposed ways of ordering British society. The immediate occasion of Hogarth's pair of engravings was a measure to limit the sale of gin,[19] while Dickens was concerned with the repressive Sabbath Bills, but both men present contrasts of healthy and depraved London life. Dickens mentions beer often enough in the first essay to make reasonable the connection with Hogarth's plates; for the drinking of beer "in content and comfort" is clearly contrasted with "outward signs of profligacy or debauchery."[20] Although the second essay does not mention the beer which is earlier associated with innocent recreation, it predicts that the restrictive Sabbath laws will produce much more "profligacy, idleness, drunkenness, and vice."[21]

Despite their technical weakness, the two cuts illustrating these two essays make evident the twenty-one year old Browne's maturity as an interpreter of the moral significance of his author's text. In particular they make use of iconographic techniques developed by Hogarth and his followers, especially emblematic detail—the church, the clock, and the inscription ("Bread Street")—to underline certain implications of the text (Illus. 4). These sorts of devices are employed by Browne in every Dickens novel he illustrated through *Little Dorrit* (as well as in many by other authors), and they increase in frequency from *Pickwick* on, reaching a high point in *Martin Chuzzlewit, Dombey and Son,* and *David Copperfield,* then diminishing in *Bleak House* and *Little Dorrit,* and disappearing entirely from the sixteen illustrations for *A Tale of Two Cities.* The particular categories of emblematic detail are various, from biblical allusions to titles of plays, sculptures or pictures representing classical mythology, references to Hogarth and Aesop, book titles of various kinds, and fairly standard emblematic objects such as clocks, cobwebs (usually indicating that the hero is somehow trapped, like a fly), maps, pictures of ships sailing smoothly or sinking—the list is almost endless. At times the use of such details may seem crude and obvious, as when David Copperfield's suit to Dora via her aunts, in "Traddles and I, in conference with the Misses Spenlow" (Illus. 5), is commented on by a trio of pictures captioned "The Momentous Question," "The Last Appeal," and "Arcadia," as well as the books *Paradise Regained* and *The Loves of Angels,* and the figurine of a girl picking the petals off a flower. It could be argued, I suppose, that the very obviousness of these details has a comic effect appropriate to David's passion for silly little Dora; but the same illustration contains two more details of greater significance: in a cage, two lovebirds sit apart while in a small bowl one goldfish seems to pursue the other. If these pairs of creatures represent David and Dora, the fact that they are fulfilling their loves in small, enclosed containers from which there is no escape is a subtle and easily overlooked comment on the realities of the new status in life to which David so enthusiastically aspires.

Examples of both seemingly simple as well as subtle emblematic details are numerous, but I shall offer only one more at present. In *Pickwick Papers,* "The Discovery of Jingle in the

Fleet" (Illus. 22) is especially interesting because it includes an emblematic detail that seems to have its origin in Dickens' text: the prisoner's wife

> who was watering, with great solicitude, the wretched stump of a dried-up, withered plant, which, it was plain to see, could never send forth a green leaf again;—too true an emblem, perhaps, of the office she had come there to discharge.[22]

Not mentioned in the text but present in the illustration, however, is a poster on the wall, apparently the famous antislavery poster, "Am I Not a Man and a Brother?" The reference is surely to the appearance of the haggard Jingle and Trotter, two rogues whose imprisonment Pickwick was eager to effect early in the novel, but whose suffering has made the imprisoned hero suddenly conscious of his common humanity with them. Whether Dickens or Browne is responsible for such nontextual details is a question I shall take up presently.

The use of emblematic details is perhaps most complex in a number of the covers Browne designed for the monthly parts and in a few of the frontispieces. These designs employ allegorical structures which comment upon the novel as a whole, although their sources are comparable to those from which the emblematic details in the regular illustrations derive. A less common kind of iconography is allusion via the partial or entire structure of an illustration, perhaps most notably achieved in the title page to *Martin Chuzzlewit* (Illus. 55–57), which (as I shall demonstrate in the chapter on that novel) refers directly to Plate I of *A Harlot's Progress* (Illus. 58), and by so doing makes an important comment upon both the novel's hero and its comic–grotesque villain, Pecksniff. This etching is but one of many executed by Browne for Dickens that are "readable" in the Hogarthian sense.

The disposition of shapes and figures in an illustration can be as iconographically simple a matter as the placement of Dombey in the center of the picture, while his neglected and scorned daughter Florence is relegated to a space outside the doorframe (in "The Dombey Family"); or as subtle as the position of the horizontal building support at the top of the picture in "Tom all alone's" (Illus. 98), as though it were supporting not merely the buildings but the sky, implying an imminent collapse of society as a whole. But disposition of figures becomes a more immediately understandable device for expressing meaning when it is used as a way of drawing parallels between two illustrations—usually, though not always, a pair in a single monthly part. Thus, the raised right hand of Mr. Turveydrop and that of Mr. Chadband in, respectively, "A model of parental deportment" (Illus. 90) and "Mr. Chadband 'improving' a tough subject" (Illus. 92) suggest a parallel between these two charlatans, which, though implied in the text, is never stated therein. This use of various sorts of parallels among illustrations becomes one of Browne's most effective ways of implying meanings, of interpreting the text.

In the last two of Dickens' novels in which Phiz's illustrations play an important part, *Bleak House* and *Little Dorrit*, yet another iconographic mode—at times in combination with the earlier ones—represents what may be the peak of Browne's accomplishment. In these two novels Browne makes heavy use of a technique commonly called the "dark plate" (though that term is misleading since certain plates are anything but dark), which allows for much more subtle uses of light and shades of dark, rather like the technique of mezzotint. It contributes greatly to the dark and pessimistic atmosphere of the text, and among other things enables Browne to suggest the insignificance and helplessness of individuals in an institutional world, with an effectiveness scarcely possible by any other method.

Browne's early development of the dark plate technique seems to have taken place outside of his collaboration with Dickens, particularly in his work for Charles Lever, and the really heavy use of emblematic detail first occurs not in *Martin Chuzzlewit* but a year or two earlier, in Thomas Miller's *Godfrey Malvern*.

And this brings us to the difficult question of the respective roles of Dickens and Browne in the invention and execution of the illustrations. For years it has been standard to assume in discussions of Dickens' illustrations that because the novelist gave his illustrators detailed instructions regarding each plate, we may consider the author to be "throned in the chair of authority, with his hand guiding the pencil of the artist at his own free will."[23] This assumption has at times been questioned, most notably in the articles of Robert L. Patten and to some extent in

John Harvey's *Victorian Novelists and Their Illustrators* (although as we shall see, Harvey is at times a champion of authorial control), but the subject has never been thoroughly aired. In order to provide such an airing, I must turn first to some rather technical matters, the question of how Browne's plates were produced; then to what I consider the very strong evidence of a high degree of independence on the part of Phiz, and finally to the typical pattern of collaboration.

The two main modes of graphic reproduction for which Hablot K. Browne made designs throughout his career are the wood engraving and the etching. Wood engraving is a *relief* method; that is, it involves cutting away the wood from around the lines intended to print black, leaving them standing in ridges; it differs from woodcutting, strictly defined, in that the latter entails cutting upon the plank grain of the wood with a knife, while the wood engraver works on the end grain of the wood with engraver's tools. Both differ fundamentally from line or steel engraving and etching, where the lines that print black are cut into the metal (*intaglio*). Whereas steel engraving is done by hand, with a burin, in an etching the lines are "bitten" into the copper or steel with acid.

Since wood engravings, like type, are in relief they can be printed along with a text, while steel engravings and etchings must be printed separately, with the moistened paper pressed into the inked grooves of the metal. There are many ways in which a design may be transferred to the woodblock or the steel (including direct drawing or etching, without any transfer), but I shall describe only those methods which Browne typically used.[24] Normally, he made use of a thin paper covered on one side with red chalk (sanguine) and placed it, chalk side down, on the woodblock, which was already covered with Chinese white; the drawing was then placed on this, face up, and the main outlines were traced over with a blunt point. The red outlines on the white surface were then used as the basis for drawing directly on the block in black pencil.[25] In this form it would go to the wood engraver, upon whose skill a great deal would ultimately depend, as can be seen readily by a comparison of the various engravers employed for the cuts (a term I shall use throughout when speaking of wood engravings) in *Master Humphrey's Clock*.

The production of an etching was more complicated, and the whole process remained in the hands of Browne and his associate, Robert Young.[26] First, a polished steel plate was prepared by applying a specially composed wax to its surface; this "ground" would then be coated with lampblack. The drawing, in more or less detail, would be transferred via sanguine paper to the etching ground in much the same way as described above for wood engravings. It is possible that at this point Browne also may have drawn directly on the ground, adding details which could not easily be traced. Once the transfer was complete the job of etching commenced: with a special needle the artist cut through the ground, exposing the steel below, wherever lines were to appear in the final print. Then followed the biting-in, a process of successive acid baths whereby the exposed portions of the steel were cut into by acid. Varying degrees of tone were achieved by stopping-out some areas, after early acid baths, with varnish. The process could be more complicated than this, for the etcher might first bite only the main lines, then remove the ground and "pull" a proof to check the progress of his work, then apply a new ground (which, without the added lampblack, would be transparent) and add with his needle certain shadings and other fine details. The number of acid baths might be considerable, though each bath might last only a few seconds; and Browne (or Young) sometimes pulled proofs at three or more stages of the biting.

This last point is confirmed by some of the proofs in the Dexter Collection at the British Library, which show several stages of biting. The method of transfer described by Edgar Browne may be corroborated in two ways. First, the vast majority of Browne's surviving drawings for his etchings are reversed from left to right, indicating that some such method of transfer with the drawing face up must have been used. Second (as no one has previously noted), in most of such reversed drawings blind indentations are visible on the recto side, sometimes closely following the drawn lines, sometimes diverging from them, and sometimes adding details to the etching which are present on the drawing *only* in this blind form. Such indentations are clearly visible as early as the drawings for the seventh part of *Pickwick*

Papers; earlier drawings, and some of the later ones for that novel (also reversed), seem to contain graphite lines pressed in heavily over the original ink lines. These pencil lines may have fulfilled the same function as the blind indentations, which became almost universal in the drawings for the later novels.

A few of the extant drawings are not the reverse of the final etching, and for this there are at least two possible explanations. Certain drawings are preliminary sketches not used in the transfer, and these are—surprisingly—sometimes drawn in the reverse of those used for transfer (which I shall throughout call the working drawings). Second, it is possible that Browne occasionally used another method of transfer, perhaps tracing the drawing and then using this tracing, face down, on the sanguine paper; a number of tracings on transparent paper for the *Master Humphrey's Clock* cuts (Gimbel Collection) indicate that he did use this method for wood engravings at times.

Understanding Browne's method of transfer enables us to distinguish between the final, working designs (since the latter will usually be reversed and exhibit the blind indentations I have described) and those which are preliminary. Thus the left–right orientation of certain Dickens illustrations—such as "Paul and Mrs. Pipchin" and the title page for *Martin Chuzzlewit*—can be seen as calculated and not the result of chance, since for these plates both unreversed preliminary and reversed working drawings exist. (The importance of this left–right positioning will be discussed in the relevant chapters.) In addition, it is possible to see that in some cases Browne seems to have added details at the last moment, for although not visible in ink or pencil, they are nonetheless present in blind indentations. Thus the "ROMA" of the map in "Paul goes home for the holidays" is present only in this form, suggesting a last-minute addition of a small yet significant detail—since study of Latin is an important stultifying force in Blimber's system of education.

Still other details present in the etchings are sometimes missing in the working drawings, and this fact brings us to the question of artistic responsibility. Some critics have offered "proof" that Dickens at least occasionally instructed Browne in the inclusion of emblematic details in addition to giving him the topic and caption of each plate.[27] In question is the illustration from *David Copperfield,* "I make the acquaintance of Miss Mowcher"

(Illus. 6), in which the dwarf is grooming Steerforth's hair and (in the text) making sly remarks to the ingenuous and uncomprehending David. The plate has three emblematic details: a ship in a storm (probably representing Emily's impending fall but also conceivably foreshadowing Steerforth's death in a shipwreck), a comic reference to Miss Mowcher's size and performance in a print showing Gulliver performing for the Brobdignagians, and a scene from *Faust*.

John Harvey has shown that this last detail, containing Faust, Margaret, and Mephistopheles, clinches the text's hint of Miss Mowcher as an intermediary in Steerforth's seduction of Emily because Mephistopheles is standing behind Faust as she is standing behind Steerforth, while the feather in her bonnet resembles that in Mephistopheles' cap. Harvey traces the source of this detail to Moritz Retzsch, but his most important discovery would seem to be that the detail was a "late addition to the plate," because "unlike the biblical scenes in 'Martha' [the companion illustration], it is absent from Browne's sketch." "Presumably," Harvey continues, "on inspecting the sketch, Dickens saw his opportunity to make clearer a suggestion that was fogged in the text, and he dictated the necessary amendment."[28] It may well be that Dickens specified to Browne that Miss Mowcher was to be a panderess, but otherwise Harvey seems to fall afoul of the evidence. First of all, as Harvey himself mentions, a detail much like the one in this plate appears in an etching Browne did a few months before for Lever's *Roland Cashel* (Illus. 8), where it apparently derives from the text, which in turn makes it clear that the original is Retzsch's engraving, "The Decision of the Flower"[29] (Illus. 9). There is even an insignificant visual parallel between the feather in Faust's cap and that in Miss Kennyfeck's bonnet in the Lever etching, and a significant one between Roland's stance and Faust's. This earlier illustration would seem to indicate that the scene from *Faust* was in Browne's mind around the time he was working on *David Copperfield*.

But in addition, Harvey is wrong about the drawing for *Copperfield* (Illus. 7): it *does* contain the *Faust* detail. As is often the case it is very rough, but it is clear that two figures, in approximately the positions of Faust and Margaret (reversed, as is the entire drawing), are intended. What the etching adds, aside from finish, is the figure of Mephistopheles, present in the Retzsch original though in a different position, distant from Faust, and absent in Phiz's illustration for Lever. We have no way of knowing for certain whether Dickens suggested the addition of Mephistopheles or Browne invented it on his own. But the former possibility seems less likely for the simple reason that the *Faust* detail in the drawing would probably be unintelligible to Dickens when first submitted to him for approval. Given the fact that Phiz had already made use of the *Faust* motif for Lever, and that the intention to use it in the Mowcher plate is apparent in the drawing, the most plausible conjecture is that Browne carried through the whole thing himself on the basis of Dickens' general instructions about the meaning of the subject in relation to later developments in the text.

It may seem excessive to argue over such a small detail at such length, but it must be emphasized that even if it were correct, Harvey's partly faulty evidence would be inconclusive. Yet it is the only evidence ever offered that Dickens instructed Browne in details down to this level of specificity. All other surviving evidence seems to point the other way: among those extant sets of directions to Phiz (and unfortunately Phiz burned most of his correspondence in 1859[30]), not one contains such specific details. Most telling are those instances in which Dickens offers extremely lengthy instructions for drawings which contain numerous such details. For the etching "Major Bagstock is delighted to have that opportunity" in *Dombey and Son,* two sets of directions survive, the second set a request to Browne for improvement on his initial drawing, but none of the emblematic details are mentioned in either set. Similarly, the instructions for the last four illustrations to *Martin Chuzzlewit* are again lengthy and specific, but with no mention of a single emblematic detail.

I find it difficult to imagine that if Dickens did not specify iconographic devices in these five cases (and there are other, less dramatic instances) where emblematic detail is so profuse, he would have done so elsewhere.[31] Not only are the devices similar to those used throughout the novels, but they are similar to those Browne used in his work for other authors, especially Charles Lever, who seems to have given Browne much less instruction than did Dickens. Thus we find Lever writing to his

Dublin publisher from Brussels during the publication in
monthly parts of *Harry Lorrequer* (1838–39),

> H. K. Brown [sic] has not yet written to me, and I regret it the
> more, because if I knew the scenes he selected, I might have
> benefited by his ideas and rendered them more graphic, as an
> author corrects his play by seeing a dress rehearsal.[32]

The mention of Phiz selecting the subjects himself and the
author altering his text to fit recalls what John Harvey has shown
about Cruikshank's relationship to Harrison Ainsworth.[33] Edgar
Browne's summary of his father's professional relationship to
Lever seems plausible: "From the beginning he [Lever] leant
upon Phiz; he was very easily satisfied with his illustrations, so
long as they agreed with the general drift of the text, he was not
solicitous about details."[34] If Browne could supply emblematic
details drawn from the traditional stock for Lever, why must we
assume that he was unable to do so for Dickens? Perhaps the
question can never be settled, but on the basis of the evidence it
seems to me harder to present a convincing argument for Dickens' complete dominance over his artist than for Browne's independence in matters of iconography.

Typical conditions under which Browne worked would make
frequent last-minute additions under Dickens' instructions unlikely. From the early years of their association the novelist and
illustrator followed a standard pattern of collaboration: for each
forthcoming monthly number Dickens would give the subjects of
the two illustrations (or four, for the final, double numbers) and
include proof copy or a bit of manuscript whenever possible.
Browne would execute these as drawings and submit them, time
and distance allowing, to Dickens, who would either approve
them or suggest alterations. If approved, the design would be
etched by Browne on a steel previously prepared by Robert
Young and then sent along to Young with the drawing and
perhaps some further instructions regarding the biting-in; according to Browne's son, Young also "came down to Croydon
nearly every Sunday, and sometimes during the week," for con-
sultation.[35] Here is a "diary" (evidently intended for a publisher's guidance) of Browne's typical procedures:

Friday evening, 11th Jan......... Received portion of copy con-
                                  taining Subject No. 1.
Sunday...................................... Posted sketch to Dickens.
Monday evening, 14th Jan. ..... Received back sketch of Subject
                                  No. 1 from Dickens, enclosing a
                                  subject for No. 2.
Tuesday, 15th Jan.................... Forwarded sketch of Subject 2
                                  to Dickens.
Wednesday, 16th Jan. .... Received back ditto.
Sunday..
Tuesday, 22nd Jan................... First plate finished.
Saturday, 26th Jan. .... Second ditto finished.—Suppos-
                                  ing that I had nothing else to do,
                                  you may see by the foregoing
                                  that I could not well commence
                                  etching operations until Wed-
                                  nesday, the 16th.

"I make ten days to etch and finish four etchings. What do you
make of it?" Browne comments at the bottom of this "diary."[36]

We may take this to be a description of the normal process,
based on Browne's work for a novel later than *Pickwick Papers*
(in the Preface to which Dickens states that "the interval has
been so short between the production of each number in manuscript and its appearance in print, that the greater portion of the
Illustrations have been executed by the artist from the author's
mere verbal description of what he intended to write").
Throughout their collaboration the availability of copy would
depend upon how far ahead Dickens was with his writing. It
seems evident that at times Browne received only a generalized
instruction, the initial execution of which failed to jibe in some
respect with the final text. For example, "The Goblin and the
Sexton," second of a pair of Christmas plates for the tenth
monthly part of *Pickwick*, was done in three distinct versions. In
the first (Illus. 10), two pencil sketched figures sit together on a
flat tombstone before a church porch; the second (Illus. 11) reverses the scene and is executed in enough detail so that it could
easily have been the final drawing. But it turns out that the text
describes the goblin as seated on an "upright tombstone."
Presumably Dickens directed Browne to bring his illustration in
line with the writing, and a drawing of the final version, in which
one can see clearly the indented transfer lines, was produced

(Illus. 12). The church porch has been changed to a church or abbey building, but the memento mori inscription and skull of the second drawing are repeated here.

For the most part, however, one would expect that such multiple versions (and, presumably, instructions) were unusual, given the time pressures under which author and illustrator operated. It is also noteworthy that Browne remarks, "Supposing that I had nothing else to do," surely implying that he usually did have other work. And well he might, considering what he was paid for the Dickens illustrations. John Harvey has shown that Browne's fee from Dickens' publishers rose from approximately £4 per etching for *Pickwick* to seven guineas for *David Copperfield*, fourteen years later, and that although the pay per etching for *Bleak House* and *Little Dorrit* was higher still (£11. 8s. 6d.), his actual pay per monthly number was less because most of the plates were no longer etched in duplicate.[37] Thus, we may calculate roughly that at his peak Browne was earning £30 per month from Dickens (from which he had to pay Young, his "biter")— hardly a huge sum for an illustrator with fifteen years' experience and a large family to support. Moreover, such income could be counted on for intermittent periods only: calculation reveals that during the twenty-four years from 1836 through 1859 Browne had thirteen years of employment on Dickens' novels. Thus it would be essential to have several jobs in progress at once (see the Appendix for a year-by-year list of Browne's work during his career as Dickens' illustrator); and thus the most amazing thing about Browne is that his illustrations—especially for Dickens, but often for other writers as well—are as technically finished and iconographically complex as they are. Considering the differences between an independent master engraver such as Hogarth and an etcher using his imagination on the creations of others, Browne is to say the least a phenomenon; for he was Dickens' collaborator and interpreter, and developed artistically as Dickens did.

CHAPTER TWO

The Beginnings of "Phiz": *Pickwick, Nickleby,* and the Emergence from Caricature

Robert Seymour, whose suicide created the opening for Browne's talents, was thirty-eight at his death, with better than a decade of experience in etching, lithography, and drawing on wood, as a creator of individually sold satirical prints, periodical caricaturist, designer of humorous sporting plates, and book illustrator. Browne was, in other words, a nonentity replacing a widely known and popular artist, and he took at first the pseudonym "N.E.M.O."—"no one"—suggesting a self-effacing hack laboring away for others. (When Dickens sixteen years later gave such a *nom de plume* to a character who very much fits this description, he may have been having a little joke at Browne's expense.) N.E.M.O. became Phiz—a more appropriate companion for Boz, as well as a logical title for one who did "phizzes"—with the third plate he did for *Pickwick*. Browne's first six etchings for *Pickwick* are as overall designs perhaps already superior to Seymour's efforts, but as Harvey has pointed out, Browne has trouble with the poses of his figures,[1] and equal trouble, I think, creating adequately distinct faces; in this respect the schoolmistress in the sixth plate of this series is as wanting as Sam Weller in the second.

The woodenness of the figures in these earliest plates is not much worse than Seymour's efforts, but with the seventh of his etchings, "Mr. Pickwick in the Pound" (Illus. 16), the young illustrator seems to have hit his stride. A comparison of

24

Seymour's *Pickwick* plates, together with those he did earlier in the year for *The Book of Christmas* (Illus. 25),[2] with Phiz's work for *Pickwick* reveals that the younger man, though by no means a slavish imitator, had carefully studied the elder's manner. Browne's work also generally reflects close affinities with older traditions of graphic satire. The figures in all of Browne's plates for Dickens' first novel are small, almost cramped, their bodies often contorted and their faces twisted into expressions which at times are insufficiently varied. Most noticeably, Phiz takes from Seymour the practice of modeling the faces by etching on them numerous curved lines that impart contorted grimaces to their expressions. Since Seymour, perhaps more directly and immediately than any other artist, provided Phiz with a mode in which to operate as Dickens' illustrator, the story of Phiz's development is the story of his movement away from that older style in a direction parallel to the development of Dickens' own art.

Almost from the very beginning, Phiz found himself called upon by the changes in the nature of *Pickwick* (including the character of Pickwick himself) to function as a different kind of illustrator. Except for the melodramatic tale of the melancholy clown, all the incidents Seymour had been required to depict were broadly comic. Pickwick was portrayed, both in text and etchings, as essentially a lovable fool, but Phiz's first commission was for two designs depicting events that for the first time involve Pickwick in incidents that require him to take morally responsible actions: Jingle's elopement with Rachael, in "The Breakdown" (ch. 9), and Jingle's encounter with the force of morality (as embodied in Mr. Wardle and Pickwick) and of the law (in Perker) in "First appearance of Mr. Samuel Weller" (ch. 10; Illus. 13).[3] The first of this pair of etchings depicts the failure of passionate, resentful action, as it shows Pickwick temporarily fallen by the way (quite literally) and taunted by the triumphant rogue Jingle, while the second depicts the impending victory of rational action, as the pursuers, now strengthened by the assistance of Perker the solicitor, are on the point of discovering the designs of their adversary.

Dickens, in the passages relevant to the first of these plates, as well as frequently elsewhere, makes great play with Pickwick's tendency to burst into violent if ineffectual rages; in the second plate, reasonable action does temporarily triumph, but Dickens has not forgotten comedy and uses Sam's good-natured insolence as a means of deflating Pickwick's and especially Perker's self-importance. Phiz emphasizes this undercutting in a way which suggests an independent use of expressive iconography: he leads our eye from the jaunty cockney, Sam Weller, on the left, through the three gentlemen to the little dog on the right, who is contemplating Pickwick's calves with vicious intent.

The artist's execution is crude, perhaps (and much improved in the 1838 re-etching of this plate), but the dog's presence is important, for it is not mentioned in the text, and although Dickens could have suggested him to Browne it is just as likely that the artist included him as a natural compositional and thematic complement to the independent-minded Sam. Thus, Phiz demonstrates from the outset a capacity for composing illustrations which may be "read" like a Hogarth engraving, significant details and composition combining to elucidate Dickens' text. Browne's 1836 and 1838 versions of his third illustration, "Mrs. Bardell faints in Mr. Pickwick's arms" (ch. 12; Illus. 14), provide an especially interesting example of this talent and its development. In the 1836 plate, with its harsh and scarcely relieved verticals, the rendering of both room and characters is rudimentary and stiff. Considered abstractly, the overall composition adequately conveys the point of the scene—Mr. Pickwick at the center holds Mrs. Bardell, harried by Master Bardell on one side while scrutinized by his friends on the other. Most interesting, however, are the rather tentatively etched details above the door: a stuffed owl and the sculptured head of what appears to be an elderly man. Presumably these constitute some kind of ironic reference to wisdom and sagacity, or perhaps the head simply suggests Pickwick's rather advanced age.

In the redesigned plate for the 1838 edition not only has Browne enormously improved the rendering of characters and scene so that the illustration comes alive in contrast to the stiff, formal feeling of the earlier one, but he eliminates the two vaguely emblematic details and introduces three new, much clearer ones: a framed picture above the mirror, showing Cupid aiming an arrow at a languid nude; on the chimneypiece, a pair of

vases with fresh flowers in them; and between these, an ornamental clock featuring Father Time with his scythe. The clock is
immediately behind Pickwick's head, while the right-hand vase
is behind Mrs. Bardell's, so that the clear implication is a lightly
ironic commentary upon the conjunction of age and (relative)
youth.

The picture of the God of Love aiming his arrow at a reclining
woman is curiously similar to a detail in an earlier book illustration by George Cruikshank. While the detail's design could resemble the earlier etching by chance, the subject of the earlier
plate makes this less likely. Entitled "The Unwelcome Intruders" (Illus. 15), it deals with an amorous adventure of the Duke of
Cumberland and depicts three men entering a room and surprising the Duke in dishabille, while a lady runs off into another
room.[4] The total composition is not similar to Browne's plate, but
the connection of the situation with the Cupid detail suggests at
the very least that Browne was influenced by his predecessor's
etching, and perhaps that he was alluding to it—which would
give extra comic point to the plight of Pickwick, who has no
intention of becoming romantically involved with his landlady.
One may also push further the interpretation of the other
emblems, as the symbol of age on the mantel is flanked on both
sides by a symbol of youth (the flowers), just as Pickwick is
caught between the swooning landlady and her kicking child. In
any case it is important to stress that Browne must have introduced all of these new emblems on his own intitiative, since
Dickens would hardly have given fresh instructions for the re-
etched plates in the 1838 bound volume. Given his great advances in drawing and etching during the course of *Pickwick's*
publication in parts, Phiz was probably not satisfied to trace and
re-etch his earlier designs, as he had to do with Seymour's.[5]

In the combination of Father Time and Cupid, Browne uses
emblematic details in a quite Hogarthian way; compare for
example Hogarth's method of juxtaposing Cupid holding a
scythe, representing the transitoriness of the flesh, with a detail
of Orpheus and his music-tamed beasts, symbolizing the illusory
nature of eternal concord on earth, in his family group, *The
Graham Children* (Tate Gallery).[6] The details in the 1838 etching hint at a more serious and broader moral context for the

episode even as they comment upon its comic aspects. In discussing the plates to *David Copperfield*, we shall see how Phiz was to use yet another detail present in this Hogarth painting, along with another from the Mrs. Bardell plate.

Part VII of *Pickwick Papers* contains the first unequivocal example of a pair of Browne's illustrations designed to present both a visual and a thematic relationship. We must remember that originally the etchings were bound together separate from the text; thus, such parallelism should have been apparent to the first readers, although the lack of any contemporary testimony to this effect raises a special problem. For if there is little evidence (despite the undoubted importance of the illustrations in influencing the reception of the novels) that Browne's and Dickens' contemporaries saw the illustrations as comparable to Hogarthian "progresses," then modern scholars who argue for a serious iconography are in the strange position of claiming to have discovered both particular meanings and possibly a whole artistic mode of which the earliest readers and perhaps even the author, if not the illustrator, were unaware. But the apparent temerity of such claims may be mitigated by the reflection that Dickens, Browne and their contemporaries lacked not so much a perception of what they were doing as any formulated critical or aesthetic theory. The continuing lack of any such critical theory more than a hundred years after the fact can be explained on the grounds that *Pickwick* represented a new genre which lasted only two decades, to be replaced by a kind of illustrated novel which consciously rejected the Hogarthian tradition.

Professor Robert L. Patten has analyzed the illustrations for Part VII at length,[7] but it will be necessary here to discuss his arguments in some detail, as an example of both the advantages and dangers of trying to read a Dickens novel as a collaboration between author and illustrator. Patten performed the great service of pointing out what no one had ever noticed in print before, and what becomes perfectly obvious once one sees it: in "Mr. Pickwick in the Pound" (ch. 19; Illus. 16 and 17) and "Mr. Pickwick & Sam in the attorneys' office" (ch. 20), Pickwick is in each case shown to be in the center of an enclosure, the object of mocking smiles or laughter from those on the other side of the barriers. I am less satisfied with Patten's use of this important insight in interpreting the novel. According to Patten, in the first of the pair, Pickwick "for correction" of his folly in drinking too much "is put in a small informal prison, separating errant characters from the larger community."[8] In contrast is the following plate, where "he is now isolated, not from the hearty villagers, but from Dodson and Fogg,"[9] thus reflecting Pickwick's moral superiority at this point. The novel's movement is from "communal harmony and benevolent good feeling to dissension and isolation,"[10] and then to spiritual enlightenment, for Pickwick's ability to join "the hilarious villagers" by laughing at himself[11] is related to the larger pattern of the novel, wherein Pickwick escapes "spiritual imprisonment" through forgiveness of Mrs. Bardell and Mr. Jingle.[12] Patten interprets the church building in the background of the pound plate as "iconographically" implying "Christian attitudes such as humility and forgiveness,"[13] while the donkeys and pigs function as emblems of Pickwick's folly and gluttony.[14]

Patten offers further valuable insights in comparing these two plates in their images of confinement with "The Warden's Room" (ch. 41), and contrasting all three with the bonhomie of the Christmas etching. But one must return to the text to determine whether a given interpretation based on illustrations in fact accords with the novel. That Dickens intended a connection between the pound and attorneys' office plates is evident from the relevant chapters, in which such connections are more explicit textually than the novelist tends to be in later years, when he lets the illustrations carry more of the burden of parallelism. First, Dickens underlines the parallels verbally by having Captain Boldwig, the ridiculously self-important landowner who puts the sleeping Pickwick in the pound, leave his victim with the words, "He shall not bully me—he shall not bully me" (ch. 19, p. 197). At the same time, the attorney, Fogg, is quoted by one of his clerks as having said to a legal victim, "Don't bully me, Sir" (ch. 20, p. 200), when it is really Fogg, like Boldwig, who is the bully. Second, when Pickwick awakes in the pound, the villagers' first response is to roar, "Here's a game" (ch. 19, p. 197), while the clerks say about their previous night's roistering, "That was a game, wasn't it," and about Fogg's hoodwinking the poor Mr. Ramsey, "There was such a game with Fogg here" (ch. 20, p. 199).

Thus both the villagers and the clerks have a "game" at the expense of those victimized by the bullies who accuse the victims of their own crime. And Pickwick is of course a victim in both cases, as well. From this standpoint the two illustrations begin to look somewhat different from Professor Patten's description. If one takes the pound plate in isolation from Captain Boldwig, Dodson, and Fogg, then the emphasis upon folly and gluttony and the view of the mob (whom Dickens calls the "many-headed") as a group of hearty villagers representing the community from which Pickwick is isolated seems at least plausible. But once the whole context is admitted this reading can no longer satisfy; folly and gluttony are there, and we can laugh at Pickwick's plight, but the mob is as much an object of Browne's satire as are the clerks, and behind the scenes Dodson and Fogg are more than agents of Pickwick's eventual "Christian" escape from "spiritual imprisonment"—though they may be that as well.

It is relevant at this point to recall Hogarth's brand of satire and how it differs from that of the graphic satirists who succeeded him in the late eighteenth and early nineteenth centuries. Hogarth's "modern historical paintings" occasionally depict virtuous individuals, such as the girl Sarah Young in *A Rake's Progress;* but in general the satirist's shafts strike everywhere, exempting no social class or political party. In the work of the later graphic satirists, however—including the very best—one is nearly always aware of extreme partisanship in political, social, and moral matters. While not suggesting that Dickens' early works closely resemble Hogarth's sweeping satire, I believe one may say that *Pickwick* (like most of the other novels) is more in the spirit of Hogarth than of his successors. Although some public or institutional figures like Boldwig, Dodson, and Fogg are conceived of as ridiculous and vicious beyond redemption, the novel is notably lacking in prominent villains or heroes. One may draw extremely simple Christian lessons from Hogarth's prints, and similarly one may read the pound plate of *Pickwick* as a simple moral tale in which the church is a Christian symbol. Equally, one could read this plate as an indictment of the church and the law, with Pickwick as their victim and the crowd as the typically ignorant, conservative peasantry; in view of Browne's later use of churches this reading is at least as likely. In both this plate and its companion, a man who is essentially innocent becomes a victim of the power quest and sadism of others; and to suggest that Pickwick's "isolation" is *primarily* the result of his own spiritual shortcomings seems to me to oversystematize, and thus oversimplify, both plates and text.

The plates for Part IX take further the problems of authority, the mob, and the law, contrasted with the virtues of private domestic life. In the attorneys' office plate, Sam Weller was seen for the first time as consoler of Pickwick and as the mediator—through his healthy skepticism toward all constituted authority and all pretensions of social distinction—between the too vulnerable Pickwick and a world made up of ignorant and venal officials, men of petty and selfish passions, and designing women. In "Mr. Weller attacks the executive of Ipswich" (ch. 24) he becomes Pickwick's protector against authority as embodied in the mob. Sam's temporary victory in this plate is contrasted with his permanent one over Job Trotter in its companion, "Job Trotter encounters Sam in Mr. Muzzle's kitchen" (ch. 25). Sam and the pretty housemaid are noticed first, then the feasting cook, butler and the former pair are contrasted with Job—his head preposterously big, like certain comic–grotesque figures in Gillray and George Cruikshank—who is isolated from the group by the vertical line formed by the door's edge; Job is also farthest from the hearth. We find as well the third of several animal emblems in the book: a kitten attacks the remains of a meat pie, while its mother prepares to join in. This activity may be a reference to Jingle and Trotter and their attempt to carry off treasures from the Nupkins household, but while fragments of food have been left out for the cats, Job is excluded from the fellowship of the servants' kitchen.

Although food and eating occur frequently throughout Dickens' novels, there is surely no other where they function so pervasively as symbols of community and love. In later novels though there are love feasts, these are often the special communion of two or three individuals in an alien environment (Tom

and Ruth Pinch's pudding, Pip and Joe's bread and butter); and
feasting is as often the expression of selfishness—Squeers and
his breakfasts at the Saracen's Head, Mrs. Gamp and Betsy Prig,
Major Bagstock. The genuine *agape* of *Pickwick* is expressed
most directly in "Christmas Eve at Mr. Wardle's" (ch. 28). This is
the first of Phiz's plates for Dickens to have had duplicate steels
etched at the time of original publication in parts, rather than a
new etching executed for the 1838 *Pickwick;*[15] doubtless because the practice was a novelty for Browne, it is the only example among all the duplicated steels for which he made two
different drawings and etched both, instead of tracing one drawing on the grounds of two or more steels. It is clear that Browne
had trouble getting all the details from Dickens' text (including
the earlier description of the Dingley Dell kitchen) into the
drawing. The problem of including four couples in the crowded
scene is solved by a triangular composition, with Pickwick and
old Mrs. Wardle at the apex, and Winkle and Tupman with their
partners at the corners, while Snodgrass and his partner are
slightly back of Pickwick. But in what was probably the first
steel[16] (Illus. 18), the fireplace is scarcely recognizable, Browne
contorts Arabella's neck and head to an extreme degree, and
gives the woman next to Wardle an imbecile expression and
undue prominence.

In his revised duplicate (Illus. 19 and 20), Browne more or less
solved these problems. He also substituted a cat rubbing against
Pickwick's leg in place of the cat and dog in the center foreground of the original. The excised cat and dog are seen by Professor Patten as symbols of the special harmony of Christmastime
at Dingley Dell,[17] but I wonder. The dog sniffs at the cat, whose
paw is raised in a cautionary way as though its claws are about to
sink into the dog's nose; if this scene has any meaning, it would
seem to parallel comically the behavior of Winkle and Arabella,
who is coyly resisting his amorous advances. In Browne's illustrations, as in many of Hogarth's plates (see for example Plate V
of *A Rake's Progress*),[18] domestic animals tend to imitate human
beings, more often than not (as the dog in "First appearance of
Mr. Samuel Weller") providing sardonic rather than cheerful
commentary.

The contrasts of private good fellowship and the snares of the
world of authority and law are suggested once again in "Mr.

Pickwick Slides" (ch. 29), which has the hero surrounded by friends who will rescue and comfort him after his fall, and its companion plate, "The first interview with Mr. Serjeant Snubbin" (ch. 30; Illus. 21). In the latter, Pickwick is no longer at the center of the composition, nor part of a friendly group. He is located on the extreme right edge, separated from both Snubbin and Perker by the door frame and the back of the barrister's chair, as though barrister and solicitor are in league against their client. Further, the half-open door links the unfledged assistant, Mr. Phunky, with the hapless Pickwick as a victim of the legal establishment.

The two steels for the Snubbin plate reveal some interesting differences that bear upon Phiz's conception of the illustration. In one steel (25B), the expression on Snubbin's face is more in accord with Dickens' request that he should look "a great deal more sly, and knowing," and be "smiling compassionately at [Pickwick's] innocence."[19] In both steels the design is composed with three overlapping triangles sharing the same base, and having as their apexes, respectively, the head of Serjeant Snubbin, his wig upon its block, and the grim bust of a judge which decorates the cabinet. Phiz has drawn Pickwick's face so that he appears to be looking at the wig rather than at the Serjeant, and the wig's centrality is consistent with the text: in employing Snubbin, Pickwick makes use of an impersonal force which has no more sympathy for him than does the wig, symbol of legal authority. Moreover, Snubbin's mild curiosity about this peculiar innocent seems to be mirrored by the expression of the amiable Mr. Perker—who is still a lawyer even if he is Pickwick's friend.

Directly above Snubbin's head is a spider web, into which flies are introduced in Steel B, indicating that it is not simply the law's mustiness which is represented. In addition, the cornice of the cabinet is ornamented in Steel B, and with the aid of a magnifying glass one can make out numerous bewigged and grinning heads with a horned one among them, suggesting that the legal forces arrayed against Pickwick are near relatives of the Father of Lies. If these subtleties of composition and detail are Browne's contribution, they surely grow out of the text and its implications: the wig is in Dickens' description of the room, yet its central position in the plate is the result of an interpretation of the relationship between law and humanity; the cobweb in the

first steel could simply reflect the general dirt and disorder mentioned in the text, but adding flies to it imparts a clearly
emblematic meaning; and finally, decorating the cabinet in such
a way that the artist alone is likely to be aware of the nature of the
ornaments suggests a high degree of commitment on Browne's
part to the craft he is pursuing—providing a running commentary, in visual language, upon the verbal text.

With increasing frequency as the novel advances, Dickens
deals with various parallels and antitheses: comic, moral,
sentimental, social, and institutional. Thus, the semi-illiterate
coachman Tony Weller can give the genteel Pickwick advice
about widows based on his own folly and consequent experience. And in "The Valentine" (ch. 32), and "The Trial" (ch. 33)
these implicit parallels can be actively "read." The central link
between chapters 32 and 33 is a love letter. As a tenant, Pickwick
has written innocent notes to Mrs. Bardell which are interpreted
through a barrister's (Mr. Buzfuz's) allegory of innuendo to read
as though they were love letters. Sam here, as elsewhere in the
novel, parodies his master, when, inspired by a comically allegorical valentine in a shop window, he writes a declaration of
love to Mary the housemaid. To stress the parallel, Dickens has
Sam sign his letter, "Your love-sick/Pickwick" (ch. 32, p. 345), a
comment upon the ridiculous position in which Pickwick has
found himself with Mrs. Bardell. Once this parallel is recognized, the similar composition in the two etchings suddenly becomes visible.

Although the second etching has many characters, it is, as
much as the first, based upon a simple spatial relationship between a central, standing, admonitory figure and, on the left, the
object of his exhortations. Sam, writing his letter, receives advice
from his father, who gestures with his right hand to support his
arguments; in the other illustration, Serjeant Buzfuz holds the
"love letter," but he too gestures—toward Pickwick—with his
right hand, and though Pickwick's expression is totally different
from Sam's, he holds his arms in a similar position. Taken together, these two plates stress the thematic counterpoint of Sam
and Pickwick which occurs throughout the novel from the
cockney's first appearance: Sam relates to his father with a bal-

anced mixture of love, respect, and independence, and he is invulnerable to the depredations of law, society, or women; Pickwick, having no father, and not yet properly fatherly himself (as he will be once he has forgiven Jingle and intervened for Winkle with *his* father) is vulnerable to women and the law.

The trial's result is depicted in the first of four prison plates, "Mr. Pickwick sits for his portrait" (ch. 39). As Patten points out, this plate recalls the two earlier illustrations in which Pickwick is confined within a small enclosure, the focus of a number of eyes; here, however, the observers are not laughing, but are memorizing Pickwick's features with a mind to confining him more securely. It is perhaps some indication of the prison episodes' importance for Dickens that for two of the prison etchings the novelist provides emblems in the text, as though especially concerned with thematic clarity. In the portrait plate, we have among the many bird-cages in Phiz's etchings, one whose significance is spelled out by the author: "'And a bird-cage, Sir,' said Sam. 'Veels vithin veels, a prison in a prison. Ain't it, Sir'" (ch. 39, p. 434). Sam also mentions the Dutch clock, implying that it too is a suitable background for a "portrait."

This plate resumes the thematic concerns of the illustration of Dodson and Fogg's office in portraying Sam Weller as Pickwick's adviser and protector, for in both Sam leans slightly over the sitting and dismayed Pickwick. By the next part, Pickwick has deprived himself of this moral support, determined to undergo alone the rigors of the Fleet. In both "The Warden's Room" (ch. 40) and "Discovery of Jingle in the Fleet" (ch. 41; Illus. 22), Pickwick expresses astonishment and perplexity. But in the former it is a reaction to the seeming anarchy of the situation and his own helplessness as a victim of his roommates' riotousness;[20] the "Rules of the Fleet" posted upon the wall (and nowhere mentioned in the text) seem an ironic comment upon the lack of order—and yet the *actual* rules of custom allow Pickwick to buy his way into a private room, for even here his money can prevent physical suffering.

In the third prison plate, Pickwick's amazement is at the presence of Jingle and the woebegone condition of this once jaunty rogue. Considering the text's requirements, this illustration demonstrates a real advance in Browne's ability to interpret his author. The placement of Pickwick in the center, looking directly at Jingle, impresses this encounter upon us as the primary one; our eye next takes in Job Trotter, who is being followed by a woman demanding payment for food and drink (a detail not mentioned in the text, and recalling *A Rake's Progress*, VII [Illus. 23]). If this is indeed how we see the details, then Browne has reversed the time scheme, for Dickens first describes the secondary details, building up to the revelation of the rogues' presence. Assuming that we read the text first, the picture causes us to reconsider the same details in reverse order, taking us from the general to the specific, and then back to consider the general in relation to the particular.[21] We first read about the ways in which the unnamed prisoners react to their circumstances, which prepares us to see Jingle and Trotter in a new light; then the revelation; then the illustration, moving us to reconsider the conditions of imprisonment, including the harrassment of prisoners for their debts incurred for mere subsistence. (There is also the famous antislavery poster, mentioned in Chapter 1.)

The last of the prison plates, "Mrs. Bardell encounters Mr. Pickwick in the prison" (ch. 44; Illus. 24) adds nothing not specified in the text, but nonetheless it can be "read," and is a good example of Phiz's early mastery of the iconography of space and form. In this plate, the horizontal band formed by the main characters is juxtaposed both to the vertical of the gateway and to the dynamic thrust of the jailer, who appears to have just pushed the ladies and child down the steps. One reads from top to bottom left, and then to the right, just as one "sees" in the text the arrival at prison, the revelation to Mrs. Bardell that she is a prisoner, and then the encounter with Pickwick. The triangular arrangement, however, makes it possible to read the illustration in two directions, as though causally: from Mrs. Bardell up to the jailer and down to Pickwick, implying that her lawsuit has brought him to prison; or in reverse, beginning with Pickwick, implying that his stubborn adherence to principle has caused him unwittingly to make a victim out of his former landlady. Yet Pickwick and Mrs. Bardell also are part of the same compositional horizontal band, linked as victims of a vicious system.

A different kind of thematic emphasis occurs in "Mr. Bob Sawyer's mode of travelling" (ch. 49) where the seedy Sawyer and his friend Ben Allen first come into contact with Pickwick. At this point the hero's transformation from bumbling fool into fountainhead of benevolence and wisdom is virtually complete, and yet suddenly we are given a violently comic episode in which Pickwick reverts to some of his early qualities, followed in the next plate by an even more broadly slapstick episode. If we accept the principle that the novel is moving toward the establishment of a pastoral Pickwickian patriarchy for Winkle, Snodgrass, Sam, and their wives, the medical students introduced at this point represent the eruption of characteristics which the novel increasingly has either overcome or denied: self-interest, self-dramatization, lack of self-control, overindulgence in corporeal (if not carnal) pleasures, and even (in Ben and Bob's eagerness to "bleed" someone) indifference to others' physical sufferings. Browne's illustration even more than Dickens' text vividly expresses the subversiveness of these figures.

There are no details in the plate which are not in the text, but the "Irish family," whose "congratulations" are of a "rather boisterous description," is interpreted as a group of tinkers—two parents, seven children, and a dog—the father, the eldest boy, and one of the girls all saluting in direct imitation of Bob's gestures with bottle and sandwich. Pickwick's indignation is, in the text, to be converted with the help of a bottle of punch into a passive participation in the merriment; but in the etching he is caught at the moment when he is at the height of bourgeois respectability, in contrast to Bob, Sam Weller, and the Irish family. Phiz has thus apparently taken a generalized reference in the text and made it into the novel's only concrete reference to the lowest classes, implying that they are both a potential threat and a source of vitality beyond the range of Pickwick's comprehension. It is as though a bit of *Oliver Twist,* which Dickens was writing at this time, has through the agency of the two medical students invaded the generally more secure world of *Pickwick.* The accompanying plate, "The Rival Editors" (ch. 50), finds both Pickwick and Sam on the side of order, interfering in the absurd conflict between the editors and ignoring the medical students who circle them, brandishing their scalpels. This is the last broadly comic episode in the novel, and can be seen as a resolution, a laying to rest of the early Pickwick, as he and Sam have the advantage over the ridiculous comic characters, and only the medical students suggest any continuation of Misrule (a term I have taken from traditional Christmas festivities, for reasons which will become apparent shortly).

As with all his subsequent novels published in separate monthly parts, Dickens had to write twice as much for the final portion of *Pickwick,* and Browne produced four illustrations instead of two. Following the procedures for all such novels save *Nicholas Nickleby,* two plates illustrate episodes in the final part, and the other two comprise frontispiece and title page, of which the first always, and the second sometimes, is of a recapitulatory or allegorical nature. The first two plates in *Pickwick's* final section are of minor importance (except perhaps in their emphasis upon eating and drinking), but the two final plates, because they become the first two in any bound edition, function both retrospectively and anticipatively. Phiz shows considerable inventiveness in carrying out what were likely Dickens' fairly general instructions. First of all, the two plates have certain broad connections: in the frontispiece, Sam and his master sit in a study, Sam showing Pickwick something in a book, while imps look in at them through a comically Gothic archway, gesticulating and laughing. In the title page vignette, Sam cheers his father, who is ducking Mr. Stiggins in a horse trough. This plate illustrates an actual episode from the novel, and is more naturalistically conceived than is the frontispiece, but both frontispiece and title page plates are linked visually by the archway through which Sam looks, for it is decorated with grotesque figures. Sam's gesture is further echoed by the figure on the inn's sign which menacingly waves a stick.

If we take the title page to represent the novel's violently active comic side, the frontispiece is, with qualifications, the reverse: a scene of contemplative repose, observed and ridiculed, however, by a group of comic subversives. The basic structure of the frontispiece is like a proscenium stage, below which an imp points sardonically at three of the main actors in the novel who are absent from the stage, Tupman, Winkle, and Snodgrass. Robert Patten has demonstrated that this frontispiece, through its visual references to books and tale-telling, its pantomime imps (one of whom is the goblin of an earlier plate, "The Goblin and the Sexton" [ch. 28B;[22] Illus. 10–12]), its globe, helmet, and shield, epitomizes the novel's use of the tale as a vehicle for conveying both experience and its evaluation.[23] But in addition, the imps and goblins embody something of the tension in this novel between comedy as a moral vehicle and as a subversive force. Why, for example, is Gabriel Grub's goblin, whose function in the novel is to bring about the sexton's regeneration, here mocking Pickwick and Sam? And why is another such figure jeering at the Pickwickians?

The sources upon which Browne probably drew may throw some light on these questions. The stagelike frame has a long graphic tradition behind it, but Browne's most direct influence in its use seems to have been his predecessor, Robert Seymour. Though at first glance the frontispiece to Hervey's *The Book of Christmas,* "Christmas and His Children" (Illus. 25), does not obviously resemble Browne's design (Illus. 26), a moment's consideration reveals some parallels. In both, the central scene—intended to epitomize the book—is framed by a proscenium arch supported by Gothic columns. The stage is in each case revealed by a draped curtain, and both stages protrude into an apron. Below Seymour's stage is a satyr's head and below Browne's two, very similar to Seymour's. On either side in both pictures are stone brackets, occupied in Seymour's etching by a harper and Father Christmas and in Browne's by the imps and goblins. The goblin on the right points to the scene within, as does Father Christmas. There is also a possible link between this goblin and Seymour's Lord of Misrule (in both the frontispiece and a plate facing p. 213 of Hervey's book), and if this resemblance is more than accidental, the implication for *Pickwick* is that reason and reflection in Sam and Pickwick are mocked by mirth and unreason—which are themselves ritualistic and seasonal rather than uncontained or destructive. There are some further minor similarities between elements in the two books, but the basic parallels at the very least suggest the extent to which Phiz was working within current as well as eighteenth-century graphic conventions.

If Browne was under the stylistic influence of Seymour in *The Pickwick Papers,* his use of iconographic methods for the pur-

pose of genuine interpretation and expression go beyond anything Seymour displayed as an illustrator. But Browne's illustrations for *Nicholas Nickleby,* which followed fairly closely in
time, are a curious mixture. Much of the same kind of Seymourean awkwardness appears in some plates, while expressive
iconography in the form of emblematic details or visual parallelism among plates is less prominent. Indeed, the general level
of quality seems lower, both in technique and invention. The
difficulties with the *Nickleby* plates may stem in part from
the same cause as Dickens' difficulties with the text, namely that
the novelist is attempting something which is new for him, a
comic novel with a single adult protagonist, yet which contains
both the picaresque and panoramic features of *Pickwick* and the
more organized thematic qualities of *Oliver Twist;* the artist is
thus perforce engaged on a new kind of venture, very different
from either the earlier *Pickwick* or the contemporaneous *Harry
Lorrequer*—a novel by Charles Lever both less serious and less
unified than *Pickwick.*

The novel as a whole is, I believe, actually less a progress in
the Hogarthian sense than is *Pickwick,* for Nicholas undergoes
no real internal development, but simply faces a series of difficulties from which he is ultimately rescued by a pair of
Pickwickian businessmen; and perhaps for this reason Browne
has less to comment upon in his etchings than in the earlier
novel, and much less than he will have in *Martin Chuzzlewit.*
There are, however, at least the seeds of social commentary in
the treatment of the moneylending villain, Ralph Nickleby, who
is at the center of the most iconographically interesting challenge
Browne was offered: the design for the serial version's front
cover (Illus. 27).

Of the seven such covers Browne designed for Dickens, two
are wholly allegorical, containing no reference to the novel's
characters or plot, while the other four combine allegory with
material directly related to the text. Since the wrapper had to be
ready by the time the first part was published, any details from
the novel would have had to originate in either specific authorial
instructions, a reading of some of the text of the first number, or
both. The overall design for *Nickleby* is based on traditional
motifs and is conceived in a general form that Browne was to use

several times. It is in the mode of seventeenth- and eighteenth-century engraved title pages which surround the words of the title with allegorical devices,[24] a form carried into the nineteenth century by George Cruikshank among others, who adapted it for comic purposes in the frontispieces or titles to such works as Egan's *Life in London* (1821) and David Carey's *Life in Paris* (1822). The idea of dividing the design into images of good fortune on the left side and ill fortune on the right, with the figure of Fortuna, blindfolded, at the top center, may have been prompted by the novel's subtitle, "Containing a Faithful Account of the Fortunes, Misfortunes, Uprisings, Downfallings, and Complete Career of the Nickleby Family"; such left–right division is later used for the wrappers to *Chuzzlewit, Dombey and Son,* and *David Copperfield.*

Although the images across the top seem conventional, Phiz's comic imagination is evident in the two fat men on stilts and in the figures at the bottom of the design, and his emblematic imagination in the middle-aged man, a kerchief tied over his hat, who is seen making his way through a swamp, surrounded by mocking imps holding lanterns, with a church in the distance. These imps are will-o'-the-wisps or "Jack-o'-Lanterns" (an alternative term which George Cruikshank was to use for an etching in his *Omnibus,* 1842), which became a favorite emblem of Browne's, and his use of it in the frontispiece to Albert Smith's *The Pottleton Legacy* (1849) and the cover for *Bleak House* indicates that it had for him the specific meaning of the temptation of riches leading one astray into a swamp of materialism. It seems probable that the central figure is intended for Ralph Nickleby, and that Browne's conception was based on the eleventh paragraph of the novel:

On the death of his father, Ralph Nickleby, who had been some time before placed in a mercantile house in London, applied himself passionately to his old pursuit of money-getting, in which he speedily became so buried and absorbed, that he quite forgot his brother for many years; and if at times a recollection of his old playfellow broke upon him through the haze in which he lived—for gold conjures up a mist about a man more destructive of all his old senses and lulling to his feelings than the fumes of charcoal—it brought along with it a companion thought, that if

they were intimate he would want to borrow money of him: and
Mr. Ralph Nickleby shrugged his shoulders, and said things
were better as they were.

(ch. 1, pp. 3–4)

In the design, the "mist" in which Ralph is enveloped thanks to
his pursuit of gold is recalled by the darkness of the swamp,
while the dulling of his senses may be represented by the scarf
tied over his ears; his apparent ignoring of the church is a further
extension of the idea of disregarding one's brother.

Certainly with *Nicholas Nickleby* Phiz worked harder than
with any other assignment, for the plates were not merely etched
in duplicate: according to Johannsen's investigations,[25] 14 were
etched in quadruplicate, 18 in triplicate—a total of 117 steels.
Such extra labor may in part account for the unevenness of the
results. Whatever the case, the very first plate to *Nicholas
Nickleby*, "Mr. Ralph Nickleby's first visit to his poor relations"
(ch. 3; Illus. 28), is a palpably theatrical scene which Browne had
trouble handling. The characters are caught at a crucial moment,
Ralph gruffly asserting his opinion of Nicholas' prospects,
Nicholas making a gesture of protest, and Kate comforting their
flustered and self-pitying mother. But except for Ralph, the
figures have no life—Nicholas' face has little expression and his
body is puppetlike, while the faces of his mother and sister are at
best ambiguous. There is more to be said for the cramped, claus-
trophobic effect of the room, which reflects the family's barely
shabby-genteel status and its dim future. Nicholas' figure seems
to be an attempt at the style of George Cruikshank which is
lacking in that artist's symmetry and grace, while Kate's face here
and elsewhere recalls the sentimental and idealized mode of the
Keepsake or *Friendship's Offering*. Although Phiz's virtuous
women remain somewhat idealized throughout his career, they
soon lose both the vapidity of expression and the raven tresses
etched so that they look like hairpieces.

The peacock feathers displayed prominently over the mirror
resemble those which appear so often in Phiz's work that it is
tempting to dismiss them as mere space fillers. They may have
been a common Victorian household ornament, but an artist with
Phiz's evident knowledge of graphic traditions could hardly have
been unaware of the symbolic meanings of such feathers. In

addition to pride, peacock feathers in a home are commonly associated with bad luck, perhaps because of the feathers' "spying eyes."[26] In the *Nickleby* plate they reflect the bad fortune that has hit the Nickleby family and foretell the worse fortune that is coming with Nicholas' employment by Squeers.

There is also an important technical aspect to this plate. At some point between the completion of *Pickwick* (October 1837) and the commencement of *Nickleby* (March 1838), Browne added to the crosshatch and other kinds of line and dot shading the use of a device known as the roulette, a small wheel at the end of a handle which, when rolled across the etching ground, produces a continuous series of dots, dashes, and the like, depending on the type of roulette. In the first plate of *Nicholas Nickleby*, its use can be seen in the carpet and on the lighter part of the ceiling; virtually every plate following has similar areas.[27] Although it is primarily a time-saver and Browne often uses it mechanically, this technique introduces a new smoothness of tone into his shading and is often employed in careful combination with other, less mechanical techniques.[28]

Despite the general weakness of the *Nickleby* plates, occasionally Browne shows evidence of having learned how to provide graphic continuity to sequences of plates stretched over more than a single part, in a novel whose action, however stilted, is less thoroughly episodic than *Pickwick*'s. Thus, in Parts III and IV he must illustrate two related strands of the story, in a sequence which might be described as a1–b1–b2–a2. The first and fourth, "The internal economy of Dotheboys Hall" (ch. 8) and "Nicholas astonishes Mr. Squeers and family" (ch. 13; Illus. 29), feature the same characters in exactly the same setting; the two sandwiched between, "Kate Nickleby sitting to Miss La Creevy" (ch. 10), and "Newman Noggs leaves the ladies in the empty house" (ch. 11), both center on Kate's London adventures while Nicholas is in Yorkshire. In addition to the connections between the members of the pair in each part, there are also links between each two adjacent etchings in the series of four, and the first and fourth plates have causal links as well.

In each of the two middle plates, Kate is being shown kindness by an eccentric but warmhearted person, but in the first Ralph Nickleby lurks in the wings while in the second the threat he represents is suggested in a secondary detail. As in the first his secret watching of Kate is ironically mirrored by a cat watching for a mouse beneath the platform, so in the second there is an actual mouse, which in addition to indicating the shabbiness of the house may symbolize Kate's defenselessness against her uncle's plots. But Ralph's spying on Kate parallels in a general way the companion plate, in which Ralph's co-conspirator Squeers is leading Nicholas into the horrors of Dotheboys Hall. In contrast, the plates in Part IV are relatively hopeful, for in the first the two women have found a male ally in Newman Noggs, while in the second Nicholas has taken matters into his own hands.

The two Dotheboys Halls plates form a before-and-after sequence: in the first, Phiz challenges Cruikshank as an artist of the grotesquely pitiable, attempting something in the vein of "Oliver asks for more." It has been remarked that Dickens' text is superior to Phiz's etching, "about which it seems difficult to say, as John Forster did about the text, that 'Dotheboys was, like a piece by Hogarth, both ludicrous and terrible.'"[29] Such a comparison seems too dismissive, but to contrast Browne with Cruikshank does reveal something about the former's virtues and limitations. For Browne does not achieve, with his ragged, starving boys, anything like the preternatural effect of Cruikshank's workhouse lads who have been reduced to a subhuman level, with their stupefied expressions and sunken eyes, and even the bony structure of their faces and the shapes of their cropped heads. By contrast, Browne's are still recognizably boys, but boys with melodramatic faces either virtuous and horrified or wizened and grotesque.

I think one grasps Browne's special talents only by considering this illustration along with its sequel. In the first, Nicholas is seen as simultaneously victim and oppressor: Squeers's stick is held with its point at his breast, so that the master–servant relationship is clear, yet at the same time Nicholas is, spatially, *above* the pupils, looking down upon them as if in his unwilling collaboration with Squeers he, too, is a "master." In the sequel we find Nicholas down in the boys' midst; he has become their ally against the Squeerses. The composition is of a kind favored by the early Phiz for scenes of violence, comic or real—a whirl of figures around one or two central ones (compare "Mr. Crow well plucked," in Lever's *Charles O'Malley*, 1840 [Illus. 30]).

Nicholas' pose may be somewhat stagy, but nowhere near as much so as Dickens' verbal handling of Nicholas' denunciation of Squeers.

Another kind of continuity is established in Parts VII through X, where nearly all the plates deal in some way with acting, disguise, or pretense. As a group these plates emphasize the extent to which acting becomes a major metaphor in the novel. Unfortunately for the novel as a whole, the effect is to make those plates in which Nicholas appears seem largely melodramatic, since they seem to imply that there is little difference between the protagonist's life and acting. But such large considerations aside, most of the plates in question are extremely effective. For example, no one is more an actor than Mr. Mantalini in "The Professional Gentlemen at Madame Mantalini's" (ch. 21), except the same man in later plates, or the Kenwigs family. The portly Mr. Crummles and his boys look far more natural in "The Country Manager rehearses a Combat" (ch. 22), especially when we consider that they do not pretend to be what they are not. In this plate, Browne implies a complex relation of acting to reality by including both a portrait of the fat host, who has some resemblance to Crummles, and a picture of Don Quixote and Sancho Panza. Thus, the illustration is a graphic version of a novel that deals with acting and pretense, and within that illustration there is yet another, based upon a book which is in turn a fiction *about* fiction, and the chivalric pretensions of Don Quixote. But the Quixote reference here applies also to Nicholas and Smike, who have set out in the world to seek their fortunes—a quest which turns out in a sense to be futile, since Nicholas ultimately must depend upon the benevolence of others.

We are actually on the stage in "The great bespeak for Miss Snevellici" (ch. 24), which presents the reality–fiction relationship in a different way. The illustration shows nothing of the actors and only a bit of the stage; because of the way they are framed by a scenic flat, footlights, the left side of the stage, and the orchestra, the members of the audience appear to be the ones putting on the performance. Much in the style of a caricaturist of individual faces, Phiz has stressed the audience's oddities, their individual eccentricities and exaggerated behavior, which is as conventionalized in its way as actors'—the overeffusiveness of the Borums, the stereotyped demeanor of the smitten young officer, the transfixion of the ginger-beer boy. All of this is in the text except for the basic graphic device, the exclusion of the actors and the theatrical framing of the audience.

The plates for Part IX further convey Dickens' and Phiz's vision of a confusion between appearance and reality. In "Affectionate behaviour of Messrs. Pyke & Pluck" (ch. 27), Sir Mulberry's two henchmen are performing for the benefit of Mrs. Nickleby, who in her stupidity—which is actually stereotyped behavior operating as a defense against reality—of course does not know it is a performance. The falsity of Pyke and Pluck (who are after all only acting out their everyday roles) contrasts with the range of genuine emotion expressed by the costumed actors in the companion plate, "Nicholas hints at the probability of his leaving the company" (ch. 29). Mrs. Crummles' costume as a queen does not prevent her surprise and consternation from seeming genuine, nor do their disguises as savage and demon conceal the glee of the two actors at lower left at the prospective departure of their rival. As usual, Nicholas has the stagiest expression of all, and he is not even in stage dress.

The most interesting plates in the remainder of the novel include several which deal with the novel's villains, and one particularly successful comic illustration. Squeers, so roundly defeated by Nicholas back in the fourth number, has a temporary triumph in "A sudden recognition, unexpected on both sides" (ch. 38; Illus. 31). One of Phiz's most complex creations for this novel, the illustration is suggestive as to the ways artist and author worked together. Its major details, including the manner in which Squeers has hooked Smike with his umbrella, the hod carriers, the schoolboy and apple woman, are all in Dickens' text, and were probably taken by Browne from a portion of the manuscript sent to him, if not from detailed instructions. The note by Dickens on the surviving drawing ("I don't think Smike is frightened enough or Squeers earnest enough—for my purpose")[30] does not tell us very much, for we have no way of knowing how much Browne finally altered the faces, the drawing being much like the etching. But Browne seems to have added details not in the text: the fishing tackle shop with its realistic sign, alluding to Squeers's "hooking" of Smike; and the notice, "Seminary for

Young Ladies / French by a Native," an oblique comment upon the Yorkshire "seminary" to which Squeers wishes to return Smike.

The details in the right half of the background are likely Browne's response to Squeers's telling Wackford to "call up one of the coaches" (p. 374), since a coach is shown waiting by the curb with a somnolent coachman on the box. But in the street itself Phiz shows an omnibus apparently racing another vehicle, whose horses are visible in full flight immediately behind. The omnibus driver is vigorously whipping his animals, while the omnibus cad standing at the rear sarcastically pretends to look at the pursuing vehicle through his purse as if it were a monocle; a face, frightened by the vehicle's speed, looks out of the rear of the omnibus. The whipping of the horses may be intended as a forecast of the gleeful "threshing" Smike will soon receive in a coach, and the anxiety of the passenger, the race of coaches, and above all the sneering look of the "cad," mirror the imminent abduction of Smike from his friends, who, however, will soon be on the trail of the Squeerses.

Three illustrations, in Parts VI, X, and XVI, feature the upper-class villain, Sir Mulberry Hawk, and his foolish young follower, Lord Frederick Verisopht. These names are less Dickensian than they are Hogarthian, reminding one of Tom Rakewell, Moll Hackabout, and Lord Squanderfield, and while all three plates make use of extreme caricatural technique rather than the subtler character drawing of Hogarth, the first two use art objects emblematically, while the second and third express meaning through their disposition of forms. Thus, in "Miss Nickleby introduced to her Uncle's friends" (ch. 19), the introduction of Innocence to Lust is paralleled by the juxtaposition on the mantelpiece of what looks like an extremely modest and shrinking figurine with a decorative clock clearly representing Vulcan (or perhaps Bacchus) in his violent and lustful ascendancy with two fair maidens at his feet. A painting above Lord Frederick's head might be an emblematic depiction of a storm engulfing a ship (or a church?), but Phiz was less careful with such details in these early years than he later became, and the painting varies so greatly among the three steels that it is impossible to be certain.

The visual structure of "Nicholas attracted by the mention of his Sister's name in the Coffee Room" (ch. 32) is such that the vicious noblemen seem to be triumphant, for they occupy the center and top of the design, while Nicholas is far below them. Dickens describes the room as having been decorated with the "choicest specimens of French paper, enriched with a gilded cornice of elegant design" (ch. 32, p. 310), but Browne's interpretation adds a new dimension not directly stated in the text. The wallpapers in the etching depict what look like *Arabian Nights* scenes, although no particular tales can be identified. The implication is that these members of the upper classes inhabit a world of voluptuousness and vicious make-believe, a world opposed and eventually defeated in the novel by the morally responsible middle classes. But there is a more specific comment in the right-hand detail, which shows one man reverently bowed down before an imperious standing figure; since they are before a castle, and their positions parallel those of Hawk and Nicholas, the lower orders' proper attitude towards the nobility (from the upper-class point of view) is suggested. Nicholas, of course, is about to rise up and challenge Sir Mulberry and to scar his face, so that the detail on the wall is clearly sardonic.

The downfall of Hawk and his gull, Verisopht, is depicted in "The last brawl between Sir Mulbery and his pupil" (ch. 50; Illus. 32). Its setting is described by Dickens in vivid but visually unspecific terms, in a passage which begins, "The excitement of play, hot rooms, and glaring lights, was not calculated to allay the fever of the time. In that giddy whirl of noise and confusion the men were delirious" (ch. 50, p. 500). The description reminds one of Plate VI, the gambling den, of *A Rake's Progress,* although such a sense of confusion is more evident in Hogarth's murky painting of the subject than in the precise lines of his engraving. But whether or not Dickens had Hogarth's gambling hell in mind, Phiz's overturned chairs and gamblers (not in Dickens' text) recall rather Hogarth's *A Midnight Modern Conversation* (Illus. 33). Although he does derive directly from the text, the man standing on the table, forming the apex of the pyramidal design, gives the whole scene something of the composition of the latter Hogarth engraving, whose apex is a similarly standing man, gesticulating with a glass.

The fevered chaos of Dickens' description is reflected in the playing cards suspended in mid-air and the unstable position of the fallen man at lower right; the solid band of figures across the center of the design also suggests something of the feverish atmosphere. We remain, however, faced with a serious question as to how well the general mode in which Phiz works suits Dickens' more subjective and impressionistic passages. Without referring explicitly to this problem, one critic has gone so far as to argue that there is a disparity between the fantastic and dreamlike subject matter of such an artist as Cruikshank and the very precise, controlled nature of his etched line; I believe the problem to be more complicated than this critic seems to recognize, but something of his argument could certainly be applied to Phiz as illustrator of Dickens.[31] Without claiming that each and every illustration accords with the mode of the particular passage being illustrated, I think it is possible to show that (at least through *Little Dorrit*) Browne strove to conceive methods that would fit with his author's stylistic development. In "The last brawl between Sir Mulbery and his pupil" both the possible allusion to Hogarth and the way Browne chose to deal with the crowd—especially in the dark tonality of the central band of figures—indicate that his methods were far from static, even if they were at this stage dominated by a caricatural mode.

Browne's caricatural method of character portrayal is perhaps most happily employed in the illustration of what must be considered a minor incident in the story, though it is one of the most memorable, and foreshadows Dickens' almost surreal comic inventiveness in later novels. The escaped madman in "The Gentleman next door declares his passion for Mrs. Nickleby" (ch. 41) is portrayed as a grotesque through the heavy use of etched lines on his face, and Mrs. Nickleby's simper is equally caricatural. Further, the shapes of the vegetables he has thrown over the wall are more evidently phallic than anything short of a much more explicit text could convey. But Browne employs other modes as well. Kate appears once again as a simpering maiden out of a *Keepsake* book, while the two birds at upper left, touching beaks in the sky, comment amusingly on Mrs. Nickleby's self-delusion about her suitor's love for her. Finally, the handling of foliage is an example of a new pictorial richness in Browne's technique.

Browne is in general less successful with the sentimental plot—the encounters of Nicholas with Madeline, the troubles of Kate, and the fate of Smike. At their worst, such plates are incompetent, as in the portrayal of Madeline in "Nicholas recognizes the Young Lady unknown" (ch. 40),[32] or are centered on awkward, melodramatic poses, as in "Nicholas congratulates Arthur Gride on his Wedding Morning" (ch. 54). At their best, they help to sum up the novel's moral themes, as in the designs related to Smike in which the action unfolds in a wooded setting: "The recognition" (ch. 58), and "The children at their cousin's grave" (ch. 65). The latter plate is the last etching in the book and the first appearance of a church since the wrapper, where Ralph Nickleby was seen to be lost to Christianity in a swamp of materialism. Here, the characters are in harmony with Nature, the Church, and with the Christian view of suffering and death as embodied in the story of Smike. It is nothing like what Browne accomplishes by use of frontispieces for summing up the central meanings of a novel (and in this one, a portrait of the author by Maclise is the frontispiece). Although the sentimental style returns from time to time, it remains a far less important aspect of Browne's development away from the caricatural than is what we might call the "sequential" mode. The two novels in *Master Humphrey's Clock*, which follow almost immediately upon *Nicholas Nickleby*, are special among Browne's assignments for Dickens, and yet they may be seen as preparations for the next novel in monthly parts, *Martin Chuzzlewit*, in which Browne's debt to and development of the Hogarthian tradition, the "progress" in all its complex manifestations, first really crystallize.

CHAPTER THREE

From Caricature to Progress: *Master Humphrey's Clock* and *Martin Chuzzlewit*

T he mode of publication—weekly instead of the usual monthly installments—with "woodcuts dropped into the text," as well as collaboration with two artists,[1] led Dickens to make new use of illustrations for the two novels which constitute the bulk of his periodical, *Master Humphrey's Clock*. Not only did Dickens have in his service George Cattermole's Gothic, architectural talents in addition to Browne's comic, sentimental, and grotesque ones, but the illustrations—more numerous and placed precisely where the novelist wanted them in the text— could serve to sustain certain moods and tones more extensively than could two etchings per monthly part. In some respects the illustrations to *The Old Curiosity Shop* and *Barnaby Rudge* are more truly integral parts of the text than any of the other illustrations in Dickens' novels.[2]

At the same time, because each cut illustrates a relatively smaller portion of the text, each one usually can bear less freight of thematic significance than the etchings for the monthly-part novels. The result is something closer to the modern comic strip than to the Hogarthian moral progress, though those two also are related.[3] Dickens could have Browne devote three cuts to the incidents surrounding Dick Swiveller's illness and the Marchioness' heroism (in chapters 64, 65, and 66),[4] when one or at most two etchings would have been provided according to the usual ratio; or, in *Barnaby Rudge* he could have his artists show, in three successive cuts, Haredale arming at home (ch. 42—Cattermole), meeting Chester and Gashford in Westminster Hall (ch. 43—Cattermole), and then standing with his foot on the fallen Gashford, pointing accusingly at Chester (ch. 43—Browne). Indeed, sequences of up to nine (or, if the definition is broadened, eighteen) cuts can be identified, with the result that if one goes through the illustrations with brief quotations from the text (as in *The Dickens Picture Book*[5]), the effect is virtually like reading a complete comic strip, with few details that are totally obscure to someone who has never read the novel.

Some statistics will indicate how this sequential specificity is possible: *The Old Curiosity Shop* is about five-eighths the length of a novel like *David Copperfield*, while *Barnaby Rudge* is about three-fourths the length of such novels; but the *Shop* has seventy-five illustrations and *Rudge* seventy-six, compared with the usual forty. Thus proportionately there are two to three times as many illustrations in the weekly installments of *Master Humphrey's Clock* as in a monthly-parts novel.

There is also a fundamental difference between what Dickens, Cattermole, and Browne achieve in the *Clock* novels and what Thackeray does with "woodcuts dropped into the text" in *Vanity Fair* and *Pendennis*. Thackeray's directly illustrative etchings and woodcuts are generally much less striking in effect than are his numerous initial letters and tailpieces, most of which are wittily emblematic as they provide symbolic commentary. In contrast, there are only twenty-five initial letters throughout the *Clock*, and few have any connection with the text; at the same time, the *Clock*'s full-size cuts are, with a few important exceptions, devoid of emblematic details. Further, in contrast to Browne's developing practice in the monthly-part novels (where he increasingly emphasizes parallels between etchings), the relation of his and Cattermole's individual cuts in the *Clock* is largely sequential rather than thematic.

After the necessarily halting start, given the change in plans regarding *The Old Curiosity Shop*, which was originally intended as a short story, the illustrations settle down into a fairly consistent pattern: two cuts per number, usually full size but sometimes one a small tailpiece, and occasionally an initial letter at the opening of a number. Early in the work the narrative and hence the graphic sequences are short, but by the fifteenth weekly number there is a six-cut sequence running through three numbers and five chapters; and from the second half of Number 19 through Number 23 a sequence of nine cuts, all by Browne, runs from chapter 24 through chapter 32. Considering that Browne was "never at home with the technique of wood cutting" because he could not envision "what changes an engraver might make in the appearance of his drawing"[6], the frantic pace involved in illustrating a weekly rather than a monthly publication, the effect of employing various engravers, and the other work Phiz had in hand at the time, the results are of surprisingly high quality, although the engravers did seem to have trouble with facial expressions. Phiz frequently seemed to treat the medium as if he expected the results to equal those obtained by etching, but the engravers often obliged by providing as subtle shading as can be produced by the method. In this respect the results are generally more successful than those achieved by his co-illustrator. Phiz was notably more skillful than Cattermole in dealing with human figures close up, and even his worst engraver, C. Gray, could not always drag him down to his level of crudity.

Although many of Browne's early cuts for *The Old Curiosity Shop* are somewhat caricatured, comic portrayals of characters, his Quilp is a notable creation. Less has been said in favor of his Nell, but compared to Cattermole's, who is either a wax doll or barely visible, Browne makes us believe in the "cherry-cheeked, red-lipped" child Quilp describes so lecherously, and yet the artist never loses the pathos of Nell's situation—indeed, it could be argued that Phiz's Nell is more flesh and blood than Dickens'. Phiz seems to have transcended the rigidity of figure which characterized his virtuous females in *Nicholas Nickleby*.

The stylistic differences between the two illustrators are especially of interest because Browne traced all of George Cattermole's drawings for the earlier numbers—and some of the later ones as well—and transferred them to the woodblock.[7] The way Dickens seems to have seen the respective functions of his two illustrators, and the difficulty he had at times keeping to that conception, is typified in the evidence regarding an engraving of Nell cowering in fear that she will be seen by Quilp, who gestures to Tom Scott beneath an old arched gateway (ch. 27). As

Dickens wrote to Cattermole, the scene was put in "expressly
with a view to your illustrious pencil. By a mistake, however, it
went to Browne instead."[8] Mrs. Leavis is probably correct in
conjecturing that Browne achieved a better effect than Cattermole would have, especially in emphasizing Dickens' description of Quilp ("like some monstrous image that had come down
from its niche") by suggesting a visual parallel between the grotesque stone carvings and Quilp himself.[9] And the use of heavy,
sinister looking architecture seems a precursor of Browne's later
treatment of buildings in his dark plates. Just how one should
read the significance of the empty niches is more questionable,
since Dickens' text specifically associates niches with monsters,
rather than with the "guardian saints" Mrs. Leavis mentions.

Dickens' intention to give the subject to Cattermole implies a
peculiar prejudice in favor of this artist and a mistaken precon-
ception about what subjects Browne is most capable of handling;
it may be symptomatic that in no surviving correspondence does
Dickens praise Browne's work as effusively as Cattermole's. The
novelist also intended Cattermole to do the first illustration for
Number 22, that of Nell and the cart which travels around town
advertising the waxwork (ch. 29); he had even enclosed a "scrap"
of the manuscript for that subject in the letter referred to above.
But for reasons unknown, Browne did that one too.

If Browne was not Dickens' ideal illustrator for the more heart-
rending episodes featuring Nell, he was certainly the one to
manage a problem of interpretation such as was given to him
with the character of the "Marchioness," the scullery maid of
uncertain origins and age. Until the novel's last chapter, we are
never told how old she is, and she seems at times a very small
child and at other times an adolescent (according to the narrator
in the final chapter, she is Nell's contemporary, thirteen or fourteen). It is tempting to conjecture that Dickens let Browne into
his secret that he intended to make her the daughter of Sally and
Quilp, omitting the crucial passage only later, when he revised
the proofs.[10] For there is a definite resemblance between the
faces of Sally and the "small servant," in the latter's first appearance (in the cut showing them outside the Single Gentleman's
door—[ch. 35]). This resemblance is not noticeable in the next
cut, depicting Dick spying upon the Marchioness' meager meal

(ch. 36), nor is it repeated. Browne subsequently shows the Marchioness as a wizened creature, looking like a little old woman (the card-playing scene, ch. 57; Illus. 34), as a fay-like being (in Dick's sickroom, ch. 64), and as a not implausibly improvable young girl (arriving with edibles for Dick, ch. 66). A few years later, as one in a set of four extra illustrations for the novel, Browne portrayed the Marchioness (Illus. 35), supposedly as she was at the sickroom stage of the book, as an attractive girl in late adolescence—less an instance, I think, of Phiz's inconsistency than of his response to the mixed intentions of the novelist in his making the Marchioness the offspring of the demonic Quilp and Sally, a workhouse orphan who has suffered great privations, and yet at the same time a suitable wife for Dick.[11]

Dickens divided the labor between Phiz and Cattermole very carefully in the later parts of Nell's odyssey through the English countryside. Between Numbers 29 and 31, Nell is brought through the hellish part of her story into a temporary Slough of Despond, and thence to the gateway of Paradise; for the reader she is brought, literally, from the fantasy world of Dickens and Phiz to the fantasy world of Dickens and Cattermole. Phiz illustrates the old man's temptation by List and Jowl (ch. 42); his rescue as Nell takes him across on the ferry (ch. 43); the night spent by the furnace (ch. 44) and the rebellious mob (ch. 45), both in the same number; and finally, Nell lying unconscious in the inn, where the schoolmaster has taken her (ch. 46). To Cattermole falls the task of depicting the church and house to which she comes to die, and Phiz has only one more cut including Nell. No doubt Cattermole, in his emphasis on buildings in this series of cuts detailing the end of Nell, came closer to Dickens' wishes than Browne could have done, although the deathbed scene is most distressing in its portrayal of Nell as a kind of proto-Flora Finching (ch. 71). One may see in the architectural emphasis an unconscious corroboration of the Freudian interpretation of Nell's death as a return to the womb—the houses clearly symbolic in this context. The suitability of these illustrations to Dickens' deeper conflicts and fantasies, especially with regard to the death of Mary Hogarth, may explain why he bestowed such effusive praise on Cattermole. One would like to agree with Mrs. Leavis that Phiz "could never have produced" anything "as sentimental and religiose" as Nell's "transference to a better world in the arms of the angels";[12] but Browne was perfectly capable of his own religiosity and sentimentality, as we can see from the angels in his frontispiece to the second volume of *Master Humphrey's Clock*. For Browne absorbed many influences besides that of caricature, including Christian iconography, German Romantic art, and the influence of some of his contemporaries among British painters, such as Maclise.

It is, however, as a caricaturist that Dickens regarded Browne at this point. It is possible that Phiz's designs for *The Old Curiosity Shop* presented Dickens with disturbing visual evidence of his text's implications. Never again do the original illustrations for a Dickens novel portray so much low life or so much exuberant energy. The character who epitomizes both is Quilp.

Despite my own Freudian leanings, I have been skeptical of Mark Spilka's description of Quilp's shape as "phallic";[13] yet Browne's Quilp brings out visually what is only implied in the text: his relation, as a dwarf, to the folklore of the "little man," "John Thomas," and the like. (The best known quasi-innocent embodiment of this figure is, of course, Rumpelstiltskin, the hunchback whose power over the miller's daughter lies in her promise to give him her baby.)

Quilp cavorts through sixteen cuts (excluding one by Cattermole and the more quiescent illustration of Quilp's death), five of which, following the text, have him thrusting himself through doors and windows, often preceded by his tall, narrow hat (Illus. 36). In another he is shown having gone through a gateway. Elsewhere he is usually engaged in violent or disreputable behavior: leaning back in his chair with his feet on the table, smoking a long, upward-pointing cigar while his wife sits by submissively; sitting on his desk while Nell stands apprehensively near by; smoking in the grandfather's chair with his bandy legs halfway up in the air; beating savagely at Dick, whom he has mistaken for his own wife; rolling on the ground, tormenting his dog; sitting on a beer barrel, raucously drinking and enjoying Sampson's discomfort; and beating at the effigy of Kit. Also in this latter illustration (ch. 16), the figure of Punch on the tombstone is like an incarnation of Quilp as Nell's pursuer; the puppet even looks as though it is making an obscene gesture at Nell.[14] The cumulative effect of Phiz's illustrations is to emphasize embedded sexual nuances and to bring to the novel the vital energy of comic rascality.

But Browne's last two depictions of Quilp mark an important break in the tone with which he is presented in the novel. The portrait of the dwarf (ch. 60), in large scale, stresses much more the malevolent, demonic side of Quilp than his subversive comic grotesqueness. This plate also includes one of the novel's few emblematic inscriptions, "[Accommodations for] Man and Beast." The insinuation about Quilp's evil and ambiguous nature is clear enough. If Dickens gave specific directions for this portrait, one might say it is as though he needed to have Quilp's evil qualities stressed at this point when he was preparing for the comic villain's downfall. With Phiz's design for Quilp's death scene (ch. 67), any trace of Punchinello fun has been eliminated.

When we realize that the number of illustrations featuring Quilp is close to half the total number of drawings for the considerably longer novels in monthly parts, we get some statistical sense of the impact of Quilp's visual presence. Surely, illustrations make it impossible to conceal from oneself the dominant role of this delightful villain.

But the visual immediacy of violence and low life in the novel is not limited to the appearances of Quilp. There are the slovenliness and drinking of Dick Swiveller; the monstrousness of Sally and Sampson Brass; the caricaturistic excesses of Mrs. Jarley, Codlin and Short, the gamblers, and even Kit and his mother; the weird vigor of the Marchioness; and the boisterous drinking of Nell's and her grandfather's companions on the raft. What I am arguing is that in *The Old Curiosity Shop* more than in any of the other novels, Phiz's illustrations—and the more noticeably so in their contrast with Cattermole's—emphasize the unruliness of the energies unleashed by Dickens' imagination. Thanks to Phiz to some extent the illustrated novel is dominated by those energies rather than by the idealizing and religious sentiments which Dickens himself evidently wished to consider the main thrust of the work.[15]

Dickens has these energies somewhat more under control in *Barnaby Rudge*, and the evolution of Phiz from an illustrator in the caricature tradition of Cruikshank and Seymour to a nineteenth-century version of Hogarth ("moralized") is well

under way. However, Phiz still shows uncertainness about his
art, so that inconsistencies of characterization are perhaps more
noticeable than in *The Old Curiosity Shop*. Other than Miggs,
Sim, and Barnaby, no character stands out as an individual creation, and the handling of Hugh is particularly uneven. Hugh's
first appearance is a full-length portrait (ch. 11), achieving very
much what the text demands; he is a "poaching rascal," who
nonetheless in his "muscular and handsome proportions . . .
might have served a painter for a model" (p. 298). In most of the
subsequent cuts, Hugh looks more like a conventional comic–
grotesque lout, although in his final appearance just before he is
executed, he suddenly takes on a rather incredible nobility of
feature (ch. 77).

It is difficult to say whether these inconsistencies are a response to Dickens' varying treatment of Hugh, a result of
Browne's artistic tentativeness, or simply the fault of the
engravers. Certainly the figure of Dennis the hangman is barely
recognizable from one cut to another, and he appears in eleven.
The illustrations with which Phiz seems to have taken most care
are the few portraits of individual characters—especially Hugh
and Miggs (ch. 9), whose reptilian face reminds us of the conventions of caricature portraits; Mr. Chester at his ease (ch. 15);
and the cuts of Barnaby with Grip the raven (ch. 12; ch. 58).

Phiz makes somewhat more play with emblematic details in
Barnaby Rudge than in its immediate predecessor, although
there is not yet much of the parallel and antithesis between illustrations that will become so noticeable in his work for *Martin
Chuzzlewit* and beyond. The first instance of such a detail in
Barnaby Rudge may provide some insight into the way Browne's
invention worked. At the end of chapter 19, Mrs. Varden finds
herself stupefied by the variety of food available at the Maypole,
and the narrator comments that perhaps even a "Peacock" might
be available for a meal. No incident from this chapter is illustrated, but near the beginning of the next chapter, in the same
weekly number, we find a cut by Browne with Dolly Varden
looking at herself in a mirror which seems to be decorated with
peacock feathers. These probably allude to Dolly's vanity, but
they may in addition imply the traditional superstition of impending bad luck, for Dolly is shortly to meet Hugh and lose her

bracelet. It is likely that Browne in this case received his idea through an accidental process of association; such an openness to random inspiration is a cardinal virtue in a man who must produce many kinds of illustrations at so terrific a pace.

Phiz next uses an emblematic detail in a cut showing Mrs. Varden and Miggs enjoying their moral self-righteousness (ch. 27), while Mr. Chester skillfully plays upon this moral vanity and Sim Tappertit ogles the more honestly vain Dolly. On the chimneypiece is an oval picture of Christ and the children (another version of which decorated the chimneypiece of Master Humphrey in Phiz's rendering, to be replaced at the close of the *Clock* by Cattermole's rendering of the Good Samaritan),[16] whose ironic relevance to the lack of humility, and unchristian self-satisfaction of the women seems clear. A few chapters later another biblical allusion is introduced in the scene where Mr. Chester disowns his son Edward for refusing to marry for money instead of love (ch. 32; Illus. 37). Here there is a large painting of Abraham preparing to sacrifice Isaac (a detail which Thackeray later used, verbally, in a parallel situation in *Vanity Fair*).[17] The ironic contrast, of course, is between Abraham's willingness to sacrifice his son out of obedience to God, and Chester's sacrificing his son out of pure selfishness; the father's raised nutcrackers and Abraham's raised knife further emphasize the contrast. A similar detail is present in Plate III of *A Harlot's Progress*, where, Ronald Paulson has suggested, it is meant to compare ironically God's and man's justice,[18] and Browne will use it again in a quite different context in *Bleak House*. Another detail is associated with Mr. Chester later in the novel (ch. 75), when Gabriel informs him of his bastard son Hugh's incarceration in Newgate, and he is amazed at the lack of "some pleading of natural affection in [his] breast" (p. 379). Upon the wall in the cut is a picture of a woman with two children at her bosom, rather unsubtly captioned "Nature."

The other emblematic details in the *Barnaby Rudge* engravings are of a comic–grotesque sort. In the depiction of Hugh and Dennis engaging in a wild, "extemporaneous No-Popery Dance" (ch. 38), a sketch is displayed on the wall of a hanged man dancing at the end of his rope, foreshadowing the scoundrels' end. And in another lowly comic cut, where Dennis pretends to admire Miggs so as to win her allegiance against her captive mistress, the neck of a dead goose hangs down off a shelf immediately next to the scrawny neck and bosom of the ludicrously vain servant girl, whose face is leering with mock-erotic vanity (ch. 70); the function of Moll Hackabout's goose in *A Harlot's Progress*, I, is surely similar.

Perhaps these particular emblems do not represent a high order of interpretation on Browne's part, but they do foreshadow greater achievements. Similarly, the two attractive frontispieces he designed for the *Clock* (to Volumes II and III), do no more than bring some of the main characters and incidents together within structures based on the idea of the clock. Phiz apparently did not feel very inspired by the last-minute request for the first of these frontispieces, for he wrote to Dickens asking for "some sort of notion of the design you wish."[19] Subsequent novels by Dickens were to provide more fertile thematic material, and in the next, *Martin Chuzzlewit*, Phiz develops something approaching a systematic iconography, both in terms of broad allegorical treatment and localized emblems in individual etchings. But on another level, he is to develop a genuinely (and sometimes literally) Hogarthian way of treating the novel as a set of moral progresses.

As *Martin Chuzzlewit* is near the center of Hablot Browne's series of ten collaborations with Charles Dickens, so it is a crucial turning point in the career of each man. Browne's essential style is established and his ability to interpret the text by means of parallelism, antithesis, and emblematic details emerges brilliantly. And Dickens has for the first time organized a full-length novel around a cluster of moral themes and the moral progress of a central as well as peripheral characters, thus providing Phiz with the inspiration that his particular kind of interpretative talent required. Of equal importance is Dickens' development as a creator of grotesques. Brilliant as a Jingle, a Squeers, or a Quilp may be, they belong more to popular comic traditions and to folklore than to the conventions of satirical comedy; Quilp, for example, remains a demon, fixed in a set of grotesque gestures, who evokes ambivalent responses analogous to audience reactions to the Vice character in medieval morality plays.[20] A Pecksniff is much more profoundly disturbing because he exists within "respectable" society, and mirrors some of its pervasive ethical confusions. He is a figure with a mask, but we never know which is self and which is mask (as Phiz's frontispiece will so beautifully bring out), and from one standpoint he is the quintessence of bourgeois respectability.

Dickens' grotesques thus become more complex, and accordingly Browne's new style loses something of the affinity with caricature defined strictly as the exaggeration of physical characteristics for the purpose of ridicule. In *Martin Chuzzlewit's* illustrations the figures are less cramped, the faces less grimacing—Mrs. Gamp a notable exception, rendered in the old exaggerated style. To modern critical sensibilities this change may seem more significant than the increasing frequency of emblematic details in the etchings; to some, the moral progress of young Martin Chuzzlewit is a paltry thing compared to the proliferation of great comic characters and the new emphasis upon vivification of the external scene. Yet *Martin Chuzzlewit* is built upon an essential superstructure of several moral progresses. Without this structure, it is doubtful whether Dickens could have achieved the triumphs of Pecksniff and Mrs. Gamp— just as without Nell he could not have conceived Quilp. Browne's visual and emblematic contributions to this structure are integral to the novel, in the sense that they affect the way we look at the whole overtly moral aspect of the work. It also seems more than a coincidence that the enormous increase of emblematically significant, external details in the etchings should occur at the same time as Dickens' increased emphasis upon external objects—the wind in chapter 2, the view of Todgers's, the Temple fountain—an emphasis which increases steadily in the succeeding novels. Since in his illustrations to Thomas Miller's *Godfrey Malvern*, a year before *Chuzzlewit*, Phiz had already begun to rely more heavily on emblematic details, one cannot attribute their presence in *Chuzzlewit* solely or even directly to the influence of Dickens; rather, it is a sign of the artistic compatibility between Dickens and his illustrator, and of the affinity of their respective careers.

Although the monthly wrapper to *Martin Chuzzlewit* seems to bear even less direct relation to the novel than does that for *Nicholas Nickleby*, in fact it sets out a group of general themes

directly relevant to the novel. Taken together with the frontispiece (appearing in the last monthly part), the wrapper's design
is important since the frontispiece applies the cover's imagery to
the specific material of the book and completes and makes intelligible the cover's iconography. Together the cover (appearing
with every part), and the frontispiece (retrospective in the serial
edition because it appeared only in the last installment, but in-
troductory in the bound volume) help yoke the novel and its
illustrations into a special kind of unity. This unity is established
by thematic rather than sequential links which result partly from
Dickens' choices of subject and partly from Browne's interpretations of those choices (Illus. 38 and 39).

The wrapper itself is allegorical, and in some ways typical of
Browne's covers for Dickens and other novelists. Like that of
Nicholas Nickleby it presents a dichotomy between good and
bad fortune, on left and right sides of the design; but it goes
further toward establishing the notion of a *progress* by carrying
through a cycle from birth to death. Thus, born in wretchedness,
one dies in obscurity (right side); born in luxury, one dies honored (left side). Browne seems to have taken some of his imagery
from the novel's full title, which includes a promise to reveal
"Who Inherited the Family Plate, Who Came in for the Silver
Spoons, and Who for the Wooden Ladles," since silver spoons
decorate the footboard of the cradle of fortunate life, while a
giant wooden ladle is thrust through the top of the impoverished
cradle. Taken by itself without the complementary frontispiece,
the wrapper expresses a view contrary to the underlying philosophy of the novel. The figure of a man in the shape of a top who is
whipped and taunted by the Fates, as well as the implication that
accidents of birth determine one's lot, suggest that fortune is
entirely beyond one's control; the novel's thematic purpose,
however, stresses the possibility of moral choice from whence
one's ultimate condition emanates.

Some of the same details are used in the frontispiece to correct
the cynicism of the wrapper and to bring the allegory into line
with the explicit moral vision of the novel. The wrapper shows
the generalized symbols of cup-and-ball toys: good fortune represented by a smiling ball (which will land in its cup), a bird of
paradise, and roses; bad fortune by thorns, an owl sitting on a
gibbet, and a suffering ball about to be impaled upon the handle

of its inverted cup. In the frontispiece, some of these symbols are altered: the hand which held the fortunate cup is revealed as belonging to a beautiful female who supports Tom Pinch's head upon a rose-garlanded cup, while the other hand belongs to a disgusting harpy who impales Pecksniff's head upon a thorn-entwined shaft. The comic Fates of the wrapper also show up again as hooded females besetting Jonas. On the whole, the parallels between frontispiece and wrapper create continuity: promises are made in general terms at the beginning, fulfilled in the text and plates throughout, and given a final summation and resolution in the frontispiece.

For many modern readers the least interesting, artistically, of moral progresses in *Martin Chuzzlewit* is that of its eponymous hero. Whether or not one considers Martin's change from a self-centered young dandy to a responsible middle-class Christian gentleman to be impressive as an example of novelistic realism, it is in large part upon this young man's development that the novel depends. While the stories (or progresses in the Hogarthian sense) of Pecksniff and Tom Pinch are equal in substance to Martin's and may well be greater artistic achievements, their evolution depends upon the conventional prodigal son story of young Martin; they parallel and throw light upon that story. At the same time, a number of secondary characters also are given "progresses," which in turn reflect upon the three main characters.

The extant evidence (i.e., full instructions for five of the plates) indicates that Dickens chose each subject to be illustrated with great care, and provided a good deal of specific direction; but that same evidence also shows clearly that Browne's freedom to interpret was considerable. Browne used that freedom to make thematic commentary by means of emblematic details, formal parallels between contiguous and scattered plates, character placement, physiognomy, and several kinds of external allusion.

Although young Martin does not enter the novel in person until chapter 5, or the illustrations themselves until Part IV of the serialized version, the ten illustrations to the first five parts, taken together, form a sequence that describes the first stage of Martin's development. This stage is intertwined both thematically and narratively with the progresses of Pecksniff and Pinch. Most immediately striking in a review of these ten plates is that the first, the fifth, and the tenth take place in the same room, with Tom Pinch in all three, and Pecksniff and Martin in two each. In the first, Pecksniff is in the center being paid homage by Pinch; in the second, Martin is in the spatial center, enjoying his own selfish indignation while Pinch mildly attempts to console him; and in the third, Martin triumphs physically over the fallen Pecksniff. Near the center Tom, a concerned and flustered pacifier of Martin, is evidently most confused about his conflicting loyalties to this pair of egoists.

The first of this trio of etchings, "Meekness of Mr. Pecksniff and his charming daughters" (ch. 2), supplements Dickens' text through its marvelous portrayal of smug self-righteousness (anything but "meekness"!) on the three Pecksniffs' faces contrasted to Tom's self-effacement, but in addition it establishes background motifs which will recur in the two subsequent illustrations of the same room. The room is dominated by Mr. Pecksniff through effigies of himself on three sides: the "Portrait . . . by Spiller" and "Bust by Spoker" (not referred to in the text until the next part, ch. 5, p. 61), and the drawings of three architectural designs bearing Pecksniff's name: a large heroic monument and two smaller buildings, one of which is mirrored in the form of the poor box (so labeled) on the chimneypiece. In its latter form, this building (which is probably intended for a workhouse) takes on the appearance of a glowering face, answering the smirks of Pecksniff, his daughters, and his portraits; and whatever evidence of their charity it may provide is also undercut by the presence next to it of a pair of scales, a conventional graphic satirist's emblem for miserliness undercutting as well the religious overtones of the cross around Charity Pecksniff's neck.

On the same chimneypiece is a small, empty vase, whose likely meaning emerges in the central plate of this sequence. In "Mr. Pinch and the new pupil, on a social occasion" (ch. 6), Tom is in charge of the house in Pecksniff's absence, and the vase now contains a flowering plant. The scales are pushed to the very corner of the mantel, the poor box and painting partly hidden. And yet they are hidden by "Pecksniff's Pump," which bears an uncanny resemblance to the master himself (and is probably inspired by the passage in ch. 6, p. 67, in which Pecksniff recommends for the budding architect "A pump" as "very chaste practice").[21] Thus, Mr. Pecksniff dominates the scene, visually, even in his absence—none of which is in the text, though the general motif of Pecksniff's portraits is the sort of thing likely to have been specified by Dickens. In the third of these etchings, "Mr. Pecksniff renounces the deceiver" (ch. 12; Illus. 40 and 41) the plant on the mantle has become barren again upon the master's return, but the portrait and bust take on a new function: with the great man now fallen, his hair tousled and his face awry, these effigies seem to smile down upon him, mocking his ignominious position. And in Steel B (numbered as 2, according to Johannsen[22]) the scales are now unbalanced, suggesting that justice has temporarily triumphed—a rather ambiguous symbol, however.

Several of the other plates in the first five parts comment by their subjects on young Martin's situation, and also are important iconographically. Thus, "Martin Chuzzlewit suspects the landlady without reason" (ch. 24), centering upon young Martin's grandfather, parallels the first plate through the theme of exclusion, for old Martin suspects and excludes Mrs. Lupin, and his withdrawal from her and most of humanity is expressed graphically by the curtain which divides the plate in two. The parallel is to Pecksniff's exclusion of John Westlock, whose figure is partly visible in the first plate. Old Martin and his grandson, their egoisms and mutual attainment of self-knowledge, are also paralleled throughout the novel.

The themes of selfishness and self-importance are reiterated in the two plates in the second monthly part, one of which centers on Pecksniff, the other on young Martin; they contain a single but important visual parallel. "Pleasant little family party at Mr. Pecksniff's" (ch. 4; Illus. 42) shows Mr. Spottletoe's attack upon the great man for arrogating to himself the role of head of the family among the fourteen relatives present. Browne has carefully differentiated the characters, giving Tigg, the hanger-on, a prominent position and having Mercy and Charity react according to their personalities, the former amused and astonished, the latter vinegary and disdainful. Tigg, Pecksniff, and Mr. Spottletoe are further emphasized because the head of each is encircled by the frame of a mirror or picture on the wall; Tigg's head is the only one on the same level as Pecksniff's, implying some equivalence between the parasite and swindler and the "moral Pecksniff," but the latter's head is the only one surrounded by a round frame, an ironic imitation of a halo. This "halo" is clearly intended for a convex (reducing) mirror, which was a common Victorian furnishing often used by Phiz in his illustrations. (Note how the mirror's image, while matching the general pattern of the scene, reverses what a real mirror would show. This reversal is likely a slip, as there are occasional errors in left–right orientation throughout Browne's work.) The reflection resembles a coronation scene, Pecksniff's upright hair looking like a crown and the outstretched arm of the enraged Mr. Spottletoe resembling the arm of a person who bestows the crown. Since Pecksniff thinks of himself as the ruler of the family the image is a fitting one, and the consistency with which Phiz handled this detail in all three steels makes it seem unlikely that it is merely an accident. (It is not, however, present in the working drawing for this plate [Illus. 43].)

It is one of the ironies of young Martin's lack of self-awareness that he in so many ways resembles those he disdains. This irony is brought out in "Pinch starts homeward with the new Pupil" (ch. 5) through the similarity of Martin's head, halfway submerged in its collar, and that of his degraded relative Chevy Slyme—the man he later so urgently wishes to avoid—in the preceding plate. Slyme in his abjectness is the embodiment of total selfishness and is admired as such by the sycophantic Tigg. Thus this plate marks a significant beginning of Martin's progress. But a different sort of parallel and contrast is provided in the second plate for the third monthly part, "Mark begins to be jolly, under creditable circumstances" (ch. 7), which introduces a new character and contrasts Martin's disagreeableness under jolly circumstances (drinking wine before a roaring fire with Tom in the previous plate) with Mark Tapley's supposed jolliness under the gloomy circumstances of leaving the Blue Dragon. Although Mark is certainly not as egocentric as Martin, his self-indulgent "humor" of needing "credit" for being jolly is hardly a selfless condition.

Browne's propensity for interpretation is evident in the

signpost, an emblem which Dickens and Browne put to various uses. The signpost in this plate points in the opposite direction from Mark's stick and hat, which together seem to express the real direction of his feelings, back toward the village; the four-way signpost is mirrored by the shape of the turnstile that separates Mark from the village. The empty, tipped-over pitcher carried by the little girl could represent either the moral emptiness of Mark's willful abandonment of his community, or the "spilt milk" over which there's no use crying. Finally, the three posters comment on Mark's action: the upper two, "Last Appearance" and "Every Man in His Humour," as theatrical notices imply that Mark is playing a role, and the specific reference to Jonson suggests that Mark's "humour" is as foolish and as in need of deflation as that of Jonson's characters; the third poster, "Lost, Stolen, Strayed/Reward!" again ridicules Mark's need for "creditable" jollity, implying that he is deserting his proper place, like a strayed dog or sheep.

The novel's first subclimax, the fall of Pecksniff in the tenth plate, is preceded in Part IV by a pair of illustrations centering on the great man in his seemingly most exalted state, making his physical fall all the more degrading. In both "M. Todgers and the Pecksniffs call upon Miss Pinch" (ch.9) and "Truth prevails and Virtue is triumphant" (ch. 10), Browne captures Pecksniff's impenetrable complacency, and in the second he also makes what is to my eyes a curious external allusion: with his hand inside his waistcoat, Pecksniff strikes a Napoleonic pose. His particular stance here, the shape of his body and head, and the hat on the table, bear a remarkable resemblance to Louis Philippe's pose in a contemporary lithograph of the king and his family.[23] The posture of self-assumed kingliness may be enough to explain the similarity, but it seems possible that Phiz's basic conception of Pecksniff was influenced by graphic representation of the French king, both in portrait and in caricature. In particular, the famous pear shape of Louis Philippe's head, often caricatured with emphasis on the jowls at the bottom and the hair coming to a point at the top, resembles Pecksniff's head; and the various distortions to which Pecksniff's face is subjected (as in the tenth plate when he cowers in a corner while Pinch restrains Martin) recall Philipon's and Daumier's malicious fun with the Citizen–King's face.[24] Apart from the obviously exaggerated expressions on the three Pecksniffs' faces as they crowd around old Martin, the only hint of an undercutting of their "virtue" is the vivified coal scuttle, which grins maliciously.

The bourgeois virtue of the Pecksniffs is only temporarily defeated in the last of the first five monthly parts, for the subsequent travels of young Martin represent what is to him the severe humiliation of having to make his way in the world on his own, without name or connection. Dickens stresses this humiliation with the appearance of the odious Montague Tigg in the pawnshop where Martin seeks anonymity, and in depicting the scene Browne has used both an external allusion and emblematic details. George Cruikshank's etching for "The Pawnbroker's Shop" in *Sketches by Boz* is surely the source for Browne's design in "Martin meets an acquaintance at the house of a mutual relation" (ch. 13). In each there is an open door decorated with the pawnbroker's emblem of three balls, and a desk counter with private cubicles. Even the arrangement of figures is the same, down to a workman in a shapeless cap. Phiz's design reverses Cruikshank's as one would expect if he had drawn directly in imitation of the original and transferred the drawing to the steel by his usual method.

In "The Pawnbroker's Shop," Dickens contrasts working-class and middle-class customers of the pawnshop, while in *Martin Chuzzlewit* the contrast is between the regular frequenter, Tigg, and the first-time Martin, who feels exceedingly degraded by Tigg's claiming him as a friend. Dickens did not describe the other customers in the scene, and this may be one reason Browne drew upon the Cruikshank etching. He also added two details in the form of a print and a painting: one is an ornately framed bacchante, suggesting Tigg's dissipation; the other is labeled "Distraining for Rent," and is evidently meant to be the much engraved painting by Sir David Wilkie—doubtless a reference to Martin's sorry financial plight.

The companion plate and the two for the following part continue Martin's decline to his lowest condition in America. First we see further evidence of his egoism in "Mr. Tapley acts Third

Party with great discretion" (ch. 14). Despite the fact that his arm is around Mary's waist, Martin is wholly absorbed in fantasies of wealth. Yet the figure of Mark and the towers of Salisbury Cathedral seem to enclose the couple and promise protection and ultimate happiness. The American plates in Parts VII and IX operate by contrast and parallel in depicting Martin's development. In the first, "Mr. Jefferson Brick proposes an appropriate sentiment" (ch. 16), Martin looks quite self-confident, despite the vicious fraudulence of the two newspapermen—underlined by the Slang Dictionary and bottle of poison—and the danger implied in the spider's web at upper left. By contrast, Mark learns something new about the American reality in "Mr. Tapley succeeds in finding a 'jolly' subject for contemplation" (ch. 17). Gazing at the nearly destroyed but now "free" slave, Mark's expression and posture belie the boldness of his signature (only initials in the text) on the *Rowdy Journal's* office door.

The empty spider web in the *Journal* office becomes a web full of flies next to a mousetrap about to snare a victim in "The thriving City of Eden, as it appeared on paper" (ch. 21; Illus. 44 and 45), which is contrasted with "The thriving City of Eden, as it appeared in fact" (ch. 23). In the first, Martin retains his optimism and self-confidence while Mark looks on skeptically; in the second Martin is utterly abject and, we find from the text, about to descend into serious illness. In a detailed set of instructions for the latter plate (which has often been reprinted[25]), it is notable how much trouble Dickens took to ensure that Browne achieved his intentions—including material which could not possibly be in the picture itself, such as the rustiness of the compasses on the stump and the intense heat of the day. Yet the two toads or frogs in the final etching (one looking at Martin and the other leaping into the water) are *not* mentioned in the instructions, and it seems possible that the jumping frog is intended to symbolize the despondent and potentially suicidal reaction of Martin to the real Eden.

During the time that Martin's progress develops apart from the other major characters, the story of Martin's cousin Jonas proceeds both in text and illustrations, and emerges visually as the most important secondary progress in the first half of the novel.

"Mr. Jonas Chuzzlewit entertains his cousins" (ch. 11; Illus. 46 and 47) is a visual embodiment of duplicity; it depicts no single incident from the text but rather conflates the reference to Jonas doing card tricks for his guests, the Pecksniff girls, with those paragraphs which make it clear that although he is pretending to woo the elder sister he is in fact aiming at the younger. If we follow a left-to-right "reading" of the plate, we first see Anthony Chuzzlewit in a sleep from which his son wishes he would never awake; next to him is the self-effacing Chuffey, sitting far from the fire. From the dark corner of the room behind Chuffey our eye moves to the strongboxes and ledgers and into the candlelight illuminating the three young persons. Jonas displays an ace of hearts to Charity, who looks at him intently, while behind his back he covertly shows an open hand of cards to Merry, who regards them out of the corner of her eye. We could not have a clearer summary of the situation: Jonas displays the emblem of love, a single heart, to the unsuspecting Cherry, while showing his hand—literally—to Merry. How much of the iconographic invention is Dickens' and how much Browne's is impossible to say, but the plate is typical of the special role illustrations play in Dickens novels: the presentation of meanings which, if made explicit in the text, might seem like clumsy moralizing, premature revelation, or both.

Jonas' next appearance follows the line set out by this illustration in one respect, for in "The dissolution of Partnership" (ch. 18) the subject is his father's death—which he believes to be the result of the poison he administered. That it takes place in the same room as the card trick suggests visually the relation between Jonas' murder plans and marriage plans. The central emblem is suggested by the text and borne out in the illustration:

> "Upon my word, Mr. Jonas, that is a very extraordinary clock," said Pecksniff.
> It would have been, if it had made the noise which startled them: but another kind of time-piece was fast running down, and from that the sound proceeded. (ch. 18, pp. 231–32)

In the etching the clock is prominent, and its hands point just before midnight (in Steel B; in Steel A it is vaguer, but looks more like one o'clock), in emblematic art a common symbol of imminent death, or the Last Judgment.[26] In a sense, the companion plate, "Mr. Pecksniff on his Mission" (ch. 19), also continues the story of Jonas, for it centers on Pecksniff's trip to engage Mrs. Gamp as a "layer-out" of Anthony's corpse.

Mrs. Gamp's alternate function as a handmaiden of birth (upon which the joke of the latter plate turns, Pecksniff being mistaken for an expectant father) is grimly established in "Mrs. Gamp has her eye on the future" (ch. 26). The midwife serves as a disturbing contrast in her grotesque jollity to the actual situation in Merry's new home. The withered branches in the fireplace, a fitting emblem for the marriage, derive from Dickens' text (although it was not unheard of for a novelist to pick up details from his illustrator). The first of this pair of plates, "Balm for the wounded orphan" (ch. 24), returns us to the Pecksniff parlor where Jonas is now the fallen man, having been struck by Tom in self-defense, while the latter perceives his first glimmerings of imperfection in his master's family. Like Pecksniff's fall in the earlier plate, this one foreshadows the character's ultimate defeat. (Browne has done something odd with Pecksniff's physiognomy here, making it much uglier in one steel than the other; it is probably intentional, since the bust of Pecksniff in each case matches the man.)

The story of Jonas becomes inextricably tied up with that of Montague Tigg from Part XI on, and the plates for this part give us a chance to see how effectively Browne could create visual parallels on the basis of the subjects he was given by Dickens. Jonas is one of the admirers—but the only gullible one—of Montague Tigg in his transformation into Tigg Montague in "The Board" (ch. 27; Illus. 48); and this transformation is parodied in "Easy Shaving" (ch. 29; Illus. 49) by Tigg's footman, Young Bailey, who has himself been transformed from the servant boy he was at Todgers's into the flashy pseudo-adult now regarded with astonishment by his old friend Poll Sweedlepipe. The themes of metamorphosis and parody are worked out intricately, for in the first etching Browne parodies the melodramatic pose of "Montague" by a still more pretentious portrait, resembling a distorted mirror image of the already distorted Tigg. The parallels in the companion plate amusingly deflate Tigg's pretense: Bailey is being shaved by the genuinely admiring Poll, although

his beard—like Tigg's respectability and his capital—is imaginary. Further, just as Montague looks fondly at his own portrait,
the puffed-up little footman gazes at a wig wearing his hat, while
from the other side a wig block and an owl stare at him in
amazement.

Tigg appears in a more sinister form in "Mr. Nadgett breathes,
as usual, an atmosphere of mystery" (ch. 38), in which Jonas is
the central figure. As Nadgett and Tigg reveal to Jonas their
knowledge of his (apparent) poisoning of his father, the glove on
the floor appears to be reaching for his throat. The consequence
of this revelation, Jonas' first attempt to murder Tigg, is dealt
with by Browne in a style different from that of the other etchings
in this novel: in "Mr. Jonas exhibits his presence of mind" (ch.
42) he has created a circular composition with Jonas at the center
of a whirling vortex, the positions of Tigg and Jonas almost
exactly reversed from those in the plate just discussed. The composition here is dynamic, yet compact and formal. Although
Browne may have been influenced by George Cruikshank's book
illustrations, Cruikshank's oval or circular designs usually freeze
the action rather than achieving the tension Browne creates. In
addition, Browne once again uses visual parallels, making Tigg's
gesture echo Anthony's, also on the edge of death, in "The dissolution of Partnership." This parallel is ironic because Jonas'
mistaken belief that he has killed his father leads him here to
attempt, and later to accomplish, the murder of Tigg.

Browne deals with a comic consequence of Jonas' earlier duplicity with Charity Pecksniff, her pursuit of the unwilling
Moddle, in a heavily emblematic style. The incident functions
more as comic relief than moral commentary; yet it is important
in providing a parallel to the career and downfall of Pecksniff by
centering on his favorite daughter, the one who most resembles
him in self-importance and hypocrisy. The "courtship" also contrasts with the genuine love relationships in the novel, Ruth
Pinch and John Westlock, Mary and Martin, as well as Tom's
unrequited love for Mary.

A parody of romantic love is the theme of "Mr. Moddle is both
particular and peculiar in his attentions" (ch. 32), while happy
domesticity is mimicked in "Mr. Moddle is led to the contemplation of his destiny" (ch. 46). In the first, Charity casts a pro-

prietary look at Moddle, who seems to pull away from Cherry even as he reaches out his hand toward her. The comic but tormenting ambivalence of this reluctant lover is thus admirably conveyed. Three book titles comment ironically upon different aspects of this romance. On the cupboard behind Moddle is *Jolly Songs,* antithetical to his morose appearance and his sorrow at having lost Merry; at his feet is *Werther,* the irony of which lies in the disparity between Moddle's implausible threats of suicide and the high-Romantic passions of Goethe's protagonist; and upon the table is *Childe Harold,* again a story about a quintessential Romantic best known for his world-wanderings, perhaps foreshadowing Moddle's eventual escape to Van Diemen's Land. Sitting on a wall bracket behind Moddle is either a cupid or a cherub, a frequently used detail in scenes of comic disappointed love (cf. the scene of Charity's jilting); here the figure is reading, an appropriate activity for the general sense of this plate that Moddle's behavior is based on books.

As is the case with several of the *Chuzzlewit* plates, there are two extant drawings for this one, from which we may infer certain things about Browne's typical practices. Both drawings are quite close to the final etching, and both are reversed, but one (Gimbel) is extraordinarily detailed, with far more indication of crosshatching and shading than is normally the case with Browne's working drawings. The other is less detailed, and the indented lines caused by transfer to the etching ground indicate that it is the actual working drawing.[27] The most likely explanation for the more finished drawing is that it was done by Phiz for himself or Robert Young as a guide to the more precise elements of etching and biting. Red chalk marks the surface, indicating that the basic lines were transferred from the working drawing in the same way as they were to the ground. Neither drawing contains the *Jolly Songs* detail, which suggests that both precede the process of etching and that Phiz might have improvised emblematic details at the last moment.

In "Mr. Moddle is led to the contemplation of his destiny" (Illus. 50), the comic lover is forced to think seriously about his impending marriage, but in the companion plate, "Mrs. Gamp makes tea" (ch. 46), he is distraught at an accidental encounter with his lost love, Merry. In the first, Phiz's imagination multiplies details which carry a good deal of the burden of comedy, for

the figures of Ruth, Tom, Moddle, and Charity are not as important in conveying the meaning as are the setting and its elements.
We gradually become aware that the scene is full of disapproving
faces: the rug just behind the couple frowns mightily, while the
fire screen in the shop grins maliciously. At the top of each door-
post a satyr or devil looks sideways at Cherry and Moddle, holding a finger to his nose. The comical recording angel, who holds a
tablet marked "Day by [Day]," may also be looking at the couple,
while the shopkeeper, peering out of the store, has a sly grimace
on his face. As if all these faces were not enough, at the left of the
door is a sign, "Maids/Wives/Widows"[28] implying that for
Augustus to make this particular maid a wife will be soon to make
her a widow because of his own despondency—something
further borne out by the poster of a lion catching a flying leaf (or a
bird?), as if Moddle were being brought down in the freedom of
his bachelorhood by a predatory creature. Finally, the customary
notice, "To Those [about to] Marry," pinned to the poster, may
conceivably have elicited the immediate response from readers,
"Don't!" although the first appearance of this joke in print is, to
my knowledge, in 1845.[29]

Two preliminary drawings for this plate (Illus. 51 and 52) indicate different initial intentions by Browne, Dickens, or both. One
shows Moddle alone, wearing dark glasses (to conceal his identity as Charity's betrothed), and conversing with a shopman outside a furniture shop. The other shows the happy couple walking
on the street from right to left, as in the final printed version, and
in somewhat the same pose, but with a miscellaneous group of
pedestrians and no Pinches or emblematic details. It seems
probable that Dickens first gave Phiz general instructions and/or
copy having to do with Moddle contemplating buying furniture,
and that Browne ultimately combined the pose of Moddle and
Charity in the one sketch with the subject matter of the other,
perhaps under further instructions from Dickens.

Because the concluding plate of Charity Pecksniff's progress
has interconnections with the other illustrations in the final,
double part, I want to defer for the moment discussing her end,
and return to the three primary progresses of Martin, Pinch, and
Pecksniff. Tom has been present in a number of earlier plates,
yet his true graphic progress (as distinct from that in the text,

where his mental conflicts and doubts about Pecksniff are presented early and in detail) does not emerge as the focus of a series of plates until "Mr. Pecksniff discharges a duty which he owes to society" (ch. 31). The scales fall from Tom's eyes when Pecksniff dismisses him, accusing him of his own recently detected crime of making love to Mary. Pecksniff assumes his imperial pose standing on a step higher than anyone else, which conveys not his superiority but his moral isolation from the others. His facial expression suggests he is an actor on a stage full of real people, for even old Martin—who has been playing a role all along—looks through the window with an expression of concern for Tom. Tom's enormous advance in wisdom is emblematized by a head of Minerva immediately over the doorstep, looking down at Pecksniff.

Tom's next appearance is a step further along the way of his progress, in "Mr. Pinch departs to seek his fortune" (ch. 36). An image introduced early in the novel's text is taken up here and once again in the title page vignette. In his introduction of Pecksniff, Dickens had remarked, "Some people likened him to a direction-post, which is always telling the way to a place, and never goes there" (ch. 2, p. 10); he later emphasizes the actual fingerpost to Salisbury and beyond, which becomes important enough as a symbol for him to exhort Browne not to forget it in the title page. In the present plate it points Tom on his journey, as it had Mark and Martin before him.

Although they at times achieve great insight, the illustrations in *Martin Chuzzlewit* usually operate on a simpler level of moral commentary than does the text at its most incisive. Thus the four horses that are to take Tom's coach to London in "Mr. Pinch departs . . ." are, unlike the ones that run away with Tigg and Jonas' carriage, tightly controlled by the coachman, although the contrast of the lively coach horses with Mrs. Lupin's staid old mare implies that Tom is starting on a road which will lead him to greater fulfillment in life.

Much of this fulfillment turns out to be vicarious, as Tom watches relationships develop between his sister Ruth and John Westlock (depicted in "Mr. Pinch and Ruth unconscious of a visitor" [ch. 39]), and Martin and Mary. Two plates, however, center on a trial to which Tom is subjected in order to prove his worth. In both "Mysterious Installation of Mr. Pinch" (ch. 40) and "Mr. Pinch is amazed by an unexpected apparition" (ch. 50), Phiz again uses the flower symbol of earlier plates. Amidst the dirt and chaos of the room in the former plate is a small vase with a single, flowerless stalk; in the subsequent plate—Tom having replaced chaos with order—the withered stalk has bloomed. And there are other Hogarthian details in the room: the candle covered by a snuffer and the adjacent clock have a spider's web between them, doubtless referring to the neglect of time and light—duty and knowledge—just as Hogarth's cobweb on the poorbox in *A Rake's Progress*, V, indicates long neglect of the poor in an acquisitive society. In the second etching, Tom has earned the right to meet his benefactor, old Martin, and upon the shelf sits a bust of an elderly man—evidently blind. This image may have come to Browne through his reading of the words in Chapter 50, "and such a light broke in on Tom as blinded him."

This bust turns up again in the very next plate, one of two text illustrations which, together with the frontispiece and title page, form the final, double part. The subjects of the plates have been criticized by Angus Wilson as "poor drama," "stagey," and representing a lower level of art than the novel as a whole sustains.[30] But if we recognize that the four plates in this last part have an almost ritualistically conventional function (evidently felt by Dickens at this stage of his development to be essential), we may feel these strictures to be misapplied. In particular, Wilson's judgment that the jilting of Charity is a "most unfortunate ending, in irrelevance and inferiority of tone,"[31] overlooks the extent to which the novel has been operating in fairly elementary moral terms all along, and that a denouement is likely to bring out this aspect of the novel with special force and directness. These four illustrations in fact make the nature of that denouement clearer than it is in the text alone and, in the last two plates, link it with the general moral concerns of the novel as a whole. The final text illustrations conclude the moral progresses of Pecksniff, Martin, and Tom (although these and Charity's progress are allegorically concluded in the frontispiece, and the *beginning* of Pecksniff's and Martin's is summarized in the title page etching).

Because the survival of Dickens' directions to Phiz about these four plates gives us a unique opportunity to examine the collaboration between author and illustrator, I shall in discussing each plate first quote the instructions.[32] For "Warm reception of Mr. Pecksniff by his venerable friend" (ch. 52), Dickens wrote to Browne relatively briefly in comparison to his extensive instructions for the second "Eden" plate.

1st Subject

> The room in the Temple. Mrs. Lupin, with Mary in her charge, stands a little way behind old Martin's chair. Young Martin is on the other side. Tom Pinch and his sister are there too. Mr Pecksniff has burst in to rescue his venerable friend from this horde of plunderers and deceivers. The old man in a [perfect] transport of burning indignation, arises from his chair, and uplifting his stick knocks the good Pecksniff down; before John Westlock and Mark who gently interpose (though they are very much delighted) can possibly prevent him. Mr Pecksniff on the ground. The old man full of fire, energy & resolution.
> Lettering.
> *Warm reception of Mr. Pecksniff by his venerable friend.*

At the bottom of the sheet, Browne penciled in:

> *Mrs. Lupin & Mary*—behind Martin's chair.
> Yg. *Martin* on other side.
> Tom & his sister.
> Old man—Pecksniff
> John Westlock & Mark

Despite the prevailing assumption that Browne always acted strictly under Dickens' directions, it is plain from the above that he had a good deal of freedom—and responsibility—to interpret the subjects, and thus, the novel. These instructions are very general, and include more in the way of a novelistic description of character and motivation than of specific graphic pointers, aside from the location of Mrs. Lupin, Mary, and Martin. Notably absent are references to the two books we see in the etching, *Tartuffe* and *Paradise Lost*. It was well within Browne's ability to insert these titles on his own, for he must have known enough of the novel, even if he had not read the entire manuscript or printed text, to understand that Pecksniff is a hypocrite (like Tartuffe), and to recognize that Pecksniff has been thrown out of paradise in the sense that he has lost old Martin's favor and fortune. (It scarcely seems necessary to adduce the bird of paradise on the cover, or the fact that *Paradise Lost* is among the books on the cover design for *Godfrey Malvern,* in order to give Browne credit for including this detail.)

We find Pecksniff fallen and reduced in size in this plate, rather like Louis Philippe in some of Daumier's cartoons, where the Citizen King is subjected to indignities and distortions of person. "The Nuptials of Miss Pecksniff receive a temporary check" (ch.55; Illus. 53) provides an obvious parallel in the fall of Mr. Pecksniff's beloved daughter, and on this subject Dickens gives abundant—if not exactly pertinent—information to his artist.

2nd Subject.

represents Miss Charity Pecksniff on the bridal morning. The bridal [table] breakfast is set out in Todgers's drawing-room. Miss Pecksniff has invited the strong-minded woman, and all that party who were present in Mr Pecksniff's parlor in the second number. We behold her triumph. She is not proud, but forgiving. Jinkins is also present and wears a white favor in his button hole. Merry is *not* there. Mrs. Todgers is decorated for the occasion. So are the rest of the company. The bride wears a bonnet with an orange flower. They have waited a long time for Moddle. Moddle has not appeared. The strong-minded woman has [frequently] expressed a hope that nothing has happened to him; the daughters of the strong-minded woman (who are bridesmaids) have offered consolation of an aggravating nature. A knock is heard at the door. It is not Moddle but a letter from him. The bride opens it, reads it, shrieks, and swoons. Some of the company catch it and crowd about each other, and read it over one another's shoulders. Moddle writes that he can't help it—that he loves another—that he is wretched for life—and has that morning sailed from Gravesend for Van Deimen's Land. [The strong-minded woman and her daughters are]

Lettering. *The Nuptials of Miss Pecksniff receive a temporary* [check] check.

The most remarkable thing about this communication is that it contains details (such as colors) and events which cannot possibly be shown in the illustration, some of which are not even in the novel's text, such as the hopes of the strong-minded woman and the consolations of her daughters. Phiz drew a vertical line in the margin next to the last four lines of the note which are extraneous to what an illustrator can depict. Perhaps this nondepictable material is not totally irrelevant, since by giving a sense of the drama behind the actual moment the author aided the artist in portraying characters' expressions and physical attitudes. However, Dickens clearly tended to get carried away: the note shows that he was going on still further and checked himself, as though suddenly aroused from his enthusiastic vision of the scene.

The parallel between the two fallen Pecksniffs is brought out explicitly only in this pair of illustrations, and Phiz enhances the parallel with emblems. A recording angel once again notes all the absurdities of Cherry Pecksniff, while two prints refer to her losses. In the first, Aesop's dog is about to drop his bone in envy of his own reflection, a suggestion of Cherry's sisterly envy of Merry, who has taken away both "bones," Jonas and Moddle. In the second, a fisherman, whose line has broken, lets a large fish fall; the word "Gone!" appears above his head. This last detail does not appear in the working drawing (Illus. 54), and was probably added in the process of etching or transfer (the fact that the letters are reversed in Steel A suggests last-minute haste). One source for the detail may be a comic design by Robert Seymour in his *Sketches,* published separately in 1834–36 and collected several times thereafter, including an edition in 1843; in it, both the situation and the caption are essentially the same.[33]

The parallel afforded by these two plates makes it clear why Angus Wilson's comments are off the mark. If anything, the allegorical frontispiece centered on Tom and the title page vignette epitomizing Pecksniff are more direct evidence of the conventions within which Dickens worked—especially in this final part. At the same time, a comparison of Dickens' instructions with Phiz's plates demonstrates just how great were both the illustrator's capacity for invention, and the degree of independence he was granted.

Frontispiece

— — —

— — —

I have a notion of finishing the book with an apostrophe to Tom Pinch, playing the organ. I shall break off the last chapter suddenly, and find Tom at his organ, a few years afterwards. And

instead of saying what became of the people, as usual, I shall
suppose it all expressed in the sounds; making the last swell of
the Instrument a kind of expression of Tom's heart. Tom has
remained a single man, and lives with his sister and John
Westlock who are married—Martin and Mary are married—Tom
is a godfather of course—old Martin is dead, and has left him
some money—Tom has had an organ fitted in his chamber, and
often sits alone, playing it, when of course the old times rise up
before him. So the Frontispiece is Tom at his organ with a pen-
sive face; and any little indications of his history rising out of it,
and floating about it, that you please; Tom as interesting and
amiable as possible

Given that Dickens had an especially arduous task in writing an
installment of double length, it is not surprising that he jotted
down these directions before actually composing the novel's
conclusion. Browne, in choosing the "little indications" of Tom's
history, went far beyond Dickens' conclusion, epitomizing some
of the novel's themes, indicating the resolution of major plot
strands (and commenting ironically upon others), incorporating
aspects of the wrapper's imagery as well. In the center, of course,
there is Tom at the organ, which is decorated with the miniature
figures of Ruth and John; above the organ pipes are Martin and
Mary, the former holding a bridal wreath, two blossoms of which
fall toward Tom. Down the left side a dance motif dominates.
Several figures connected with marital bliss are joined by the
Blue Dragon himself, and two pint pots dance with Mark and
Mrs. Lupin. A female figure with a bandbox head labeled
"Gamp" capers with two teakettles as she is observed by three
suffering elderly patients and three squalling infants, all
presumably victims of her professional skill. Poll Sweedlepipe
dances with a vivified dummy and birdcages, while behind him
stands Young Bailey, defiantly smoking his cigar (one of the few
details not in the working drawing).[34] Behind three dancing
couples at the lower left are a weeping Moddle and a teasing
Merry with Jonas (probably) at her side.

Two groups at the bottom represent the destinies of Jonas and
Pecksniff. The latter is besieged by snarling images of himself
which in turn clutch at smiling Pecksniff masks—a striking way
for Phiz to show Pecksniff tormented by his own hypocrisy. The
most interesting creation is the smiling figure of Pecksniff holding money bags, who also has a threatening Pecksniff face for a

belly. The placement of this face is such as to include the genital region, and it would seem to represent the base passions— gustatory and sexual—of the real Pecksniff. The theme of self-confrontation is repeated for Jonas, who is surrounded by his own reflection in mirrors that hold bags of money. Above this, Pecksniff is shown again, hanging in a horizontal position from a block and tackle borrowed from an earlier illustration in which Mark and Martin attend, unrecognized, the honoring of Pecksniff for what are really Martin's architectural designs ("Martin is much gratified by an imposing ceremony" [ch. 35]). Now literally hoist with his own pretense, Pecksniff watches helplessly while vivified implements of the builder's trade cavort below him. Above this scene Jonas once again is besieged, now by skeletons, medusae, and Fates, who hold out money bags and glasses (of poison) to him. Between the suspended Pecksniff and Jonas is Charity as an old maid holding a cat; she is looked down upon by a moon and an owl (the latter recalling the owl in the bad fortune side of the monthly cover).

From the top center of the frontispiece and down the right side we find those "indications" of Tom's story asked for by Dickens. Though not shown in strictly chronological order, they depict the main episodes in Tom's career: Pecksniff leering at Mary in church; Tom working away at his drawing board while Pecksniff admires his own effigy; Jonas on the ground and Tom on the stile; a foolish-looking Tom being mocked by Mercy and Charity; and Tom consoling a young woman who is either Mary Graham or Mercy. Several inscriptions comment on the Pinch–Pecksniff relationship. "P's Pump," a reference back to the fifth plate, is surmounted by a sign inscribed "Sacred"—either an ironic reference to Pecksniff's view of himself or a serious one to Tom's love for Mary. Two Latin mottoes refer to Tom's uncritical view of his master in the first half of the novel: "Sic vos non vobis" (you labor, but not for yourselves) describes Tom's condition of virtual slavery as Pecksniff's "young man," while "Si monumentum requiras [sic] circumspice" would seem to have multiple significance. This allusion to Christopher Wren's monument in St. Paul's cathedral (meaning "if you wish to see his monument, look about you") is an ironic comment upon Pecksniff's architectural pretensions and it may also echo Dickens' reference to the Latin inscription which appears on the cornerstone of the school

whose design Pecksniff plagiarized (ch. 35, p. 415). It also may
be a pun, however, related to the other tag; Pecksniff regards
monuments of himself (a bust and a statue), but the real monument to Pecksniff is Tom Pinch, for whose virtues and talents
Pecksniff receives the credit.

While the frontispiece centers upon Tom but includes allusions to much of the novel, the vignette title (Illus. 55) deals with
Pecksniff; its location opposite the frontispiece in the bound volume makes it complementary to that plate. As the one depicts
Tom in his most typical and admirable condition, so the other
portrays Pecksniff in his most characteristic and contemptible
role. And, as the frontispiece looks back over the novel, the title
page anticipates the fundamental behavior of its greatest
figure—although at the same time, this vignette is fully com-
prehensible only to someone who has already read the book.
Once again, Dickens' directions to Phiz demonstrate how much
was left to the illustrator's discretion.

Vignette for title page

— —
— —

The finger post at the end of the lane, which has been so often
mentioned. You can either have Tom Pinch waiting with John
Westlock and his boxes, as at the opening of the book; or Mr
Pecksniff blandly receiving a new pupil from the coach (perhaps
this might be better); and by no means forgetting the premium in
his welcome of the young gentleman

Will you let me see the designs for these two?

Note how Dickens arrives at the subject: he knows that he wants
the fingerpost as an emblematic focus, and after considering a
specific scene from the novel decides that he prefers one which
does not occur in the book and is an epitome rather than a pure
illustration. Browne's rendering of the subject provides meanings which are not specified in these directions. First, the fingerpost itself is broken—specifically the board pointing in the
direction from which Pecksniff has come, implying that to follow
him is to go nowhere, and also recalling the description of
Pecksniff as a "direction post" which "never goes there" (ch. 2,

p. 10). Upon the post is a sign reading "£100 / Reward" (or in the drawing and one steel, "100£," a matter of some moment to collectors), which alludes to the premium demanded, and to the criminal, because fraudulent, nature of Pecksniff's dealings with his pupils.

But the most important thing about this title page is its ingenious use of a Hogarth engraving as a source. There is another detail not specified by Dickens, a basket overflowing with game and fish which the naive new pupil has evidently brought to Pecksniff, since a slip with the latter's name is attached to the hare's hind legs. Browne draws from Plate I of *A Harlot's Progress* (Illus. 58), in which a young girl arrives from the country hoping to be met by her cousin but is instead greeted by a notorious bawd and procuress. At the lower right of Hogarth's engraving is a basket with a goose in it, whose head protrudes over the edge as does the fish's tail in Browne's etching; attached to the goose's neck is a note reading, "For my loving cousin in Thames Street in London." Two other details clinch my identification of the source: in both plates there is a horse cropping grass to the right of the young person (our left), and in both a studded traveling-trunk stands near the basket.

But none of this would be very important were it not for the similarity of the central characters. Pecksniff and the bawd stand in identical positions, the former holding the pupil's left hand in both of his, and the bawd reaching out to chuck the girl under the chin; both the pupil and the girl hold an object of value—a purse and the premium (so labeled). Both girl and pupil have a demure expression, with downcast eyes, while the bawd and Pecksniff simper engagingly at their victims. Although the young man in Phiz's picture is not supposed to be Martin, the point should still be clear that both innocents travel to meet a "loving cousin" and instead meet a disgusting hypocrite who will make use of them for his/her own profit, while pretending to be a benefactor; that Pecksniff is, in relation to Martin, actual cousin *and* exploiter increases the irony of the parallel. Further, the city–country antithesis of the two pictures emphasizes the point that while Pecksniff pretends his home is an Edenic retreat, it is really as corrupt as the London in which Hogarth's innocent finds herself.

Ronald Paulson's analysis of the Hogarth engraving suggests another aspect to the parallel. Postulating that we normally read

pictures as we do texts, Paulson says that Hogarth "shows, from
left to right, the York Wagon and the young girl who has just
dismounted, the girl in conversation with a procuress, and the
waiting figure of the aristocratic keeper: past, present, and future."[35] Reading Phiz's vignette from left to right, we get the
word "Plans" displayed prominently in the gig which will take
the young man to Pecksniff's; close by, the coach that brought
him, already hurrying away, with the letters "art" visible (one or
more letters preceding these covered by the postillion's body);
then the trunk, the boy with his premium, Pecksniff, a broken
signpost pointing to the right, a bunch of trapped and
slaughtered animals (comparable to the goose in Hogarth's
engraving), a milestone, and a small sheep. Past, present, and
future: the young man's plans for a career in a branch of art; the
present, seemingly amicable relationship with Pecksniff; and the
future, when he will have passed in the direction of the broken
fingerpost, to become a (sheared) sheep, as Pecksniff's victim.

The highly finished working drawing (Illus. 57) is reversed,
and thus one might think that the ultimate left–right orientation
is merely the accident of the particular process of transfer Phiz
used for etchings. But there exists a pencil and wash drawing
(Illus. 56), much less finished and thus no doubt an early sketch,
which faces the same way as the final etching. The evidence is
therefore strong that in his initial conception of this design
Browne intended the final left-to-right arrangement, thinking—if
I am correct—of the appearance of Hogarth's print, and carefully
working out the finished drawing in reverse so that he could
transfer it by his usual method and have the etching print properly. How conscious the left-to-right *chronological* order was, we
cannot know, but Browne does seem to have planned carefully to
preserve the resemblance to Hogarth's engraving. That the similarity had not been noted before 1971 suggests only that by
Dickens' and Browne's time most readers had lost the ability to
read pictures.

Despite a number of minor inconsistencies from month to
month, Browne's suite of one wood engraving and forty etchings
for *Martin Chuzzlewit* must be judged a major advance in his art
of interpretation. He breaks with the more limiting aspects of the

caricature tradition, and simultaneously makes greater and more incisive use than before of significant details and careful drawing of facial expressions. One cannot say that his illustrations reflect every aspect of Dickens' art; there is no way for the brilliant linguistic experiments of Mrs. Gamp, Pecksniff, and the Americans to be conveyed visually, nor does Dickens give Browne a chance to interpret "Town and Todgers's," this novelist's first great attempt at a surrealistic rendering of the city's alienation, although we may see a parallel between his new emphasis upon vivified objects and the sudden increase of emblematic details in Browne's plates. This latter aspect of the illustrations is related most closely to Dickens' own emblematic tendencies, however. It is Dickens who describes the pictures of the Prodigal Son and Wise Men which decorate the walls of the tavern where Martin breakfasts after being renounced by Pecksniff (ch. 13, p. 162), and he mentions in the text the withered branches at Mercy Chuzzlewit's first homecoming. In one instance, at least, Browne's use of a particular emblem precedes Dickens', for the scale placed next to Pecksniff's poorbox in the first plate shows up in the text much later, when Martin says of his relationship to his grandfather, "and there is no such balance against me that I need throw in a mawkish forgiveness to poise the scale" (ch. 14, p. 184)—a demonstration, at the very least, of the complementary relationship of author and illustrator.

Browne's plates for *Martin Chuzzlewit* show how allusion, detail, and composition can amount to a visual language as complex and satisfying as Dickens' own. In later novels the Dickensian vision of the city (at its height in *Bleak House* and *Little Dorrit*) will be intensified by Browne's daring use of the dark plate technique. But the prime function of Phiz's illustrations will remain what they have been in *Martin Chuzzlewit:* to emphasize and clarify thematic structures which may not be stressed explicitly in the text, and to maintain a continuity between the monthly parts by keeping the characters before the readers' eyes.

CHAPTER FOUR

Dombey and Son: Iconography of Social and Sexual Satire

Dickens' seventh novel is at once less complicated and more complex than his sixth. Instead of *Martin Chuzzlewit*'s proliferation of subplots and groups of characters mirroring one another in rather abstract ways, in *Dombey and Son* Dickens carefully relates moral, social, and psychological themes, purposefully rather than in hindsight. His penetration beneath the brilliant linguistic surface is also deeper. Although the novel pivots on the moral progress of Mr. Dombey, the fact that his evil has social ramifications means that his individual development does not become the primary point of reference. And Mr. Dombey is at once the source of Paul's and Florence's difficulties in childhood and his own ensnarement in a tangled set of conflicts regarding power and sex. Browne's most important illustrations bear on these topics, and at their best they interpret and illuminate in ways more subtle and profound than do those of *Martin Chuzzlewit*.

The new dimensions and assuredness of Dickens' initial formulation of his themes are strikingly visualized in the cover design for *Dombey and Son* (Illus. 59), especially in contrast to that for *Chuzzlewit*. As usual, we cannot know how much guidance Dickens gave Phiz in the particular allegorical conception of the design, but he must have revealed a good deal about his plans for the novel; the wrapper includes references to Dombey's commercial career and the ultimate fall of his business, to his marriage, to the birth and schooling of Paul, to a young man setting out to sea and being shipwrecked, to the Wooden Midshipman, and to one of the last episodes in the as yet unwritten novel, Florence's care for her shattered father. Although Dickens felt there was a little "too much in" the design, it is on the whole fairly unrevealing of the plot and conceived in traditional imagery and structure.[1] There is no reason to think that Browne could not, given the requisite hints about Dombey's personality and the commercial themes of the novel, have composed out of his own imagination and stock of visual ideas the central allegory as we have it.

The fool with cap and bells, lying on the ledger, is a traditional figure Phiz reverted to more than once in his monthly covers; here, the fool's pipesmoke "dreams" the rising and falling structure of the design. The proud Dombey sits above on a throne, but his cash box and day book are supported by an edifice of ledgers which is no more substantial than the precarious structure of playing cards paralleling it on the right. A structure on the point of collapse will be hinted at in the *Bleak House* cover, but here it is the most effective element in a design which is otherwise full of details that could have meant little at first to the original readers. When the novel was completed, Browne produced an allegorical frontispiece more closely related to the body of the novel, yet it omitted the commercial theme altogether. Thus it is difficult to say whether we should consider the two designs complementary or must rather conclude that there is some disjunction of purpose. The commercial theme as such is never adverted to again in the plates to this novel, whose subjects, as usual, Dickens specified; but careful reading of the plates and their interconnections shows that they do emphasize and complement Dickens' social vision.

From the beginning Dickens was almost as concerned with the illustrations as with the text; as he wrote to John Forster,

> The points for illustration, and the enormous care required, make me excessively anxious. The man for Dombey, if Browne could see him, the class man to a T, is Sir A＿＿＿ E＿＿＿, of D＿＿＿'s. Great pains will be necessary with Miss Tox. The Toodle Family should not be too much caricatured, because of

Polly. I should like Browne to think of Susan Nipper, who will
not be wanted in the first number. After the second number, they
will all be nine or ten years older; but this will not involve much
change in the characters, except in the children and Miss Nipper.[2]

The implication that the Toodles *might* have been caricatured,
were it not that Polly is a wholly sympathetic character, is evidence of how Dickens' changing purposes operated upon Phiz's
development as an illustrator, for indeed the style of the etchings
is less caricaturistic than in *Martin Chuzzlewit,* one result of
which is that the grotesques—in particular Major Bagstock and
Mrs. Skewton—stand out in sharp contrast to many of the other
characters, although at times, as with Mrs. Pipchin, Browne was
seemingly not *enough* of a caricaturist for Dickens.

Up to the point of little Paul's death, in Part V, the illustrations
form a unified sequence, but thereafter they reflect the novel's
bifurcation into the worlds of Dombey and the Wooden Midshipman, with Florence moving between them. A single theme
dominates the early plates relevant to the first of these worlds,
while those in the second offer thematic counterpoint. Paul is
naturally the central figure in the early plates, but Browne attempts more than merely to record his development: in Part I the
illustrations contrast the Toodles and Dombey families at the
same time as they show the relationships which grow up between them.[3] Without its companion, "Miss Tox introduces 'the
Party'" (ch. 2) would seem no more than a stilted lineup of the
Toodles, Miss Tox, and Mrs. Chick; but as soon as we look at
"The Dombey Family" (ch. 3), the importance of the first plate
becomes apparent. In both plates Polly stands left of center holding a baby in the same position, and in both the muffled chan-
delier, a "monstrous tear depending from the ceiling's eye" (ch.
3, p. 16), is present. But the first plate characterizes the Toodles
by their physical closeness and contact; in the second plate the
Dombeys are epitomized by the spaces between them. Paul is
close only to his nurse, who stands at a respectful distance from
her employer. Florence is separated from Paul by her father, and
from her father by a wide space; as Mrs. Leavis points out, she is
even outside the door frame.[4] While the precise scene is not
described in the text, no one before Alan Horsman had recognized that Dickens, in choosing this version over the one Browne

drew with Dombey standing, elected to have the artist differ from the text.[5] It is as though the illustrator's attempt to present the author's original conception forced the author to recognize that he had not adequately expressed his own inner vision. Phiz's version rather than Dickens'—which was not altered to fit the illustration—is the one that remains in our memory.

The thematic contrast of the first two plates is carried farther in the illustrations for Part II, "The Christening Party" (ch. 5) and "Polly rescues the Charitable Grinder" (ch. 6). While the first pair compares the newest Toodle and the newest Dombey, in the second the infant Paul is juxtaposed to Polly's oldest son, Biler, who is about to be saved by his mother from a hostile mob of children. Since both boys are under the aegis of Mr. Dombey (who has arranged for Biler's education and thus for his consequent humiliation), perhaps the point is as much an ironic parallel as a contrast: on the surface the difference between the loved and pampered child of a rich man and a coldly patronized poor man's child is shown, but on another level we see in both the tendency of the Dombey influence to blight and wither.

This tendency is illustrated in the first of several plates dealing with Paul's childhood, "Paul and Mrs. Pipchin" (ch. 8; Illus. 60), perhaps the most celebrated etching in the novel, if only because Dickens is on record as having been violently disappointed with it.[6] Dickens seems to have objected because Paul is sitting in the wrong kind of chair, and Mrs. Pipchin should be stooped and much older, although according to Mrs. Leavis the whole atmosphere is not uncanny enough, the witchlike and magical qualities of the text insufficiently realized.[7] Yet Browne was presented with special problems as an interpreter. The description of Mrs. Pipchin is, if taken straight, quite extravagant: she is a "marvelously ill-favored, ill-conditioned old lady, of a stooping figure, with a mottled face, like bad marble, a hook nose, and a hard grey eye, that looked as if it might have been hammered at on an anvil without sustaining any injury"; she is an "ogress and child-queller" who likes hairy, sticky, creeping plants, and whose "waters of gladness and milk of human kindness had been pumped out dry" (ch. 8, p. 72). The description of the scene depicted in the fifth plate concludes that "the good old lady might have been—not to record it disrespectfully—a witch, and

Paul and the cat her two familiars, as they all sat by the fire together" (pp.75–76). Dickens may have been upset because the plate (whose drawings he evidently did not get to see) failed to match his own inner vision.[8] Browne can certainly be faulted for not getting the chair right, but one must ask how an illustrator is to deal with semifacetious suggestions of the uncanny and supernatural when he is illustrating a purportedly realistic novel. Surely he is faced with the problem of embodying a sense of the author's description without suddenly shifting his style into a more fantastic one.

The drawings for "Paul and Mrs. Pipchin" give evidence that Browne worked hard to get this illustration right. The initial sketch (Dexter) is a free ink drawing, with the figures facing the same way as in the printed etching;[9] the number of comparable drawings extant is small enough so it seems reasonable to assume that when Phiz did make such a sketch he was especially concerned about the left–right arrangement, as in the vignette title for *Martin Chuzzlewit*. In this case a look at the working drawing (Illus. 61), reversed as usual, reveals that the placement of the figures makes some difference. With Paul on the left, as in the etching, he catches our attention first, and only then do we notice Mrs. Pipchin; with the figures reversed, Mrs. Pipchin dominates: looking from left to right we see first her creepy plants, then her looming figure, and only third little Paul. The printed version and the initial drawing cause us to see Mrs. Pipchin more through Paul's eyes; the author's description of her then may be understood to take some of its fairytale quality from that viewpoint. Browne seems to me to have been as successful as possible in his attempt to combine a realistic with a fantastic atmosphere, and it should be mentioned that Mrs. Pipchin's expression is a good deal more frightening and witchlike in Steel B than in Steel A, though it is the latter which most resembles the working drawing—suggesting that Browne was still experimenting with La Pipchin down to the last minute.

The companion etching, "Captain Cuttle consoles his friend" (ch. 9), takes us from the harshness of Paul's Brighton environment to the protections of the Wooden Midshipman. Visually, the parallel is between Paul sitting in his chair looking up apprehensively at the old "child-queller," and Sol Gills sitting in his chair being comforted by his nephew and Captain Cuttle. Although the basic point may be one of contrast, both Paul and Sol are "old-fashioned" in slightly different senses: Paul, we discover, seems precocious because he is so close to and intuitively so aware of death; Mr. Gills is old-fashioned in the present sense of being, as he says, behind the times. In both there are overtones of enfeeblement and decline.

Dr. Blimber's school finishes off, in the next three plates, what was begun by Mr. Dombey in dismissing Polly, and continued by sending Paul to Mrs. Pipchin. For "Dr. Blimber's Young Gentlemen as they appeared when enjoying themselves" (ch. 12), Dickens' surviving instructions show us how much Browne was able to contribute to his collaboration with Dickens. The larger part of the memorandum concerns a paraphrase of his evocation in the preceding chapter of the Doctor's disagreeable method of education; the rest gives a very brief account of the subject:

> These young gentlemen, out walking, very dismally and formally (observe it's a very expensive school). . . . I think Doctor Blimber, a little removed from the rest, should bring up the rear, or lead the van, with Paul, who is much the youngest of the party. I extract the description of the Doctor. Paul as last described, but a twelvemonth older. No collar or neckerchief for him, of course. I would make the next youngest boy about three or four years older than he.[10]

Phiz deviates from the instructions and text by including seventeen rather than the ten boys said to be in the establishment at one time, and the only possible excuse for this might be that the smaller number would populate the design too sparsely; in the drawing (Elkins) six are lightly drawn, suggesting a late addition. Besides making this change, Phiz has fully apprehended the drift of Dickens' meaning and added four country urchins, two of them ogling the funereal procession with amusement, the others rollicking alongside Blimber's boys, some of whom view them with envy; in addition, there are bathing-machines on the beach, a child flying a kite, and another riding a donkey with an older companion—all examples of the kind of childhood fun that

Blimber's pupils are supposed to be too dignified and un-
childlike to enjoy.

The last etching in which Paul appears, "Paul goes home for
the holidays" (ch. 14), emphasizes a different aspect of Paul's
experience at Blimber's. Here, the composition stresses how little Paul, the "old-fashioned child," has become the object of love
and pity for everyone in the school, and the students are transformed temporarily; rather than threatening they are here all
devoted to Paul, with Florence the center of nearly all eyes. By
adding the three boys at top left, greedily going for the ices and
cakes while the rest of the party are engaged with Paul, however,
Browne hints at how very transitory is the school's transformation under the boy's influence.

The remaining three subjects in the first six monthly parts are
devoted to the aftermath of Paul's death: the first, "Profound
Cogitations of Captain Cuttle" (ch. 15), contrasts with Paul's
farewell in foreshadowing Walter's actual sea journey, while
"Poor Paul's Friend" (ch. 18) and "The Wooden Midshipman on
the look out" (ch. 19) deal with Florence who turns away from
her father after Paul's death.

Despite the number of child subjects in the first twelve illustrations, taken as a group these etchings bring out strikingly that
Dombey and Son is populated by a large number of monstrous or
dangerous women, and that sexual hatred and frustration lurk not
far below the surface. Though it is centered upon the Toodle
family, the very first plate features both Miss Tox and Mrs. Chick
who preside over the scene like a couple of harpies. In the third
plate, Susan Nipper, Miss Tox, and Mrs. Chick again chill the
atmosphere, and the spiritually castrated Mr. Chick looks like a
guilty schoolboy trying to control his urge to whistle. In "Paul
and Mrs. Pipchin" we have the famous witchlike widow, a "disappointed" woman who hastens Paul's decline. But the themes
of sexual conflict and female domination begin in full with
"Major Bagstock is delighted to have that opportunity" (ch. 21;
Illus. 62 and 63).

The Major introduces Dombey to Mrs. Skewton and her
daughter Edith Granger at Leamington Spa in a plate which is
special if only because two sets of instructions from Dickens
survive, the second a comment on the illustrator's preliminary

sketch; two drawings survive as well. As is generally the case with the later *Dombey and Son* plates, apparently Browne was given no text to work from (by his own account, Dickens had not yet written the text). Thus in a sense the instructions are a kind of ur-text. Dickens wants "to make the Major, who is the incarnation of selfishness and small revenge, a kind of comic Mephistophilean power in the book," and he proceeds to describe each of the figures' personalities, but little of their appearance. In outlining the subject, Dickens says nothing about arrangement of figures, and even gives Browne the choice of portraying them in "the street or in a green lane . . . if you like it better."[11]

Evidently the first lengthy set of instructions was inadequate to convey Dickens' inner vision, for he returned Browne's preliminary sketch[12] with polite but firm directions to dress the Native "in European costume," and to "make the Major older, and with a larger face." As he was to do with several of the plates involving Dombey, Edith, and Carker, Browne made this very much his own creation by adding details which are not merely incidental. The tableau of characters—Edith, Withers the page, Mrs. Skewton, the Native, Bagstock, and Dombey—is ordinary enough in arrangement, though there is a greater power of portraiture evident in the uncaricatured figures of Edith and Dombey than would have been true a few years earlier, and the grotesques are fine indeed. But Browne has added two groups of characters not requested by Dickens in either memorandum. Between Withers and the Native, in the background, are two women and a man, walking toward the distance; the woman on the left, like Edith, wears a bonnet and carries a parasol, and is looking back at her in a way that implies curiosity and perhaps disapproval.

This woman may be no more than a visual parallel to Edith, but at the far left of the etching another group serves a more functional purpose: a man raises his hat to a woman on horseback (as does Mr. Dombey to Edith and her mother on the opposite side) who looks down at him; she is followed by a liveried servant. This group works like one of Phiz's typical background emblems, providing implicit commentary on what is taking place in the foreground. The woman is in a dominant position, above one subservient male and ahead of another, and if I am correct in thinking that she wears a hunting costume, then Dickens' remark about Edith—that she "flies at none but high game"—has been given direct visual expression. There is also a foreshadowing of "Mr. Carker in his hour of triumph" (Illus. 71), in which Edith has humiliated Carker, and a statuette of an amazon on horseback strikes down a male warrior. Since much of the novel is devoted to Dombey's attempt to crush his second wife's spirit, our sympathies do tend to rest with Edith, but this illustration (along with subsequent plates) helps to state the theme of male–female conflict, with the woman a match for the man.[13]

The plate with which this one is paired, "Mr. Toots becomes particular—Diogenes also" (ch. 22), forms a comic counterpoint. As Mr. Dombey is about to woo Edith with the purely ulterior motives of possessing a wife and producing another male heir, so Toots is trying to kiss Susan Nipper in order to get closer to her mistress, Florence. Susan herself is by now transformed from "Spitfire" into a loyal companion for Florence, and in these illustrations she is much prettier than in earlier plates. Ultimately she is the comic, virtuous avatar of the strong-minded woman, transforming Toots's romantic love for the unattainable Florence into a sensible affection for herself. Dickens was perhaps not fully aware of the extent to which sexual conflict developed as a major concern in the novel; but Phiz's plates establish the theme as integral. This plate also offers a useful example of how ephemeral the emblematic details could be to the man who did the final biting of the lines into the steel plate, for surely the inclusion of both a thermometer and a barometer on the wall was supposed to represent the rising heat of the situation, and Miss Nipper's stormy temperament (in his later, extra portrait, Phiz included a picture of an erupting volcano and a box marked "Lucifers" to symbolize this temperament); however, neither steel clearly indicates that the thermometer is high, or the barometer falling, as we might expect, although the barometer's needle is in the same position as in the fifth plate of *David Copperfield*, where it *is* clearly marked "stormy."

From Part VIII to Part X, a further sequence of five plates develops the theme of sexual conflict along the Dombey–Edith–Carker axis of the novel. In "Mr. Carker introduces himself to Florence and the Skettles family" (ch. 24), the novel's most sinister villain shows his teeth to Florence and, graphically, to us for the first time. Browne could never have incorporated most of the text's details into his illustration: Carker whispering to Florence that Walter's ship has not been heard of yet (and the insinuation that Carker is thinking about Florence as a possible wife for himself) and the unspoken communication between them about Florence's complex feelings toward her father, whom she loves but knows would not be pleased to hear from her. Instead, Browne stresses general things about Mr. Dombey's confidential agent not mentioned explicitly in chapter 24. Carker holds a close rein on his horse so that the animal is totally dominated, as Carker will dominate both Dombey and Edith. Carker's nastiness is also alluded to comically. In chapter 22, Dickens had referred to the naturalness of Diogenes' antagonism to Carker: "You have a good scent, Di,—cats, boy, cats!" (p. 224). In the etching, the natural world's instinctive reaction to Carker's evil slyness is brought out not only by the little dog running toward him, but also by the ducks flying away and the donkey raising his ears in terror. The geese, with their upright necks, also parody the dreadfully snobbish and stiff-necked Skettleses in this illustration.[14]

The next two monthly numbers and their illustrations deal largely with the progress and fruition of Mr. Dombey's courtship, and Phiz achieves some of his most telling effects. In "Joe B is sly Sir; devilish sly" (ch. 26), Carker observes Dombey with the same concentration he has devoted to Florence, but here the one observed is unconscious of the observer. It is one among many plates in which looking-at and spying-upon are central motifs, usually with Dombey as the unconscious cynosure of many hostile eyes and thoughts. From his reading of the text or his understanding of the general account Dickens may have given him of the situation, Phiz has seen fit to include a painting on the wall of the "wooing" of Uncle Toby and the Widow Wadman in *Tristram Shandy*, almost certainly derived from C.R. Leslie's painting of this subject, now in the Victoria and Albert Museum.[15] The application is clear, and startling: the joke around which the courtship in Sterne's novel revolves is that the Widow wants to make sure Toby's war wound is not such as to incapacitate him sexually, but Toby is incapable of understanding her hints. Phiz perhaps does not mean to question Dombey's virility, but the notion of sexual incapacity becomes entirely apposite when one realizes that Dombey is not able to command Edith's submission, that his wish for an heir is never fulfilled, and that he is—in appearance at least—cuckolded by Carker (and up to nearly the last minute Dickens intended a literal cuckolding).

The companion plate, in which matters have progressed further, "Mr. Dombey introduces his daughter Florence" (ch. 28; Illus. 64), is notable for the skill with which Phiz has delineated the characters without a touch of caricature except in the case of Mrs. Skewton, who is, after all, caricatured in the text. Browne directs no emblematic ammunition against her here, but in 1848, as one of a set of eight "extra" portrait illustrations to *Dombey and Son*[16] (Illus. 65), he depicts her in much the same pose, but in more detail, as a pathetic grotesque with one scrawny, stockinged foot emerging from beneath her skirts, a bonnet with wilted flowers, and a thin hand toying with a heart locket. On the floor is a magazine open to "La Mode," and on the couch a book, *The Loves of Angels*, which has an ambiguous meaning to say the least—is Mrs. Skewton "angelic" in her sweetness or her deathliness? The vase of flowers under glass suggests the extreme care necessary to keep her looking more alive than dead, while the cupid decorating the mirror regards her archly, as though to say, "You'd better not look in here, my dear." (The motif of the looking glass ominously predicting a woman's death is sketched several times in Browne's 1853 notebook.) At the very top of the composition is a Watteau-like pastoral scene of men and women in seventeenth-century dress, and immediately over the old lady's head, a clock with Father Time in a most threatening pose looks down upon his nearly conquered victim.

I mention here an illustration executed after the novel was first published because it provides some additional evidence that Browne could take the trouble to interpret Dickens independently of the author's monthly instructions—and that he had the skill and understanding to do so. In the remainder of the *Dombey* plate in question, Browne includes two details which relate to characters other than Mrs. Skewton: the nearly covered portrait of Dombey's late wife continues the motif of eyes secretly observing Dombey, for she appears to peek out from behind the cloth. Further, Browne here makes the dog, Diogenes, explicitly hostile to Dombey, whereas in the text he is merely lively because he is happy to see Florence—a change which suggests the underlying alienation between Florence and her father.

The sequel plate in the next part, "Coming Home from Church" (ch. 31; Illus. 66), Browne's first for Dickens to be printed horizontally, is a triumphant culmination of what is best in his work up to this time. It is also an especially important example of the integration—even the inseparability—of text and illustration. Dr. Harvey has praised this plate, citing in particular the emphasis upon Dombey's separation from the crowd and his inferiority to it in "vitality and character," as well as the telling details of the Punch and Judy show, which is in the text, and the funeral procession going in the opposite direction, which is not.[17] The crowd is more than simply vital, however, for the people immediately near the portico look at Dombey with amusement as well as something vaguely menacing, and the image of Dombey in earlier plates as the unaware object of prying, knowing eyes is further advanced.

One of these figures clarifies what is otherwise an obscure passage in the text, at the end of the paragraph being illustrated:

> And why does Mr. Carker, passing through the people to the hall-door, think of the old woman who called to him in the grove that morning? Or why does Florence, as she passes, think, with a tremble, of her childhood, when she was lost, and of the visage of good Mrs. Brown?
>
> (ch. 31, p. 316)

Two curious questions, intelligible as soon as we look at the etching and notice that "good Mrs. Brown" is seated just to the right of the portico. Carker and Florence must have experienced a subliminal impression of the old harridan when they passed through the doorway. It is most likely that Dickens had instructed Browne—who had yet to portray her—to include this figure; we do not even learn that "Mrs. Brown" and the old woman in the wood are one and the same until later. The perfection with which picture and text are integrated here is indicated by the fact that the passage quoted above seems not to have bothered generations of Dickens readers, and the presence of good Mrs. Brown was not remarked in print until 1969.[18] T.W.

Hill says this plate is "almost all Phiz's creation,"[19] and one would like to credit Browne at least with the funeral procession, which is the same kind of spatial parallel as the background details of the plate depicting the Leamington introduction, and the same kind of conceptual analogy we find in a later plate, "Another wedding," which I believe comments satirically on this one.

The first such parodying occurs, however, in the comic plate, "The Midshipman is boarded by the enemy" (ch. 39; Illus. 67 and 68), in which the Bunsby–MacStinger story echoes certain aspects of Edith and Dombey's situation. The predatory women and the "forced" marriages are paralleled; Browne offers considerable iconography both to illustrate this theme and to tie the two couples together. There are, for example, prints of a sea-battle and a foundering ship, an overturned globe, the upset vestiges of such masculine activities as smoking and drinking, and what is apparently the skin of a huge predatory bird with frightening talons. But further, when we recognize that Mrs. MacStinger holds nearly the same position and strikes the same pose as Edith in the companion plate (discussed below), we realize that the tiny Medusa head near Mrs. MacStinger and the caption, "Medusa" (on Steel 25A only) make up a fitting emblem for both women—for do not both reduce men to powerlessness by a mere look?[20] Dickens himself refers to Edith as Medusa during her interview with Florence, just before the great showdown with Dombey: "She did not lay her head down now, and weep, and say that she had no hope but in Florence. She held it up as if she were a beautiful Medusa, looking on him, face to face, to strike him dead" (ch. 47, p. 462). The influence here could well have been one of the artist upon the author, for this passage occurs in an installment two months after the plate in question.[21]

The effect of such parallels between comic and serious plates is not so much to ridicule the more serious elements in the novel as to help unify the narrative structure by stressing the theme of sexual conflict. To view "A chance Meeting" (ch. 40) alongside its companion is to receive sudden enlightenment. Dickens has already been making great play with parallels in juxtaposing the stories of Edith and Alice. Browne's illustrations extend the parallels further, beyond the emphasis upon high-life and low-life prostitution to a vision of the terrifying power of woman. To

put the matter another way: through the parallel between Alice
and Edith, Dickens expresses his social vision of the cash-nexus
between human beings, but through the illustrations Browne
stresses the underlying view of woman as a potentially destructive force. Edith and Alice in "A chance Meeting" are drawn
with so little attention to scale that they appear to be giantesses;
but this serves to emphasize the almost mythic power of women.
And the parallel of Edith and Mrs. MacStinger, implied in their
similar positions, further promotes this theme. One could argue
that Phiz is equally justified in neglecting scale in "Florence
parts from a very old friend" (ch. 44), making Mrs. Pipchin another giantess, for she too is one of the monstrously powerful
women in the book, both child-queller and (it is implied)
husband-queller, halfway between the serious and the purely
comic figures in conception.

The first in a series of plates depicting the course of Dombey's,
Edith's, and Carker's headlong flights to self-destruction, "Mr.
Dombey and his 'confidential agent'" (ch. 42), is of special interest for the care with which Browne sets forth visually the drift of
Dickens' text. Carker regards covertly the painting on the wall
which happens to resemble Edith; but Browne has added another painting depicting a seminude woman at her outdoor bath.
A close look (particularly at Steel B) reveals at left the head of a
man who is evidently watching the bathing woman; the most
likely allusion is to Actaeon coming upon Diana at her bath.
(Phiz used this allusion twice, with more graphic clarity but less
emblematic significance, in Lever's *The Daltons*.) That Actaeon
was torn to pieces by his own hounds as a consequence of his
spying may allude to Carker's ultimate self-destruction resulting
from his interference in Edith's life. Another apparent contribution of Browne's is the small dog near Carker's feet; since it is a
lapdog, looking up at Dombey with its tongue out, it seems to
function as an emblem of Carker himself, fawning upon his master; consistent with this emblem, Carker's teeth are here con-
cealed, while in all previous plates they are very much in evidence.
Browne's emblematic imagination seems to have been stirred
by the theme of sexual conflict, for in the next pair of plates he
displays not only his skill as an etcher, but his ability to make use

of melodramatic conventions to good effect. In "Abstraction & Recognition" (ch. 46; Illus. 69), the statuesque figure of Alice Marwood stands in the dark gateway, but the highlights and the aura of light about her head make her the dominant figure; her mother, though witchlike and sinister, is under Alice's sway, and she blends and recedes into the shadows. The most interesting compositional achievement is the way Browne balances the "abstracted" Carker and Rob against the "recognizing" Alice and her mother, leaving space between the former lovers in the center of the etching for a collection of significant posters on the wall. Phiz has come some distance in making such details credible, for these posters look like a random and tattered group, blending with the street scene and the ragged poverty of mother and daughter.

As with all the *Dombey* plates there are two steels, and in them the posters vary slightly. The source of such variations may be inferred from the extant drawings: a sketch (Gimbel) facing the same way as the final etching but containing most of the poster inscriptions, and the reversed working drawing (Elkins), in which these inscriptions are absent. There is also an early proof (Gimbel) in which the words are again absent, indicating that they may have been etched in reverse directly onto the steel at a late stage. The more obvious posters read "Observe" (Steel B only), alluding to the immediate subject of the plate; "Bal Masque," suggesting Alice's concealment; "Cruikshank/Bottle," in reference to the Hogarthian set of eight plates published in 1847, depicting the fall of a family, through drink, into poverty. The others are rather more complex. "Down Again / 6" (Steel B only) is, literally, a merchant's announcement of a drop in prices, but here it foreshadows the fall of Carker, who will be brought down thanks to Alice's vengeful scheming. "To Those About to Marry" would now undoubtedly carry the implied injunction, "Don't," but has a more somber overtone in this novel than in its earlier use in *Martin Chuzzlewit*. "Moses" would be the famous clothing merchant, who wrote poetical advertisements and took advertising space in the third part of *Dombey and Son;* but in the immediate context it probably has a broader meaning as well: with Edith about to run off with Carker, it evokes the Commandments against adultery and coveting one's neighbor's wife.

The remaining poster, "Theatre/City/Madam," is the most interesting allusion in the group. Massinger's *The City Madam* was
produced in London as recently as 1844,[22] and it contains enough
similarities to *Dombey* to make inescapable the conclusion that it
is the source for certain elements most relevant to the present
illustration. A wealthy City merchant, Sir John Frugal, whose
lack of a male heir is "a great pity," has a wife, who, like Mrs.
Skewton, pretends to be younger than she is. Sir John also treats
his younger brother Luke much as James Carker treats John:
Luke has squandered the large fortune left to him, and his debts
have been paid by his brother, who employs him, treats him like
a servant, and reminds him of his disgrace. Luke embezzles
money and urges the other clerks to emulate him, and like John
Carker speaks of himself as an "example"; but unlike John he
turns out to be a total scoundrel. In addition, a bawd, Secret, is
reproached by her prostituted daughter, Shave'em, for not caring
"upon what desperate service you employ me, / Nor with whom,
so you have your fee."[23] The parallel with Alice and her mother is
clear, and since it seems unlikely that so many parallels could
have been coincidental, it is probable that Dickens either consciously drew upon Massinger's play, or, at the very least, that he
or Phiz recognized its relevance. As well as giving us an insight
into Dickens' knowledge of Jacobean drama (and remember that
he refers to the final situation between Carker and Edith as an
"inverted Maid's Tragedy"),[24] this illustration shows at how fundamental a level picture and text could complement one another.

    The relation of "Abstraction & Recognition" to its companion,
"Florence & Edith on the Staircase" (ch. 47; Illus. 70), is primarily sequential, rather than formal, in that Edith's flight follows
from Carker's plans made during his "abstraction"; but the pairing implies a link between Alice and Edith as each raises her left
hand to her mouth. Again, Browne has posed his characters
theatrically without falling into absurdity. But in this plate
perhaps more than in any other, full significance of the illustration is conveyed by the emblematic details taken together. The
position of the topmost detail, an oval painting of a young woman
holding a dove at her bosom, suggests a guiding principle for
reading the plate. Browne's use of a similar image in later years is
probably reliable evidence of its meaning here. At some point

before 1859 (when he moved away), the Croydon Board of
Health asked him to design a new seal for them. He first submitted a full-length drawing of a young woman holding a dove much
as in the detail for the staircase plate; it bears the caption "Purity," and beneath, "Sans Tache."[25] The placement of an emblem
representing spotless purity at the very top of the present etching
implies a hierarchy of values, and Browne's device conveys not
only purity, through the dove, but spiritual love, since the bird is
succored at the girl's breast.

In the lower half of the design we find two pieces of statuary
flanking Edith and Florence that respectively refer to Dombey's
treatment of Florence and to Edith's conduct and the situation
she has become enmeshed in. The left-hand statue depicts a man
about to sacrifice a young woman with his knife; the probable
allusion is to Agamemnon and Iphigenia, a father sacrificing his
daughter to what he thinks are higher principles. The other
statue represents Venus holding the apple she had been awarded
by Paris, and the implications are bitterly ironic: it is Carker who
is Paris in the novel, choosing Edith over the other two women
he has favored in the past, Alice Marwood and—as we are liable
to forget—Florence Dombey. Above Edith, the wall plaques are
Thorwaldsen's popular reliefs, "Night" and "Morning," both of
which show children borne aloft by maternal angels; they evoke
the twice-thwarted motherhood of Edith. The remaining
emblem is a figurine directly below the emblem of Purity depicting a woman riding on a quadruped which to all appearances
might be a bear or some member of the cat family. T. W. Hill,
without any explanation, says this is "Una and her lion," a reference to The Faerie Queene; the assumption is reasonable, since
Una (Truth) would consort very well with an image of Purity.
Part XIV of Dombey and Son included, among other advertisements, a page by Felix Summerly's Art Manufacturers which
refers to "PURITY, OR UNA AND THE LION, a Statuette. Designed and modelled by John Bell." However, the reference
continues that the statuette is "a companion to Dannecker's
Ariadne, or 'Voluptuousness,'" and it is to this second sculpture
that Phiz's detail in fact bears its strongest resemblance. The
motif is that of Ariadne on her panther, and to carry out the
allusion produces interesting results: Dombey would be
Theseus, who deserted Ariadne, while Carker is Dionysus, arriv-

ing on his panthers to abduct her. The ironies are considerable, however, since it is Edith who, physically at least, abandons Dombey, and Carker's function as a Dionysus is largely in his own "voluptuous" mind rather than in Edith's response to him.

But how successful is the plate as an illustration? To modern sensibilities the message of the emblematic details may be painfully labored, even if the implications of Venus and Ariadne are far from simple; yet one should consider how such an illustration might function in a novel read as a serial over a period of nineteen months. In addition to enhancing continuity through the repeated depiction of central characters, such illustrations could underline moral and psychological themes upon which the novelist might otherwise feel obliged to expatiate at length. Dickens' and Browne's collaboration in such matters seems to have been at least partially intuitive. Sometimes the collaboration would work and sometimes not, but its function was more important to a long, somewhat sprawling novel in parts than to a more tightly organized work half the length or less, such as *A Tale of Two Cities*—in which Browne does not employ a single emblem—or *Hard Times* and *Great Expectations*, which have no illustrations.

The next plate to continue the Dombey–Edith–Carker triangle, "Mr. Dombey and the World" (ch. 51), pleased Dickens,[26] and is another example of how picture and text may be closely integrated. The "stare of the pictures," and of Pitt's bust, as well as the eyes in the world's "own map, hanging on the wall," all derive from Dickens' text. Among the pictures that Phiz has included are the portrait of the first Mrs. Dombey, once again peering out from behind a cloth, and a staring miniature of little Paul; he has also introduced an especially sardonic and satyr-like Father Time immediately behind Dombey's back (perhaps a reference to Dombey's failure to control time in the case of Paul), an amused face on the urn next to Mr. Pitt, and, upon the fireplace, two heads and a naked woman (or a Sphinx?) also regard Dombey. The reminders of Paul and Time imply something more than the shame of cuckoldry, but the withered and drooping flowers are suggestions of sexual impotence, while the Major's way of gesturing with his stick seems aggressively phallic in contrast to Dombey's present languidness. The peacock feathers attached to the mirror—again, hanging down, instead of

displayed erectly—have three appropriate emblematic meanings: they are another example of "eyes" looking at Dombey,
they inevitably evoke the idea of Dombey's overweening pride,
and they symbolize the misfortune which has come to the House
of Dombey.

We continue the progress of Edith, and particularly of Carker
and Dombey, through to their conclusions in three more plates,
those for Parts XVII and XVIII, and one (not including the sum-
marizing frontispiece) in the last, double part. "Secret intelligence" (ch. 52) shows Dombey eavesdropping as Mrs. Brown
wheedles from Rob the Grinder the whereabouts of the eloped
pair, while Alice stares at Dombey with an expression of sup-
pressed hatred. The hovel is effectively drawn and Mrs. Brown's
cat hints at her witchlikeness, but one may feel that the shading
is scratchier than usual and that the dark plate technique, reserved in this novel for Carker's flight, would have been more
effective. One subtle set of details, surely of Phiz's invention, is
the bowl of vegetables, the paring knife, and parings on the floor;
their sole purpose is to serve as a metaphor for the process of
peeling off Rob's resistance layer by layer, until the core of truth
is revealed.

The companion, "Mr. Carker in his hour of triumph" (ch. 54;
Illus. 71), has been given considerable if incomplete attention by
critics.[27] On a general level the etching is a suitable partner for
the preceding plate in direct visual parallelism (both men on the
far left, both women on the right) and the inverted thematic
parallelism of Dombey–Alice and Carker–Edith, each woman
having used her partner in the illustration as a despised means of
destroying the man with whom she has been linked. Mrs. Leavis
points out that the melodramatic poses of Carker and Edith fully
suit the high-flown rhetoric of the text, but it should be said that
in comparison with the working drawing (Illus. 72), Edith's
figure and expression resemble a stuffed dummy's—which indicates that translation from drawing to etching is not always perfect. But a number of other elements make this a most important
illustration.

However dubious at first may seem the suggestion by John R.
Reed that Edith's gesture toward Carker's groin is castrative, the
emblematic details in this plate do in fact emphasize her destructive tendencies—and perhaps those of women in general,

specifically in connection with their sexual allure. In the first plate of Hogarth's *Marriage A-la-Mode,* one of the paintings belonging to the Earl who is arranging his son's marriage portrays Judith just after she has killed Holofernes. Although the large picture (larger than most of Phiz's emblematic details) behind Edith of Judith and Holofernes does not resemble this one, another, at right angles to it and barely distinguishable because of the reflected candlelight, shows a Judith in very much the pose of Hogarth's; there is an even greater resemblance between the large picture behind Edith and the frontispiece Hogarth did for William Huggins' oratorio, *Judith*—the outstretched left hand of the figure in that frontispiece is echoed by Edith herself. It is as though Phiz wished to make sure that we noticed the parallel between Edith and Judith.

As Dr. Reed has noted, both the sword of Judith and the spear of the amazon point at Edith's head, and may suggest Edith's self-destructiveness. If one is hesitant to attribute such an insight to Phiz, one can imagine that Dickens said something to his illustrator about Edith's ruinous course and Browne interpreted this accordingly. For the amazon herself Browne in fact drew upon his own stock of graphic ideas, the statuette closely resembling a detail in an illustration to G. P. R. James's *The Commissioner* (1841–43), where it comically represents the housemaids who have in a "Revolt of the Petticoats" set upon the men who insisted that their boxes be searched. But this does not exhaust Phiz's invention. On the chimney piece there are ceramic figures of courtiers and ladies (two pair, ironically suggesting the two couples, Edith–Dombey and Alice–Carker), and a curious clock at the bottom of which the figures of a reclining Venus and Cupid are discernible, while from the timepiece above an unclear figure hovers rather ominously. There is possibly no precise allegory intended here, but the notion of Time suspended over Beauty and Love seems appropriate, if not brilliant. One may also interpret the two mirrors, both facing Edith, as symbols which imply that she is fully recognizing what she herself is, in the process of spurning Carker.

Following directly from Edith's Judithean confrontation with Carker—interrupted by Dombey's arrival—is the flight of Carker in "On the dark Road" (ch. 55). It is an impressive composition, brilliantly catching the motion of the carriage, with a line of trees receding off into the vanishing point at right resembling a column of men implacably following the fugitive. The solitary cross marking a lonely grave forecasts Carker's impending death; no such detail is mentioned in the text where it would be intrusive, but in the etching it forms a natural part of the whole scene. Its unobtrusiveness is aided by the new "dark plate" technique, which increases greatly the possibilities for tonal variation—especially, but by no means exclusively, in scenes of darkness—and thus a sense of space. Although this is often cited as Browne's first dark plate, in fact the first seems to have been the frontispiece to the 1847 edition of Harrison Ainsworth's *Old St. Paul's* (Part XVIII of *Dombey and Son* having appeared in March 1848), which, along with a title page vignette, was added to the John Franklin illustrations of the 1841 first edition. Franklin's etchings were nearly all done with this technique, which may well have inspired Browne to adopt it though with differing effect.

The dark plate becomes ubiquitous among Browne's etchings in the late forties and through the fifties, and it is as well to explain the technique at this point. In its most basic form it provides a way of adding mechanically ruled, very closely spaced lines to the steel in order to produce a "tint," a grayish shading of the plate. It is this simple method that Browne occasionally used for authors other than Dickens. But in general he made more subtle and complex use of the dark plate. Some of the proofs in the Dexter Collection show the outline of the general subject bitten in without the tint, and the process would thus have been something like this: the subject was etched through the ground in the usual way, then the plate bitten, the ground removed, and proofs taken. The lines already fully bitten in the steel would be packed to prevent further biting, and the steel again covered with a (transparent) ground. A ruling machine, adjustable for distance between the lines, would then be drawn over the ground, cutting through it and exposing the steel below; this might be done only horizontally, or diagonally as well, or in two opposing diagonals, so as to produce tiny lozenges. Further shading by means of etching needle and roulette would also be done at this stage.[28] The highlights, areas which were to remain white, would be stopped out with varnish, and then the biting could commence. Those areas which were to be lightest in tint would be stopped out after a short bite, the next lightest after a longer bite, and so on down to the very blackest areas—which would never, except where wholly exposed by the needle, become totally black, but would shimmer with the tiny lights of the unexposed bits between the ruled lines; the darkest sky in "On the dark Road" has these little lights, while the dark parts of the puddle have none, apparently having been exposed to the acid by the needle rather than the ruling machine.

It is breathtaking to consider how much time and effort must have gone into the production of such steels, and no doubt Robert Young deserves some of the credit for the effectiveness of the dark plates. Those by Franklin for *Old St. Paul's* may at first strike one as more finely done: Franklin uses more closely spaced lines, resulting in an almost velvety texture of grays and blacks, but he never makes the kind of dramatic use of the method that Browne does, and thus by contrast Browne appears a bold experimenter. Strangely, the technique does not seem to have been widely used by illustrators, and manuals of etching of the period scarcely ever mention the ruling machine as an available aid. I suspect the technique was just too much trouble for commercial illustrators, and yet too mechanical for those etchers with pretensions to high art.

Carker's actual death is reserved for the allegorical context of the frontispiece, and we are left with two more plates which bear significantly on the Edith–Dombey–Carker situation and the theme of unhappy marriage and female predation. "Let him remember it in that room, years to come" (ch. 59) depicts the moment before Florence's reconciliation with her father, but in a way it illustrates much more; it is probably not accidental that the particular passage in which Florence comes into the room occurs not at page 595, where the illustration is placed in the first bound edition, but four pages later. In between, the text dwells upon Dombey's thoughts, centered around the sentence which forms the plate's title, and brings him almost to the point of suicide just as Florence enters. The details of the illustration emblematically encompass much of this extended indirect monologue. Society (including the worldly Major), which has abandoned Dombey, is represented in the rolled up map of the world and the disapproving bust of Mr. Pitt. The screen shows three images which contrast with Dombey's condition: children at play, a pastoral scene of a young man playing the flute to a young woman, and a rather undefined scene outside a church, possibly a wedding. If the latter is correct, the three panels embody the sequence of a happy boy–girl relationship from childhood through courtship and marriage. The candle on Dombey's dressing table, nearly burnt down, is a traditional image suggesting Dombey's approaching death. In this context, Florence's appearance with sunlight behind her perhaps should not be taken quite literally, for it gives one the impression that she is a visionary apparition rather than a real person. And so it must strike anyone reading the novel for the first time in a bound volume (assuming the illustration is placed as in the original bound edition), since such a reader will not know for four pages whether Florence actually appears or this is her ghostly image.

The companion plate, and the last to depict an actual scene in the novel, relates visually and conceptually back to an earlier plate, "Coming home from Church," by treating marriage comically and ironically as a trap set by predatory women. Although the adjective in its title, "Another wedding" (ch. 60; Illus. 73), is intended to refer to the recent marriages of Florence and Susan, the depiction of the wedding of Jack Bunsby and Mrs. MacStinger recalls Dombey's wedding. It is one of only three horizontal plates in the novel, and it clearly parallels the first one (the second is the dark plate of Carker's flight) in showing a wedding procession with the bride and groom at its head walking arm in arm, observed by casual onlookers in the background. Phiz's mastery of the crowded scene is by now evident, as each of the twenty-three human faces has its own distinct expression, and yet the composition and handling of shading focuses attention upon the main actors in the comedy.

Individual details either reflect the main idea of capture and imprisonment—or worse—or comment upon some aspect of the marriage. And at least one may refer directly back to Edith: the poster, "Wanted/Some Fine/Young Men/Hector/Amazon," recalls the amazon statuette which symbolized Edith's dominance in "Mr. Carker in his hour of triumph," as the detail, "Medusa," referring to Mrs. MacStinger, was echoed in Dickens' subsequent description of Edith. A further link with other strands in

the novel is the poster for "Black-Eyed Susan," a play by Douglas
Jerrold about the marriage of a jolly sailor. We should remember
that Susan Nipper (a name not unlike MacStinger in import) has
often been described as possessing black eyes, and in taking over
and marrying the malleable Toots she has matched Mrs.
MacStinger's capture of Bunsby, if somewhat more benignly.
Several animals are emblems for Jack Bunsby in his present woe-
ful state: the cows and sheep being led through the street (a
procession which mirrors the main subject much as the funeral
does in "Coming home from Church"), and the carcasses of animals (including two detached hearts) hanging up outside
Smashem the butcher's next to the Jolly Tar, suggest that the
capture is to be followed by a slaughter, at least symbolically; the
pig, tethered by the hind leg and striving to escape his little
owner, reflects Bunsby's present state of mind; and the caged
birds over the hung up sailor's hat predict his future state as a
married man. The chickens, on the other hand, are probably a
humorous reference to the party of women following in the train
of the happy couple.

But this is not all. Among various other posters, the list of
turnpike tolls for horse, mule, and donkey suggests that Bunsby
is henceforth a servile beast. "She Stoops to Conquer"—
recalling that initially Bunsby managed Mrs. MacS. rather than
the other way around—and "La Mariage [sic] Forcé" hardly require comment, while other posters use naval imagery: the
"Wanted" poster already described, and one reading "Clipper/
Schooner/Wasp" (cf. Mac*Sting*er) on one steel, "Clipper/
Schooner/Triumph"—appropriate in a different way—on the
other. Finally, as the ultimate emblem of Jack Bunsby's fall and
capture, his walking stick, symbol of masculine authority (it is
much in evidence in the plate "Solemn reference is made to Mr.
Bunsby"), ingloriously sits in the muddy street, while he is
allowed to hold only that symbol of female authority, Mrs.
MacStinger's umbrella (cf. Mrs. Gamp), and her reticule.

In claiming that "Another wedding" is a parody of other marriages in the novel (and especially of Dombey's). I do not mean
to diminish the comic power of the Bunsby–MacStinger subplot.
But I am suggesting that without this and certain other illustrations, the links between comic and serious story strands and the
dominance of the woman-as-predator theme would not be as

readily evident. Browne seems to have invented the emblematic details to illustrate this theme, but it is probable that Dickens also stressed the theme to him. In the passages describing Bunsby's wedding, the text repeatedly refers to capture, sacrifice, and victims, and to the danger of all women: "The Captain saw . . . a succession of man-traps stretching out indefinitely; a series of ages of oppression and coercion, through which the seafaring line was doomed" (ch. 60, p. 609).

Considered by absolute standards as either art or interpretation, the frontispiece to *Dombey and Son* (Illus. 74) is not a great work; it has "too much in it," as Dickens complained of the wrapper, leading to an effect—on first sight, at least—of fragmentation. Conceptually, however, it is related to concerns central to Dickens' artistic vision. The novel's final passage has Dombey and a new little Florence and Paul (his grandchildren) on the beach, and it evokes the first Paul, who "lay upon a little bed beside," while the new Paul is "very strong" and can "run about" (ch. 62, p. 624). The sea imagery which so dominates the first part of the book up to Paul's death—signifying at once life, death, and afterlife—is only faintly revived in the conclusion, but it forms the basis of Phiz's frontispiece. From the evidence of the instructions for the *Chuzzlewit* frontispiece, it appears likely that the general conception of the one for *Dombey* was specified by Dickens, but the particular working out left to Browne. As he so frequently did with allegorical compositions, Browne divided this etching into distinct sections (employing different characters and imagery), and he united the lower half with sea imagery.

As in the wrapper, the sea is at the composition's base, but the position of the shore is above; there are no other obvious connections between wrapper and frontispiece. Certain characters are given an allegorical watery fate, depending on their moral deserts, but the treatment ranges from the serious to the slapstick. Major Bagstock, for example, flounders in the waves, about to go down, while Miss Tox at the water's edge acts concerned. What Phiz is probably conveying here is the touch of corruption in Miss Tox's character which temporarily caused her to admire the Major. But, cleansed by the waters (from which she is rescued by a cupid in a scull), she is ultimately saved by her selfless love for Dombey. These figures in the sea are linked to the large central group of Florence, Paul in his beach chair, and four angels, some of whom look up and wave to the children. Paul and Florence are here as in chapter 8 (p. 78), on the beach "with Florence sitting by his side at work." Compositionally this central group is linked with the angels at top center, toward whom two angels ascend, holding an infant Paul in their arms. A motherly angel welcomes him; she may represent Paul's mother in heaven, for Polly Toodles' assertion that "good people turn into bright angels and fly away to Heaven" (ch. 3, p. 18) is not necessarily regarded by Dickens as mere folk-superstition.

If the angels are Dickens' idea, Phiz's conception of them seems to be his own, but very much influenced by late Romantic art, in particular the work of Moritz Retzsch. There are similarities between the large group of angels in the *Dombey* frontispiece and an outline engraving in Retzsch's *Fancies and Truths* (published with English text in 1831, in Leipzig), "The Sleep of Infancy" (Plate 6). To be sure, Retzsch's subject is sleep rather than death, and the arrangement is not identical; but the basically triangular design with a harp-playing angel at the apex is similar, as are the embracing, younger angels at the harper's left. Further, Retzsch's single harp is decorated at top right with a flower and at top left with a star, while Phiz's right-hand harp terminates in a flower, the left-hand one in starry rays; and the way of surrounding the group with clouds is quite similar.

Two other images of death in the frontispiece present it as terrible rather than benign: Mrs. Skewton, looking terrified as she drops her fan, is accosted from behind by both a grinning Father Time with an hourglass which has run out, and a skeleton with a spear, traditional figures of death which were ubiquitous in the nineteenth century and earlier. Directly opposite this group, at the left, Carker's fate is depicted: an avenging spirit threatens him with a lightning bolt while he is pursued by a locomotive engine. (Interestingly, Phiz has anthropomorphized the engine much in the style of contemporary satirists of the 1845 railway panic.[29]) The two angels behind Paul and Florence appear to look at this horrible scene and shield the children from it, a connection which helps somewhat to unify what is altogether a rather diffuse allegory. It is perhaps also significant of Dombey's gradual moral progress that the black clouds (or smoke) arising from the train surround Mr. Dombey, but then are covered by white ones in the angelic scene at the top. From the two cherubs kneeling at the right of the central group a parallel column of white clouds ascends.

With the frontispiece there appears a title page vignette showing a sneaky Grinder reading to an oblivious and magisterial Captain Cuttle. At first glance, this etching appears to illustrate a minor incident (ch. 37, p. 386) that bears no connection with the frontispiece facing it in the bound volume. Yet a definite, if ambiguous, connection exists. The cloud of smoke from the Captain's pipe is not merely incidental, for it all but obscures the map on the wall behind him, leaving visible only its title, "The World." Apart from a visual parallel with the clouds in the frontispiece, this would seem to imply that Captain Cuttle as a representative of the Wooden Midshipman—the company of the virtuous—blocks out The World—the materialistic civilization that produces Carkers and Dombeys, the opinion of which obsesses Dombey until his final conversion to the other party. But in the context such a meaning must remain double-edged: the Captain's innocence is also naiveté, as he is unaware of Rob's deceitfulness and is incapable of fathoming Carker's masks. Whether or not we can attribute this ambiguity to a conscious intention by artist or author, it does seem to expose profound moral ambiguity in the novel itself.

This particular illustration is important for its illumination of an almost subliminal aspect of the novel, not necessarily for the brilliance of the artist's conscious insight. Even the theme of the predatory female has a complexity which probably was not fully recognized by Dickens or even Browne. The explicit theme of *Dombey and Son* seems to be that mercenary and power-hungry men like Dombey and Carker make victims of women; there is no consistent recognition in the text of the paradox that such men are simultaneously the prey of these women. It is the illustrations which bring out the complexity, through comic parallels and emblematic details. I do not mean to suggest that Phiz had greater insight than Dickens; rather, he sometimes saw different things, just as the need to choose subjects for illustrations sometimes led Dickens to see possibilities in his novel not made explicit in the text. And this phenomenon is one of the chief reasons why as Dickens critics we disregard the illustrations only at our peril.

CHAPTER FIVE

David Copperfield:
Progress of
a Confused Soul

Dickens' "favorite child," *David Copperfield*, is un-
equivocally a *Bildungsroman* centered on the progress of
a single protagonist, to which all other strands are subordinate
and usually relevant to the main plot as cautionary tales or ideal
models. The illustrations function in several ways. They make
comic or serious comment on the characters and events through
emblematic details and allusions, underlining implications of the
text; and they also anticipate developments—not simply events,
but feelings and attitudes—which are no more than hinted at in
the text.

A third function that I attribute to the illustrations is perhaps
more debatable. Critical opinion about the novel has tended to
be radically divided. There are those, such as Gwendolyn
Needham, J. Hillis Miller, and Q. D. Leavis, who—whatever
their divergence of interpretation—see the novel as a unified,
artistically successful treatment of David's development from
self-centered immaturity to moral adulthood and wholeness of
self in his marriage to Agnes;[1] and there are those who see Agnes
as an evasion, on Dickens' or David's part, of the realities of
social position, love, and personal development.[2] I am not pro-
posing that the illustrations can resolve this debate, for the critical divisions originate both in the *Weltanschauung* of each critic
and in what is perhaps the ultimate ambiguity of the novel. But
Hablot Browne's work for *David Copperfield* does form part of
the evidence of what the novel *is*, both because of Dickens'

113

selection of subjects and because of what may be considered the interpretations and judgments of the novel's first critic, Phiz.

Some of the etchings for *David Copperfield* are characterized by a slacking off of technical precision, a flattening out of perspective, a frequent sketchiness of line, and less care in filling in backgrounds. None of the faces, with the exceptions of Uriah Heep, Mr. Micawber, and Aunt Betsey Trotwood, have the memorableness of those in *Dombey and Son*. Yet the level of iconographic invention is high, and there is a continuity of imagery that makes the illustrations worthy of close attention. The wood-engraved cover for the monthly parts has a curious relationship to earlier and later cover designs, because unlike those for *Dombey*, *Bleak House*, and *Little Dorrit*, it contains no definite references to any of the novel's characters. Yet it is one of the most coherent of the wrappers, and is thematically parallel to a number of others. Like its immediate predecessor, the design is organized in terms of a series of figures ascending on the left and descending on the right, to and from a single figure at the apex. But here the stream of figures is continuous, from birth at lower left to death at lower right, with the cycle beginning over again in the child playing horsey with the tombstone (a scene which Browne had etched six years earlier in the frontispiece to Thomas Miller's *Godfrey Malvern*, where it derives from the text). The total sequence recalls the Seven Ages of Man, with a mocking Fortuna at the top, as well as modern fools with hobbyhorses, and castles in the air.

The range of traditional iconography is wide, for the stairway of life is a common late Renaissance *topos*, while the fools and their hobbyhorses may derive from certain of the engravings to Quarles's *Emblemes*, probably the most familiar emblem book in the eighteenth and nineteenth centuries. Browne had already used Quarlesian images in *Dombey*'s frontispiece (angels in boats appear several times in the *Emblemes*). The single detail which appears to bear specifically on events in *David Copperfield* is the child playing with the gravestone, which foreshadows both Clara's death and David's shock at discovering that life goes on. But this allusion may be no more than coincidental. (The inclusion of a mother, child, and nurse in the plate is not necessarily a specific reference to David, his mother, and Peggotty.)

The first five monthly parts comprise David's early childhood, up to the flight to Dover and liberation from Murdstone, and the first and last plates of this sequence are concerned directly with David's terrifying stepfather. "Our Pew at Church" (ch. 2; Illus. 75) is one of Browne's most complex illustrations for this novel, or indeed for any of his commissions; its meanings go beyond the passage of text to which it directly corresponds. From among David's "earlier recollections" Dickens has chosen the church rather than a sentimental domestic scene with David, Clara, and Peggotty for Browne to illustrate. The passage referred to describes David's confusion and boredom in church, and ends with the child falling asleep, and "off the seat with a crash," to be "taken out, more dead than alive, by Peggotty" (ch. 2, p. 12). But Phiz has transferred David's sleepiness to the congregation so that the little old pew-opener, the beadle, most of the church band, and several other parishioners are fast asleep.

The subject of this etching resembles Hogarth's engraving (based on his own earlier painting), "The Sleeping Congregation," and although "Our Pew at Church" is a far more crowded and complicated picture, there are definite visual similarities. In both, the clergyman myopically reads his text from a Bible propped up on pillows; and in both a young woman is a principal focus, Mrs. Copperfield with her hands crossed and her eyes demurely cast down, and Hogarth's wench with her hands similarly crossed and her eyes closed in sleep. As Hogarth's clerk slyly regards the sleeping woman out of the corner of his eye, so Mrs. Copperfield is the object of male attention in the person of a black-haired, bewhiskered gentleman who can be no one but Murdstone contemplating the "bewitching young widow" and her small annuity as well, no doubt. The clinching evidence that Browne had Hogarth's engraving in mind is that whereas Hogarth's sleeping female has her prayer book open to the marriage service, indicating where her thoughts and dreams really are, in Phiz's version it is Mr. Murdstone who thinks about marriage, and it is his prayer book which is open: in one of the steels (1A) the letters "MARR" are clearly discernible.

It is altogether curious that Murdstone should be here, since he is nowhere mentioned in the passage that is presumably being illustrated; but his presence is explained several para-

graphs later when David suddenly asks Peggotty whether one
may remarry when one's spouse dies. The source of his wonder-
ing becomes clear when his mother comes in with a "gentleman
with beautiful black hair and whiskers, who had walked home
with us from church last Sunday" (ch. 2, p. 13). One may presume
that Dickens told Browne to include Murdstone, although the
illustrator could have inferred his presence simply by reading
the manuscript of this chapter; either way, the effect is to imply
that the narrator, the grown-up David, has momentarily repressed his recollection of Murdstone in the church on the day in
question, and further, that the child David repressed any awareness of Murdstone as a prospective stepfather, and yet was
prompted by an intuitive insight to question Peggotty about
marriage. Thus text and picture are inextricably related, with the
allusion to Hogarth's marriage-crazy young woman a subtle
added dimension.

Browne has further elaborated the situation in a number of
details. On the one hand, the sleepiness of the congregation is
metaphorically represented by the cobweb upon the light fixture
at upper left and the spider hanging from the angel's trumpet, as
though the figures in the scene are permanently immobile and
the church neglected; only the five little boys who look at a bird's
nest with two eggs in it and mock the unconscious beadle lend
any touch of life to the somnolent scene. Yet the stolen nest may
also symbolize the innocence of Mrs. Copperfield, soon to be
violated by the cunning Murdstone, and the spider and web assume sinister overtones as emblems of deceit and capture. The
most prominent biblical emblem employed in the plate is Eve
tempted by the serpent (a symbol which also links David's
mother iconographically with the doomed Emily). Still more
ominous are the two ostensibly reassuring inscriptions on tombs
in the church floor, "Requiescat in Pace" and "Resurgam."
Common enough in real churches, these epigraphs take on a
special significance in view of David's fear of his father's grave
and the "raising of the dead" when Peggotty tells him "You have
got a pa" (ch. 3, p. 32). This association would seem to be evidence for Mark Spilka's contention that Murdstone is, symbolically, the "*murd*ered man (or *murd*erer) beneath his grave*stone*,
who has risen to assert his rights."[3] Finally, the lamb of God is
shadowed beneath the clerk's hand and, given its subordinate

position relative to Eve and the serpent, may refer to the as yet innocent David.

A drawing of this subject (Illus. 76) is very close to the etching in most respects, but a few changes suggest Phiz's last-minute improvisation. No spider hangs from the trumpet nor do cherubs grimace on the Bodgers monument; instead of the sleeping clarinetist and his neighbor dropping the prayer book off the balcony, a rather large, comic musician plays a long wind instrument—which would make no sense, as the scene is during the sermon. In addition, the only visible biblical detail is of Eve, the lamb having been added with a blunt point for purposes of transfer. A further example of how Browne went on revising his illustrations up to the last minute can be seen in the vertical railings of the stairway leading to the pulpit: in the drawing their lines are straight, and in the etching wiggly, but the change is clearly visible in blind indentations on the drawing.

The companion plate, "I am hospitably received by Mr. Peggotty" (ch. 3), subtly suggests a contrast between the aloof arch of the imposing church and the protective hull of the humble boat house. The three subsequent illustrations are full of emblematic details, most comic but a few portentous. Thus, the waiter's treatment of David in "The Friendly Waiter and I" (ch. 5) is mirrored in pictures of the fox and crane, and of Sancho Panza on "Barataria," where he is prevented from eating (an especially common subject in political satires of earlier decades, and used a number of times by Phiz), while a poster advertising an auction sale implies that Murdstone is disposing of David like a piece of merchandise. In "My musical breakfast" (ch. 5) a picture of a bearded king dancing with his harp before a group of women doubtless represents King David. One may recall that David was despised by Saul's daughter, whom he reproved that "I will yet be more vile than thus, and will be base in mine own sight: and of the Maidservants which thou has spoken of, of them shall I be had in honour" (II. Samuel 6, 22); similarly the boy David has been despised, but he is now honored by two impoverished old women. Also in this plate the recurring cracked mirror and peacock feathers forecast more trouble.

The confrontation between "Steerforth and Mr. Mell" (ch. 7) is full of significant details, most of them comic and immediate, but not until David's return to his home in "Changes at Home" (ch.

8) do we find another plate which we may in some sense "read."
It is a carefully composed etching whose major and subsidiary
details tell a story related to, but not simply repeating, what is in
the text. It focuses upon the brief moment when David enters to
find his mother nursing his new baby brother, and the way
Browne has positioned Clara's chair with its back to David stresses his recent status as outcast, while the decorative wings on the
clock behind him suggest the rapid passage of time. The space
between mother and boy is charged with the tension of an un-
completed action. Mother and infant are centered in such a way
as to recall the stock image of Madonna and Child, consistent
with the rather heavy religiosity of Dickens' text; they are also
watched over by an angel on the fireplace surround, hinting at
perhaps both holiness and impending death. But we are brought
back to earth by the overturned reticule with its sewing implements spilled out on the floor, a reminder of Clara's acceptance of
her Murdstone-assigned role as a flighty child and incompetent
housekeeper.

I find it difficult to agree with Q. D. Leavis' assertion that the
portrait over Clara's head is herself in younger days, since not
only does it fail to resemble her, but the fashion of dress—both
historically and socially—seems inappropriate.[4] The portrait's
emphasis on the lady's breasts suggests a connection with
motherhood, although in the working drawing the breasts are
represented only as blind indentations. To the extent that the
portrait has anything to do with Clara, there may be some sense
in its juxtaposition with prints of the Prodigal Son and Moses in
the Bullrushes. But David is a prodigal son only from the
standpoint of the Murdstones, who consider him to be willfully
bad; Clara regards him so only to the extent that they have been
able to influence her. The print of Moses, on the other hand,
suggests both David's being found again, so to speak, by his
mother, and his own unexpected discovery of his baby brother.

"Changes at Home" exemplifies the intermittent heavy-
handedness of Phiz's emblematic art in *David Copperfield;* yet
he is truly being responsive to the author, for what is an illustrator to make of such effusions as David's "I wish I had died. I
wish I had died then, with that feeling in my heart! I should have
been more fit for Heaven than I ever have been since" (p. 80),
other than to use religious imagery? Phiz is most successful

when his emblems bring out ideas which if stated baldly in the text would strike the reader as mawkish. When both text and etching are so terribly explicit, one feels inundated with sentiment. With no more than one (possible) emblem, "Mrs. Gummidge casts a damp on our departure" (ch. 10) seems more successful artistically in its representation of the infantile adult couple (Barkis and Peggotty) and the precocious child couple (David and Emily); there is a spirited horse and fine, open handling of the boat house and the sea, and only the chain linked to a broken piling in the left foreground may comment unobtrusively on the perils of marriage, which the rest of the novel is at some pains to elaborate.

One of the best known of Browne's illustrations is the first of the pair concluding David's childhood tribulations. Browne originally offered a drawing for "I make myself known to my Aunt" (ch. 13) that showed Betsey Trotwood sitting "flat down in the garden-path" with astonishment when David announces who he is. The etching (Illus. 77) (for which I have not located the final, working drawing, though the other two, as well as a preliminary first version [Illus. 78], are in Elkins) combines the figure of Betsey in the second version (Illus. 79) with the more appealing figure of David as he is in the first. It is a good solution, since Betsey's essential dignity is retained without scanting her personal eccentricity. When asked what is Betsey's reaction to David, I would wager that most readers of the illustrated edition would reply in terms of Phiz's etching rather than the text.

The companion plate, "The momentous interview" (ch. 14), shows Betsey bringing David through to his liberation from the Murdstones, and is most interesting in its single emblematic detail. It may tell us something of Dickens' attitude toward his character that between the earliest graphic appearance of Murdstone (when he is not mentioned in the relevant text) and his deflation by Betsey, he and his sister do not appear once in the illustrations; it is as though Murdstone's appearance in the role of chastiser, for example, might jar too painfully with the tone Dickens wanted for the plates. On the other hand, he may have felt that Murdstone portrayed would be Murdstone prematurely deflated by caricature. In this plate Betsey is a buffer between the hirsute stepfather and his oddly attired stepson, and even Miss Murdstone shows little fight under Betsey's withering gaze. A picture on the wall portrays Joseph's brothers bringing the bloody coat to their father in order to shift the blame for their presumed murder of Joseph onto a wild animal. The envy of Joseph's brothers for his coat of many colors is probably a humorous allusion to the protective swaddling in which Betsey has had David dressed; but there is a more important parallel between the brothers' envy and the jealousy Murdstone has felt over his wife's love for her son. Beyond this, the attempted murder of Joseph parallels the accusation by Betsey that Murdstone has caused the death of both wife and baby and also attempted to destroy David; the casting of blame upon an animal is also analogous to Murdstone's insistence that it is David who was the source of evil in his family.

As David himself says, what follows the encounter with the Murdstones in Dover is a "new life," with the Wickfields. At this point new, subordinate strands are introduced for the first time, as David's story itself divides between his love for Dora and that for Agnes, while the stories of Annie Strong and David's first love, little Emily, the prostitute Martha, and the ruthlessly ambitious Uriah Heep operate as cautionary parallels. Some of these strands are difficult to separate, but certain sequences can be traced which, through their subjects and iconography, imply thematic parallels not always made explicit in the text.

"Somebody turns up" (ch. 17) finds David in his new, middle-class existence, now a young gentleman, someone to be deferred to by the Heeps, although actually as much a victim as ever. His pride at being "entertained as an honoured guest" (p. 181) by the fawning Heeps is indicated in the pleasure with which his prissy little face and figure seem to be enjoying Uriah's obsequiousness; it is understandable why he is not glad of Micawber's interruption, but his annoyance is shown in the door knocker's grimace at that gentleman rather than in his own face. Yet the real nature of the event taking place, the corkscrewing of facts about himself out of David—the metaphor is Dickens' own—is indicated by the corkscrew hanging on the wall, the stuffed owl which implies the predatory watchfulness of the Heeps, the mousetrap, and even the ceramic cats, which, together with the real cat next to Mrs. Heep, could represent the

Heeps' ability alternately to fawn and purr, and to hiss, spit, and scratch, or destroy a "mouse." Similarly, David's pride once more goes before a fall in "My first fall in life" (ch. 19), where the sign, "Trespass," and the geese running away from the horses suggest what is happening to David as he loses his seat to the horsey gentleman, and the ease with which he is routed.

Uriah as the double of David, the other side of his respectable ambition to be a gentleman, is suggested in two etchings. In "Uriah persists in hovering near us, at the dinner party" (ch. 25), the ostensible meaning implies that Uriah threatens Agnes with his lecherousness and his ambition to marry the boss's daughter; but Browne's introduction of the statuette of an angel standing protectively behind a child (itself probably inspired by the chapter title, "Good and Bad Angels") makes matters less simple. In the text, David's "good angel" is Agnes, his bad one, according to her, Steerforth; but in the illustration the angel and child visually parallel the positions of Uriah and Agnes, implying that Uriah is at once a threat to Agnes and possibly also another "bad angel" for David. If we take this plate with its companion, "I fall into captivity" (ch. 26), a parallel emerges between David and Uriah: each wants to marry the boss's daughter, and the main difference seems to be the social acceptability of the suitor.

This doubling is, I think, carried further in "Mr. Wickfield and his partner wait upon my Aunt" (ch. 35), where Uriah, who is taking over Mr. Wickfield's business, is paired visually with David. In addition, the picture of the sun rising over Dover Castle not only contrasts Betsey's comfortable country home with the smoke of London outside the window, but, because it is directly over Wickfield's head, implies Uriah's rising "sun": his ambition to replace the old man in business, and perhaps to become his "son" by marrying Agnes (such a pun is suggested clearly in one of the plates for *Little Dorrit*, and goes back at least to Gillray).

David's courtship and marriage to Dora is probably the activity to which the hero devotes the most passion in the novel, and it is given a series of important and carefully worked out illustrations, most of which are thick with emblematic details. In the one already mentioned, "I fall into captivity," perhaps the only strictly emblematic detail is the diorama of birds under glass, suggesting the exceedingly preserved and sheltered life of Dora. But a piano is also present which in view of the rest of the series may represent Dora's eternal singing of "enchanted ballads . . . generally to the effect that, whatever was the matter, we ought always to dance, Ta ra la, Ta ra la!" (ch. 26, p. 277). A piano turns up again in "Traddles and I in conference with the Misses Spenlow" (ch. 41; Illus. 5) where, as I have noted in my first chapter, it is adorned with numerous emblems of Dora and of David's love for her.

The musical emblem becomes a guitar (the actual instrument played by Dora) in "Our Housekeeping" (ch. 44), rather unceremoniously used as a hatrack, and positioned beneath a caged pair of lovebirds who are now apparently quarreling, in contrast to those in an earlier plate. In "My child-wife's old companion" (ch. 53), where Dora's death is announced by Agnes, the guitar, its strings broken, represents Dora herself (the emblem is to be used again by Browne in *Bleak House*, where it represents Lady Dedlock in her impending flight toward death).

Of all the Dora illustrations, those depicting the marriage and her death are most elaborate. In "I am Married" (ch. 43; Illus. 80), marriage is presented as a joyous occasion, a miracle, as the mural of the changing of water into wine at Cana suggests, but a good deal more is conveyed through the miscellaneous crowd. At the far right two women stand with infants behind the font, presumably awaiting their children's christening; in front of the font is a young girl with a small child of two of three years. Next to the large monument at right a pair of young lovers seem oblivious to all but each other, but behind them a woman clearly intended to be a spinster turns her nose up and her mouth down at the proceedings (which include another young man who is looking at her pretty companion). From the gallery above, Peggotty, in widow's weeds, looks down, and beneath the gallery, directly behind the font and the waiting mothers, is a casket covered with a sheet, implying a recent death. The panorama of the stages of man's life—echoing the cover—is thus expressed, from birth through childhood, love and marriage, to death. And the inclusion of all these within such a small compass may foreshadow the brevity of David's marriage to Dora. Much as in "Our Pew at Church," the relative moribundity of the Church of England is suggested by the elderly, indifferent clergyman and the cobweb decking the right-hand monument. The web has trapped a fly, and since Phiz used this emblem in *Pickwick* and *Martin Chuzzlewit* to signify entrapment or entanglement, there is perhaps a somewhat cynical implication that David (or Dora?) is being trapped into an imprisoning and destructive marriage. (The cobweb is a last-minute addition, present on the drawing [Elkins] in blind only.)

Browne's function as a commentator is clear in "My child-wife's old companion" both in the composition and the details, which together summarize, but do not specifically repeat, the several thematic notes struck in the related pages of text, from David's agonized and guilty thoughts, with attempted religious self-consolation ("I have remembered Who wept for a parting between the living and the dead"—p. 543), to the last interview with Dora, Jip's death, and Agnes' simultaneous announcement of Dora's:

> He comes very slowly back to me, licks my hand, and lifts his dim eyes to my face.
> "O, Jip! It may be, never again!"
> He lies down at my feet, stretches himself out as if to sleep, and with a plaintive cry, is dead.
> "O Agnes! Look, look, here!"
> —That face, so full of pity and of grief, that rain of tears, that awful mute appeal to me, that solemn hand upraised towards Heaven!
> "Agnes?"
> It is over. Darkness comes before my eyes; and for a time, all things are blotted out of my remembrance.

We may be thankful that the illustration does not depict that "solemn hand upraised"; the calmer air of the moment just before David becomes aware of Agnes' presence seems more appropriate and less bathetic. The religious element is introduced unobtrusively in the cross of the church steeple and the moon (suggesting Dora's purity?) above it, and the boatman on the Thames may refer to Dora's crossing over to the afterlife. These details also recall Agnes' role as David's good angel, and while the prominence of Dora's portrait of course refers to her as the absent subject of the plate, its position between the two characters recalls that she has stood between David and the so-called "real heroine." The other details allude to David's relationship to

Dora, and to her death. The eighteenth-century figurines on the mantel suggest the "romantic" love of their courtship, the embracing cherubs on the fireplace surround, the idyllic immaturity of their love. The empty clock case indicates death and loss, while the dog mourning over its master's body is a direct reference to Jip. In the just extinguished candle end we have a traditional image of the end of life; but the most condensed and easily overlooked emblem is a butterfly perched on the inkstand, in one steel (34A) only, and missing in the working drawing. By itself, the butterfly might be merely a symbol of the human soul and its transitoriness; but although it retains this connotation, in conjunction with the inkwell and the attached quill pen it reminds us of the incompatible union of the striving author and the child-wife flitting from one thing to another and unable to help David's work and ambitions.

David's difficult relationship with Dora is explicitly commented on in the text by the situation of Annie Strong, her rakish cousin Jack Maldon, and her elderly husband, Dr. Strong. In the illustrations, the juxtaposition in one monthly part of "Our Housekeeping," which depicts the troubles of David's marriage, with "Mr. Dick fulfils my Aunt's prediction" (ch. 45), in which the solidity of Annie's marriage is affirmed, is undoubtedly intended by Dickens to underline the contrast between David's marriage of "unsuitability of mind and purpose" with Annie's perfect father–daughter marriage. But the first plate which features Annie and the Doctor, "I return to the Doctor's after the party" (ch. 16), presented long before David or the reader has any idea of how this May–December marriage will fare, in context seems to relate more directly to the story of Emily, the fallen woman, whose own prominence in the illustrations is remarkable. Not only does Phiz stress heavily the insensibility of the Doctor by having him fail to look down at the lovely creature before him, and his gullibility by including the detail of a brick labeled "Babylon" (which itself may allude to sensuality and loose living), but he stresses the temptation and possible fall of Annie by showing a moth circling a candle's flame.

Apart from this plate, altogether eight illustrations (one-fifth of the total) are devoted to the waywardness and near-destruction of a fallen woman; three of these eight include Martha, the remorseful prostitute, whose tale is a cautionary one for Emily and who aids David and Mr. Peggotty in saving her from a terrible fate. It seems to me that by the subjects he thus has chosen (and three more plates, including the title page, portray Emily as a child), Dickens reveals an undercurrent in his own conception of David's life, the importance of Emily and of the fallen-woman *topos*. Furthermore, of these eight plates two include the seducer, Steerforth, two involve visits of David to Steerforth's mother, and one includes Steerforth's valet, all of which tend to underline the fascination of David with this upper-class Adonis, with his magnetic sexual power and domination over women.

Steerforth and Emily first meet in Part VII, but the pair of illustrations in Part VIII together form Browne's first important graphic interpretation of the tension-charged atmosphere between the upper-class seducer and the fisherman's daughter, betrothed to her cousin, Ham. I have already discussed in my opening chapter "I make the acquaintance of Miss Mowcher" (Illus. 6) as a prime example of Browne's independence as an interpreter; it is also one of the best examples of the use of emblematic detail to anticipate action not yet specified in the text. In it, we see David as both an extreme innocent and an unquestioning admirer of Steerforth. In its companion, "Martha" (ch. 22; Illus. 81), David is again a naive, somewhat bemused onlooker, so deeply clothed in shadow as to be easily overlooked at first glance. The arrangement of figures and emblems, however, makes naivté on the reader's part less likely: we are well aware that Martha's fate may be Emily's. The two girls are connected visually, first of all, by the luster in their dark hair.[5] Although Martha's kneeling position is specified in the text, Browne takes this further by mirroring it with the pose of Mary Magdalene anointing the feet of Christ, in a picture over the mantel.

This last detail brings out several analogies when one recalls that the sister of Mary Magdalene was named Martha, for this suggests both a link between the latter two, and a sisterly link between Martha and Emily. Further, Ham Peggotty is closest to imitating the position of Christ in the picture, which reminds us of Ham's charity in not scorning Martha and in adding to the purse of money Emily gives her. As Martha kneels almost directly beneath the picture of the Magdalene, so Emily stands beneath a print of Eve and the serpent. The clear implication is

that Emily is being tempted to evil, while Martha is on the path
to reform through her own remorse and others' forgiveness, although she does not yet recognize the path. Such parallels and
foreshadowings again involve Browne in presenting iconographic commentaries which would seem terribly heavy and
moralistic in the text; and it is worth considering that such practice is analogous to the marginal commentaries in editions of
Pilgrim's Progress or the Bible, which were familiar and would
feel natural to readers of Dickens' and Browne's time.

Emily's story is continued in "We are disturbed in our cook-
ery" (ch. 28), in which the slimy Mr. Littimer appears and asks
about his master's whereabouts; only the rather comical print of
Damocles with his sword about to descend hints at the impending disaster of Emily's flight with Steerforth. The sword has de-
scended already in "Mr. Peggotty and Mrs. Steerforth" (ch. 32)
which contains a set of significant details commenting upon the
action in general terms: the large portrait of Steerforth as a small
child provides (in the innocence of the child and the carefree-
ness of the butterfly beside him) a contrast to the present situation, while just below the portrait is one of those Father Time
clocks common in Browne's etchings. Here the figure most
clearly illustrates the transitoriness of human existence by his
resolute step. A less hackneyed image is the kitten attempting to
get at the caged bird, for although one might think this refers
simply to the abduction of Emily, Hogarth's use of similar
emblems in *The Graham Children* suggests that it is also relevant to the theme of time passing. In Hogarth's painting, as
Ronald Paulson describes it, "a tiny figure of Cupid with a scythe
like Father Time's rests atop the clock at the left, and opposite
him a cat eyes the bird in its cage—these, flanking the happy,
smiling children, constitute an admonitory allegory" on the
transitory nature of youth, beauty, happiness and innocence, the
illusion of a world where birds aren't killed by cats.[6] Phiz makes
the allegory more complex by drawing a kitten which, like the
infant Steerforth, will have to grow up in order to do harm to
other living creatures. Finally, the male and female busts may
simply represent adult sexual life, but Johannsen identifies the
male one as Apollo,[7] and it does resemble conventional heads of
that god. The allusion might either suggest Steerforth's excep-

tional male beauty or the pagan gods' tendency to become enamored of mortal women—just as Steerforth has stooped from his social height to choose a fisherman's daughter.

The other, later illustration with Mrs. Steerforth is less successful, but before the denouement of Emily's story, Martha appears in two illustrations as, so to speak, Emily's cautionary double. "The Wanderer" (ch. 40), in which Browne experiments with effects of light and shade, has mainly the function of underlining the dramatic effect of the text, in which Martha's "haggard, listening face" appears momentarily at the door as David talks to Mr. Peggotty about his lost niece. Much more striking is "The River" (ch. 46; Illus. 82), the second dark plate Browne did for Dickens and the only one in *David Copperfield* (all forty of the etchings for Lever's *Roland Cashel*, overlapping in time of appearance with *Copperfield*, were produced by this method). Its uniqueness in this context is among several factors contributing to its success. It gives us the scene of a last-minute prevention of the standard watery fate of prostitutes, a fate which, the accompanying plate makes clear, could also have been Emily's. Phiz's conception of Martha at the river, and the technical differences between the two versions, seem to me more interesting than Dickens' hysterical narrative at this point. Phiz translates a strong and bold drawing (Illus. 83) in pen and wash into two carefully executed etchings which vary considerably in the handling of light and dark. Dickens rarely provided opportunities for sweeping, panoramic outdoor scenes, and when liberated from the confinement of interiors, narrow streets, or mild country views, Phiz seems to have indulged his propensity for dramatic landscape. (Ainsworth and Lever were to give him freer rein in this regard.)

As is often the case with dark plates, one steel is generally much darker than the other, and the lighter one (31A) depends more on subtle tonal variations in the mechanical tint, achieved by stopping-out, while the darker has a great deal more shading added by the etching needle, apparently over the tint. The effects are quite different, with the first steel subtler and smoother, and the second more strikingly dramatic in its contrasts and strong lines. In both versions the figure of Martha is given an unusual degree of solidity through the use of light and dark and, in 31B only, the modeling of her features. Surrounding objects, bits of junk and flotsam, are subordinated to her predominantly bright figure, as are David and Mr. Peggotty. The hazy presence of St. Paul's in the background may suggest—as it does more emphatically in one of the dark plates to *Bleak House*—the distance of official religious institutions from such outcasts. Otherwise, Phiz has followed the text and made good use of the smoking factory chimneys specified by Dickens.

The rescue of Martha from the river is followed in the text by the rescue of Emily from prostitution, and so in the illustrations. "Mr. Peggotty's dream comes true" (ch. 50; Illus. 84) was apparently a bit uncertain in the making, as the drawing (Elkins) suggests; in it not only does David wear a hat, but a female figure seated in the chair and slumped over the table is probably intended for Rosa Dartle, who has been haranguing Emily when the two men enter.[8] This drawing is an awkward version, but it is understandable that Phiz should have included Rosa, since the text itself fails to indicate whether she managed an exit before the end of the chapter. Parallels to other plates are numerous. First, Emily recalls the main, kneeling figure of "Martha" (Illus. 81), whose face is similarly hidden. Then there are conventional allusions to Emily's lost innocence in the broken flowerpot, cracked mirror (into which she seems to be looking as her uncle holds her), and broken pitcher; Rosa's remark that Emily must "drop her pretty mask"—that is, be the prostitute that Rosa considers her, instead of the wronged woman she thinks herself—is rather awkwardly reflected in the domino mask and masked-ball program, since Emily surely has not come from a party, although perhaps these items are to be taken literally as the leavings of a previous, disreputable occupant.

From another point of view than Rosa's, however, the dropping of the mask might represent Emily's return from her pose as mistress of a grand gentleman to her real self, emblematized in the signs of her cherished past and happier future: the seashells that have fallen from her trunk, mementoes of her beloved home, the picture of a fisherman and a little girl, and that of a ship sailing on fair seas. This last may have its origin in the text's reference to "common pictures of ships on the walls," but recalling that in an earlier illustration Emily's fate has been foreshadowed by a picture of a ship in a storm, it is likely that the present one refers to her future, when she is happily reunited with her uncle. That the mask may signify the return to one's true self is suggested by its presence in the first illustration for the next monthly part, "Restoration of mutual confidence between Mr. and Mrs. Micawber" (ch. 52), where it clearly signifies Micawber dropping his role as Uriah's toady, exposing the villain and returning to his own natural expansiveness.

The relative positions of Emily, Dora, and Agnes in David's life are brought out both in Dickens' choice of the last three subjects for the final, double part (the first is a minor comic plate showing the fates of Littimer and Heep), and in Browne's interpretations of those subjects. Unique in Phiz's work is the inclusion of miniature versions of the frontispiece and title in that last regular plate. "A Stranger calls to see me" (ch. 63; Illus. 85) brings Mr. Peggotty back to England from Australia after some years, and David and Agnes have in the meantime been peopling the world with Copperfields; this is the literal and sentimental subject of the plate. But for once the emblematic details, laid out symmetrically against the wall behind David and Agnes, take precedence over the characters. The two angel statuettes on the mantel remind us of Agnes' role for David throughout the novel, and their centrality here suggests her ultimate triumph as the "real heroine," while the rollicking cherubs adorning the clock may imply the number and angelic status of the many children this couple have produced in ten years. But poor Dora, whose inability to give birth has been associated with her child-wife qualities, looks down smilingly upon the married pair; perhaps she is blessing the union as she did with her last earthly breath, and perhaps her picture and those of Blunderstone Rookery and the boat house with a figure on the beach (who must, in view of the title page, be Emily, improbable as this may be) merely represent the past which David has outgrown. But in another sense David and Agnes are permanently haunted by his earlier loves—including Mrs. Copperfield, whom Dickens has after all made an explicit prototype of Dora.

My interpretation of the plate is offered in all seriousness, although I cannot make a case for Dickens or Phiz having consciously included such meanings. It does make sense for Dickens to have Phiz illustrate for the frontispiece the moment before his hero's birth, when Aunt Betsey is looking in the window of the Rookery, for the novel is written as David's autobiography. The use of Little Em'ly sitting winsomely on the beach as the subject of the title page is also suggestive: the two in conjunction indicate the extent to which Dickens viewed David's development, and thus the drift of the novel as a whole, as centered in his protagonist's earliest years. Browne's bringing together of the three most prominent strands of David's life—early childhood, Emily, and Dora—in the details of the final plate helps to reinforce the importance of the past.

The illustrations downplay the notion of Agnes as the dominant female force in a broader way. While no more than half a dozen plates include or clearly refer to Agnes, when we include those containing emblematic allusions or portraits as well as the two Annie Strong plates which have an overt thematic connection, there are ten having to do with Dora; and including all those which allude to her seduction by Steerforth there are no fewer than twelve concerned with Emily, not even counting the two centering on Martha with Emily absent. Surely the prominence of Dora and Emily in the illustrations might cause one to question those interpretations of the novel which identify the apotheosis of David's love for Agnes as the novel's major concern. We may have to search in the text for an ultimate answer, but the illustrations—a combination of Dickens' choices and Browne's interpretations of them—should cause us to look back at the novel without preconceptions based on Dickens' rather hasty dismissal of Dora to the world of angels.

Finally, it may seem odd to readers for whom the Phiz illustrations form an inextricable part of their consciousness of Dickens that I have made only two passing references to Mr. Micawber; and I must acknowledge here that Phiz's Micawber is *the* Micawber of our visual imaginations. Yet it is Browne's depiction of the ladies of David's life, from Clara, Emily, and Betsey through Dora and Agnes, that constitutes his major contribution to the visual progress of David Copperfield.

CHAPTER SIX

Bleak House and *Little Dorrit:* Iconography of Darkness

The illustrations for *Bleak House* are far more uneven in quality than those for the three preceding novels. Most of the comic plates—with a few important exceptions—are technically weak, even sloppy, and many of those which feature the novel's protagonist, Esther Summerson, are relatively uninteresting, though usually done with care. Mrs. Leavis finds Browne's work here "disappointing" because the illustrator "does nothing to actualize the Chancery fog," and there "is little in the way of background and almost no interesting detail," and she decides that in any case illustrations for this novel and those that follow "would have been unnecessary but for the habit of having illustrations," because of the extent to which Dickens' own art had matured.[1] Further, she finds those illustrations which do make use of emblematic detail to be inappropriate to Dickens' art, since the "Hogarthian satiric mode" is no longer Dickens'.[2] Yet *Bleak House* contains some of Browne's finest and most complex work in that Hogarthian mode, fully appropriate to Dickens' own effects. Both in combination with and transcending this mode, the illustrator employs the dark plate technique to convey graphically what is for the Dickens novels a new intensity of darkness. Some of this intensity is retained in the illustrations for *Little Dorrit*, but in other ways Browne's work for that novel definitely shows a falling-off which is then almost embarrassingly apparent in his last collaborative effort with Dickens, *A Tale of Two Cities*.

The complexity of Dickens' conception, the many interweaving plot strands and symbolic and thematic parallels of the text, is reflected in some respects from the outset in the complexity of Browne's emblematic conception in the *Bleak House* monthly cover (Illus. 86). Because this design includes a number of identifiable characters, Browne must have had quite explicit directions, or at least some explanation of Dickens' purposes. The novelist had completed the first number by mid-December 1851, and so could have shown Browne the manuscript (chapters 1–4) well before it was published in March 1852; it is conceivable that Browne saw in addition at least a portion of the second number—which was already in proof, with the illustrations completed, by 7 March—before he finished work on the wrapper design.[3] But three of the vignettes involving specific characters could not have been derived from a reading of the first six chapters, and this together with the fact that the vignettes are connected both visually and in relation to the plot indicates that Dickens explained his intentions in some detail. On the right side of the design we see Lady Dedlock taking a walk beside her carriage (an incident not occurring until Part IV, ch. 12); linked to this panel by a generalized depiction of a young couple with a distressed cupid between them is a third panel, of Nemo the "law-writer" (actually Captain Hawdon, Lady Dedlock's former lover and Esther's father). Although he is mentioned by Miss Flite in chapter 5, Nemo's opium addiction, indicated in the design by an apothecary's bottle on the table beside him, is not referred to until Part III, chapter 10.

These three vignettes together adumbrate the story of Lady Dedlock and Captain Hawdon, estranged in their youth, and now presented in the novel in early middle age. As I pointed out before, there may have been something of a private joke between Dickens and Browne in the fact that the scrivener is called "Nemo," since this was the *nom de crayon* Browne first adopted as illustrator for *Pickwick*. Like Browne, the Nemo of *Bleak House* works at a lowly paid task, hiring out as a free-lance to others, and willing (as Snagsby puts it in chapter 10) to "go at it right on end, if you want him to, as long as ever you like" (p. 95).

The other details in the crowded, though not confused, design relate in one way or another to Chancery, which provides the unifying theme for the wrapper as well as for the novel. The notion of Chancery as a gigantic game is expressed by Richard Carstone's remark that it is "wanton chess-playing," the suitors like "pieces on a board" (ch. 5, pp. 41–42). The two other game metaphors employed in the cover are battledore-and-shuttle-cock, with lawyers as players and suitors as shuttlecocks, and, across the top of the design, a panoramic game of blindman's bluff, with the Chancery attorneys and officials, appropriately, the "blindmen," and a host of terrified men, women, and children their fleeing victims. The image of the stumbling blindmen suggests that Browne read the first chapter, in which we find "some score of members of the High Court of Chancery bar . . . tripping one another up on slippery precedents, groping knee-deep in technicalities, running their goat-hair and horse-hair heads against walls of words" (p. 2). It has recently been shown that the battledore-and-shuttlecock vignette resembles a cut by George Cruikshank for Gilbert à Beckett's *The Comic Blackstone* (1846);[4] despite the resemblance, however, the portrayal of human beings as shuttlecocks goes back at least as far as Gillray, and was used twice by John Doyle ("HB"), in 1831 and 1840. Although Cruikshank's cut takes priority as a probable direct source because of its more recent date, many motifs from HB cartoons do turn up in Phiz's illustrations, including the chess game played with human pieces of the *Bleak House* cover.[5]

The blindman's bluff image includes at the right a man thumbing his nose at the proceedings, perhaps representing the author's standpoint, or, since he wears shabby clothing, expressing the contempt of a pauper ruined by Chancery toward a court which can do him no more harm. The placement of this vignette at the top puts the most extensive metaphor of Chancery's blindness, incompetence, and random destructiveness in the most prominent position, and also suggests a structural relationship to the rest of the wrapper. Two men, some money, and papers spill over the inside border of the design which is formed of thin sticks acting as an espalier for a grapevine. This vine, winding in and out of the various panels in the wrapper (just as Chancery insinuates itself into life in *Bleak House*), is evidently barren, a suggestion of the moral sterility of the Court; and the fragility of the supports implies—given the clear hint of collapse in the top-most vignette—that the whole structure is liable to come crashing down, a foreshadowing of the author's warning in chapter 32

of the possible spontaneous combustion of the system of government and law. (We may recall a similar hint in the structures
of ledgers, cash boxes, and playing cards in the *Dombey and Son*
wrapper.)

The only element structurally opposed to the blindmen is the
depiction in the bottom center vignette of Bleak House itself and
its owner, John Jarndyce; but the prospect is not really a very
hopeful one, for Jarndyce, wearing the hat with ear-straps mentioned in chapter 3 (p. 16), has his back turned to both the sinister
game above him and the representative figures who surround
him. These include a "telescopic philanthropist" embracing two
black children; a man blowing a toy trumpet while seated in a
cart whose label, "Bubble / Squeak," hints at the commercial
bubbles of philanthropic projectors and the squeak of their noise
(it also implicitly compares them to the cockney hash); two arguing women; and two fools, one holding a roll of plans marked
"Humbug" and another bearing a sign, "Exeter Hall," the site of
evangelical meetings. Jarndyce's habitual denial of the unpleas-
ant is embodied in the weathervane pointing east, representing
his defensive fiction that the "wind is in the east" whenever he
hears anything distasteful about the philanthropists he supports.

Chancery is represented not only in the game metaphors but in
two other vignettes, which together with the chess and
battledore images make up the four corners of the inner design.
At upper right Mr. Krook the mock Lord Chancellor writes "C R"
on the wall for "Chancery Rex," suggesting that Chancery, understood in its broadest symbolic sense, rules modern British
society. The corresponding left-hand vignette presents a bewigged man digging up papers with a shovel, which evokes
Krook, the collector of papers; we are reminded that Dickens
from the beginning conceived of him as the man "*who has the
papers*" resolving the mystery of Lady Dedlock and the case of
Jarndyce and Jarndyce.[6] Finally, just as the suitors pursued by
Chancery spill over and threaten to land on Bleak House, so the
dirt unearthed by the digging figure spills over its boundaries
and seems to descend on Esther's head. To understand this symbol, we must turn to the vignette centering on Esther, perhaps
the most puzzling element in the *Bleak House* cover.

Esther stands with her face in profile to us, looking down at a
fox which assumes a supplicatory or anticipatory position, one

paw raised; facing Esther is an impish man dancing through a foggy swamp, carrying a lighted lantern in one hand and holding a globe on his head with the other. The globe is a widely used symbol of the material world, and a man bearing it on his head often represents Man burdened down with materialism, although here that is not quite the case. For the lantern and the swamp suggest the will-o'-the-wisp, a prominent emblem used in nineteenth-century graphic art to represent temptation or the pursuit of foolish and self-destructive undertakings.[7] The two emblems combined in this way imply the temptations of the material world. Phiz had already used the two together in another etching, the allegorical frontispiece to Albert Smith's *The Pottleton Legacy* (1849), in which the materialistic temptations of the *ignis fatuus* are made explicit (they had already been implied in the *Nickleby* wrapper), and a figure nearby bears a globe on his head (Illus. 87).

But what of the fox? Recalling the weathervane fox above John Jarndyce may help to clarify matters, for this latter fox points directly to the one standing alongside Esther. It has been suggested to me[8] that the weathervane fox crystallizes Jarndyce's irritation with his society, and thus in a sense, like the East Wind, represents him. If this is so, then the fox next to Esther may be a kind of protective figure, guarding her against the world (symbolized not only in the globe but in the dirt being shoveled down upon her by the Chancery figure). Moreover, one possible reason to make this protective animal a fox is its conventional association with prudence; in emblem books foxes are often shown listening at the side of a frozen river to see if it is safe to walk upon the ice.[9]

The range and complexity of emblematic representation of the novel's themes are considerable in the *Bleak House* cover, and it should be remembered that the novel's original readers were confronted with this design—and thus were confronted with a visual summary of the novel's thematic concerns—once a month for nineteen successive months. Whether or not a reader took in all the details, he could hardly escape the wrapper's points made about Chancery in the three game metaphors, nor the position of John Jarndyce in the novel. The wrapper's design also hints at the past relationship between Lady Dedlock and the law-writer, an obvious reference when viewed with hindsight. While *Bleak*

House's wrapper may not be the most unified in strictly visual terms, iconographically and structurally it complements Dickens' own achievements in the most emblematically unified of all his novels, in which Chancery, fog, mud, disease, and Tom-All-Alone's act as powerful organizing images.

After this promising start, the series of etchings begins weakly; the one attempt at fog, in "The little old Lady" (ch. 2), is puerile, and only with "The Lord Chancellor copies from memory" (ch. 5) does Phiz hint at the power of his best plates in this novel. In terms of plot sequence, the action depicted here is completed only at the end of the tenth part, with Krook's death in "The appointed time" (ch. 32), in which the junk dealer's black doll (of the earlier plate) appears to be shocked at the event. But in its ominous quality, "The Lord Chancellor copies from memory" also foreshadows the dark plates of the novel's second half. Phiz has taken his cue for most of the details from the text, but he adds a demonic mask which reminds us of Miss Flite's remark that Nemo was said to have sold his soul to the devil (ch. 5, p. 40). The Lord Chancellor's pointing finger introduces a motif which will occur more importantly twice again, as we shall see; and Esther's almost completely hidden face, in this and the two preceding plates, is also a motif—one might almost say an emblem—which continues through the novel and links Esther visually with her mother.

Before discussing the long series of illustrations which connect Esther, Lady Dedlock, and some of the novel's themes, I want to take up the four plates in which Browne employs Hogarthian techniques with the greatest variety and force. Among the novel's sinister, grotesque, or comic figures, there are a number whom Browne seems to handle unenthusiastically. Mrs. Pardiggle, the Smallweeds, Tulkinghorn and Bucket, for example, are given nothing like the vividness and individuality of Phiz's Pecksniff, Gamp, Dombey or Bagstock. But these deficiencies seem to me more than made up for by the inventive handling of Turveydrop, Chadband, and Vholes, three characters who embody the corrupt qualities of *Bleak House* society: dandyism, false religion, false politics and law. Phiz shows his full powers only beginning in Part V, dated July 1852, when he is between assignments for Lever, having completed *The Daltons* in March or April; he will not begin *The Dodd Family Abroad* until September. (He had also been engaged on Ainsworth's *Mervyn Clitheroe* until March 1852, and worked on Smedley's *Lewis Arundel* during both 1851 and 1852, so it is understandable that he may have felt a bit tired and overworked at the start of *Bleak House*.)

"The Dancing-School" (ch. 14; Illus. 88) is the second of fourteen horizontal plates in *Bleak House*; with its long, sweeping dance floor and its twenty-five distinct figures the plate requires all of the unusually large space allotted to it. Stylistically it is in the mode of some of the best plates for *The Daltons* and *The Dodd Family Abroad*, though surpassing in satirical impact anything in Lever's novels. There is relatively little modeling (though some careful shading) in the faces of the characters, but the figures are carefully balanced and arranged (e.g., Prince Turveydrop's pupils form a diagonal from the smallest at left to the tallest at right, with the dancing master in the center), and the lines are controlled. The most significant aspect of the characters' placement involves two mirrors, one at either end, on parallel walls. Into one a very small pupil on tiptoe is barely able to gaze and admire her pert little face; in the other the back of Mr. Turveydrop's ornately styled coiffure (wig) and his spotless collar are reflected. Just as the chapter is entitled "Deportment," so this plate really focuses on the Master of Deportment, who stands taller than any other figure and oversees the labors of his son as though he somehow deserves credit for them. Mrs. Leavis' argument that Dickens becomes his own illustrator is given some credence by the marvelous description of Mr. Turveydrop, "a fat old gentleman with a false complexion, false teeth, false whiskers, and a wig" (ch. 14, p. 135); Browne can convey little of this in the mode in which he works.

But the illustration's function is a different one. Apart from the way its composition emphasizes the relative pretended and real positions of father and son, the plate comments upon Turveydrop's narcissism by paralleling him with the vain little girl; and it also unobtrusively makes visible the connection between Mr. Turveydrop and the Prince Regent, his supposed model, referred to early in Esther's meeting with him. Esther feels that he sits "in

imitation of his illustrious model on the sofa,"[10] and Mr. Turveydrop recalls when "His Royal Highness the Prince Regent
did me the honour to inquire, on my removing my hat as he drove
out of the Pavilion at Brighton (that fine building), 'Who is he?
Who the Devil is he? Why don't I know him? Why hasn't he
thirty thousand a year?'" (ch. 14, p. 137). A comparison of the
Model of Deportment in this plate with an engraving by George
Cruikshank of King George IV at the beginning of his reign
(Illus. 89) will make it clear that Phiz is consciously using an old
device from the days of "6d plain, 1/-coloured" political and social prints, the parodying of a well-known portrait to suggest a
parallel between a contemporary and a figure from the past.[11]

It is especially interesting that the Cruikshank portrait—to my
eye almost a caricature, though apparently intended to be taken
straight—shows George IV standing with the Royal Pavilion in
the background. The reference to a print of the Regent on a sofa
is less easy to pin down, but it may enter into a later illustration
by Phiz, in which Mr. Turveydrop's connection with the Regent
is explored in far-reaching ways. That Dickens was reminded of
the early nineteenth century's most famous British object of caricature is suggested by his note to himself in the number plan for
the dancing school chapter:

Deportment.

Mr Turveydrop—*Prince Turveydrop* George the Fourth, old
Turveydrop's model of . . .
                    Deportment.[12]

The graphic allusion to George IV in "The Dancing-School" is
picked up again, this time solely in illustration, in Part VIII.
Although this number, comprising chapters 22 through 25, contains many important serious episodes—such as Richard's decision to give up the law for the army, Jarndyce's request that
Richard and Ada call off their engagement, Gridley's death, Mlle.
Hortense's offer of herself to Esther as a maid, and Jarndyce's gift
of Charley Neckett to Esther for that same purpose—Browne was
directed to illustrate two scenes notable for their acid, grotesque
comedy: "A model of parental deportment" (ch. 23; Illus. 90),
and "Mr. Chadband 'improving' a tough subject" (ch. 24; Illus.

92). A glance at the two plates will reveal a connection between them which could hardly have been missed by those who read the novel in parts, when the two would have been placed together at the opening. Although no parallel between Turveydrop and Chadband is made explicit in the text, such a parallel is obvious in Phiz's depiction of the two men: each, with right hand raised, is in the process of bestowing what Esther calls "benignity" (ch. 23, p. 232) upon an assortment of followers and skeptics; in each plate a pair of true believers and a single doubter are similarly placed, Esther facing Turveydrop and Snagsby facing Chadband from the extreme left, while Caddy and Prince kneel close to the Model and Mrs. Snagsby and Mrs. Chadband sit near the "oily vessel."[13] Other details link these two etchings with "The Dancing-School": the mirrors of the earlier illustration have their counterparts in both plates, and the lyre decorating a wall of the dancing school is repeated in miniature on a chest in the Chadband illustration.

The broad significance of the parallels seems clear. Turveydrop and Chadband are just two characters who embody the theme of hypocrisy and false belief, but these two are linked by the special blatancy of their use of others' faith in them as a means to the gratification of selfish desires; yet without the graphic parallel one's impression might be that these fat men are merely two among a miscellany of grotesques who come off and on stage like music-hall performers. And there are at least two other graphic links between the illustrations, for each character is mirrored or parodied by a picture on the wall near the top center, and at the right hand of each there are upon a table objects which emblematize the character's major preoccupations. But further, the presence of such details is related to Browne's knowledge of his forerunners in graphic satire, and their special significance can best be inferred by examining those sources.

Few of the qualities usually associated with George IV as king or as prince regent are brought out in Dickens' treatment of Turveydrop; of the "First Gentleman's" licentiousness, gambling, drunkenness, gourmandizing and foppery, only the last two are present in his fictional emulator, and only the foppery is given much emphasis. Yet when we trace the derivation of old Mr. Turveydrop's image we find that the artist has subtly retained in attenuated form some stereotypical Regency qualities in the

Model of Deportment. The immediate source appears to be George Cruikshank's wood engraving of George IV as Prince of Wales, "Qualification" (Illus. 91), the first illustration to William Hone's pamphlet, *The Queen's Matrimonial Ladder* (1820), which traces the course of the Prince's marriage to Caroline of Brunswick up to the year of his accession to the throne.[14] Despite the obvious differences, these two pictures contain three notable visual similarities: the position of the torso and legs of each figure; the almost identical placement of the head of the Prince and that of Turveydrop in front of a decorated tripartite screen; and the presence of similarly shaped objects upon a table near each figure's right arm.

But before going into these parallels, we must complete the derivation by going back to the source of Cruikshank's malicious caricature, Gillray's already sufficiently cruel portrait of the same man, "A VOLUPTUARY *under the horrors of Digestion*" (July 2, 1792; *BM Cat* 8112).[15] Not only are the poses in the two caricatures nearly identical, but Cruikshank picks up details from Gillray and either repeats or alters them tellingly. In both designs empty bottles are piled beneath the Prince's chair and a dice box and dice are in evidence. But one of the upright decanters in Gillray is replaced in Cruikshank by an overturned and presumably empty bottle, while the dishes of mutton bones are replaced by two candles, burnt down to their holders and guttering—signifying the burning out of the Prince's life as the empty bottle suggests both repletion and exhaustion. Although Gillray in other prints frequently dealt with the Prince's notorious amours, this aspect is adverted to in his "VOLUPTUARY" caricature only by the bottles of nostrums for venereal disease; the artist was probably planning the ironically contrasting print which appeared a few weeks later, "TEMPERANCE *Enjoying a Frugal Meal*" (July 28, 1792; *BM Cat* 8117), in which the King and Queen dine on eggs and sauerkraut amidst emblems of miserliness, and he thus would have wished to emphasize gluttony in the first etching of the pair. But Cruikshank in his adaptation gives full play to lechery, showing on the screen Silenus upon an ass, a winged goat, and three voluptuous women (parodies of the Three Graces) dancing around a satyr's effigy, while a woman's bonnet hanging on a corner of the screen further intimates the Prince's main interest.

Where Cruikshank replaces the evidences of gluttony with emblems of a lecherous and spent life, Phiz in turn adorns Mr. Turveydrop's dressing table with implements of this character's main obsession, adornment of self: a mirror, and bottles of cosmetics which resemble in shape the candlesticks of Cruikshank's cut. In the Chadband plate, the corresponding table holds a dish of food, a decanter, two glasses, and an open Bible—together emblems of a gorging and preaching vessel (to use Dickens' terms). But there is another technique of iconographic expression in both plates which hints that Dickens' illustrator had in mind not only Cruikshank's caricature of the aging Prince, but its source in Gillray. Above the Prince's head in the Gillray is a portrait of Luigi Cornaro, "the author of . . . a discussion of disciplines and restraints which might be exercised in pursuit of longevity."[16] The irony of this allusion is paralleled in the companion satire of George III and Charlotte by an empty frame labeled, "The Triumph of Benevolence," and a picture entitled, "The fall of MANNA."

An ironic contrast of this kind is evident in the picture of John the Baptist directly above Chadband's head; the pose of the figure is similar to Chadband's, but nothing could be more pronounced than the contrast between Chadband's overfed and well-clothed body and the gauntness and rags of St. John (and of little Jo). The corresponding portrait in the "deportment" plate reflects Browne's sources even more directly. It appears to show Mr. Turveydrop as a younger man, scarcely less obese, but more luxurious and indolent in pose; in view of Esther's reference to the print of the Regent on a sofa, this may be intended for the Gillray original rather than the Cruikshank copy which shows an aged Regent in spite of its purporting to depict the Prince of Wales. In either case this picture, like that of John the Baptist, parallels the technique of contrasting portraits in Gillray's print; but there is enough resemblance in dress and pose between Turveydrop and the Cruikshank, and between the portrait and the Gillray, to suggest that Phiz may have been thinking of *both* caricatures. To parallel further his own Turveydrop plate with the Chadband one is to further imitate his own imitation of Cruikshank's imitation of Gillray—clearly, Browne was aware of his artistic heritage.

We may approach the interpretative significance of Browne's allusion by considering first what he makes of the folding screen. Cruikshank's bacchic and priapic emblems are transformed to decorous courtiers, ladies, and cupids, an attenuation of sexuality which is in line with Trevor Blount's view of Turveydrop as a "dehumanized neuter,"[17] but I think there is even more to it. Desexed as he may be, Turveydrop is not wholly asexual, as witnessed by the way Esther shrinks from his tribute: "'But Wooman, lovely Wooman,' said Mr. Turveydrop with very disagreeable gallantry, 'what a sex you are!'" (ch. 14, p. 138). Beneath Mr. Turveydrop's impotent exterior lurks the remnant of a nasty sexuality which is emphasized by knowledge of Browne's graphic sources. There is also a possible parallel between the Model of Deportment's mistreatment of his late wife and the mistreatment popularly imputed to the Regent in regard to Caroline of Brunswick—the subject to which *The Queen's Matrimonial Ladder* is devoted. Ironically, while the middle and lower classes abhorred the Regent, by contrast in *Bleak House* two of the best, gentlest souls, Prince Turveydrop and Caddy Jellyby, blindly believe in Deportment. Thus in a sense the dandyism Dickens excoriates in the novel as typical of the upper classes has also infected the humbler orders of his age.

The parallel to Mr. Chadband suggests that this oily individual represents another case of the same thing—the deluding of the lower middle classes through a form of Christianity which is essentially no different from the religion of Deportment. Three details provide further comment on the specious preacher. Immediately beneath his outstretched arm and imitating its angle is a toy trumpet, which suggests that Chadband is blowing his own tinny little horn, like the self-puffer on the cover design. Above the chimneypiece are two symbols which suggest the spuriousness of Chadband's religious pretensions: a fish, one of the conventional symbols for Christ, is preserved under glass, but its mouth is open and its eyes regard Chadband with astonishment. And on the mantel itself a human figure resembling Jo huddles under a bell jar; on either side are shepherd figures with sheep.

These elements represent the isolation of Jo from pastoral aid, the traditional church being indifferent to him and the pseudo-clergyman Mr. Chadband preaching at him for self-aggrandizement rather than out of compassion.

This series of three plates, from the dancing school to Chad-band is, as an example of Browne's use of the Hogarthian techniques of allusion, emblematic detail, and visual parallel between illustrations, on a level of artistic and interpretative accomplishment with the title page of *Martin Chuzzlewit,* the etching which shows Edith Dombey's final confrontation with Carker, and the first plate of *David Copperfield.*

In the depiction of Mr. Vholes, the eminently respectable solicitor for whose parasitic survival the archaic procedures of Chancery must be maintained, Phiz indulges in his last big splurge of emblematic invention for Dickens. The techniques of "Attorney and Client, fortitude and impatience" (ch. 39; Illus. 93) are perhaps less brilliant than those of the Turveydrop–Chadband series, but a close examination of this etching's details and process of creation reveals much about one aspect of Phiz's art.

Q. D. Leavis has criticized this Vholes–Carstone plate on the grounds that it depicts Mr. Vholes in terms of a "Hogarthian satiric mode" which is no longer Dickens', and that Phiz "conveys nothing of the sinister ethos that emanates from Mr. Vholes in the text of the novel."[18] Mrs. Leavis' assumption is that the only proper function of illustrations like Browne's is to mirror the import of the text, but, as I have shown, an illustration may present a point of view and bring out aspects which are not overtly expressed in the text. Mrs. Leavis also fails to differentiate multiple purposes in Dickens. In describing Vholes's office, Dickens himself employs Hogarthian techniques, first conveying the decay and dirt, the "congenial shabbiness" of Symond's Inn, and then the "legal bearings of Mr. Vholes." The office is described in detail worthy of Hogarth, and then the narrative takes another turn and speaks of the "great principle of English law," i.e., "to make business for itself" (ch. 39, p. 386). Throughout the page-long discussion of the "Vholeses," Dickens uses metaphors which border on the emblematic: the law is a "monstrous maze," Vholes and his tribe, cannibals, and the

lawyer is "a piece of timber, to shore up some decayed founda-
tion that has become a pit-fall and a nuisance" (p. 386). In the
interview with Richard, Dickens describes some blue bags
stuffed in the way "the larger sort of serpents are in their first
gorged state," while the office is "the official den" of predators
(p. 387). And most Hogarthian of all, and a detail which turns up
in the illustration, "Mr. Vholes, after glancing at the official cat
who is patiently watching a mouse's hole, fixes his charmed gaze
again on his young client" (p. 388).

One can hardly blame Phiz for picking up this last detail as
well as that of the maze, and elaborating these conceits into a
multiplicity of images representing the predatoriness and confusion of the law; and there is nothing discordant between this
elaboration and Dickens' own treatment. The three extant drawings indicate that Browne took a good deal of trouble with this
plate. One, which I think is the earliest (Illus. 94), shows Vholes
at his desk much as in the ultimate etched version, but the desk is
open beneath, and thus not the kind which would echo hollowly
like an empty coffin (specified by Dickens). Richard stands with
his back to Vholes, tearing his hair (as on page 387); even at this
stage, most of the emblematic details are clearly visible, indicating that they were a part of the original conception. In a second
drawing, the figures are placed as in the final version, but the
details are somewhat sketchier and Phiz apparently was dis-
satisfied with Vholes's face, which is much less predatory in this
version; another head, more like the one in the previous drawing, is sketched in the margin.[19] The drawing which was used for
transferring the subject (Illus. 96) is much like the etching, only
rather sketchy, and the head of Vholes is still not like the final
one, which seems to come from the first drawing.

The significant details are so numerous that in order to discuss
them coherently it seems best to divide them into three broad
categories:

1. *Emblematic representations of the law's confusion and delay.* These include a prominently displayed page of an open book
showing a maze, a reference to Chancery and the Jarndyce and
Jarndyce suit that echoes the text; a clock covered with cobwebs,
suggesting the endless delay of the law and of Mr. Vholes's work

for his client; a box of papers labeled "De Maine Estate," probably a pun on *demain*; and a skein of what is doubtless red tape,
which stretches in a tangle on the floor and around the foot of the
law's victim, Richard Carstone. The latter detail could also fit
into a second category,

2. *The predatoriness of the law and its effects upon its victims.* Taking off from the textual detail of the cat and mousehole,
Phiz includes a mortar and pestle (recalling Tom Jarndyce's remark, related by Krook, that being a Chancery suitor is like "being ground to bits in a slow mill"—ch. 5, p. 38); a snuffer and
candle, suggesting Richard's rapid physical decline; a bellows,
probably referring to the inflaming effect of Chancery, particularly as Weevle remarks to Guppy about Richard that "'there's
combustion going on there . . . not a case of Spontaneous, but . . .
smouldering combustion'" (ch. 39, p. 391); and an ornamental
pair of foxes reaching after grapes, a metaphor for the perpetual
frustration of suitors. The paper at bottom center, reading "Law
Stationer / Chancery Lane / Fools Cap," may refer to Richard's
reduction to the state of a fool by Chancery. More specifically
symbolizing Vholes's predation are a spider's web with a fly
about to be caught in it, a net and fishing rods, a picture of a man
fishing, and two lion heads on the fireplace. (Some of these
emblems have already appeared elsewhere in Browne's work,
most recently in "The Money Lender" in *Roland Cashel,* in
which spider's web, net, and fishing tackle, as well as a fly trap
and stuffed fish, are present.)

3. *Direct representation of the law.* Most prominent is the
portrait of a judge with his spectacles off, whose eyes look quite
blind; a time table, recalling the delays in Court; and several
boxes of papers for various cases, whose names are clearly
emblematic: "Black v. White," an ironic comment on the fact that
Chancery cases are never clear-cut; "Holdfast, esq"; "I Flint,
esq"; and "Sharpe," all alluding to the tenacity, greed, and
heartlessness of Chancery suitors and, especially, attorneys.

Dickens and Browne evidently wished to overwhelm the
reader with the sinister qualities of Chancery and Vholes, and
the Hogarthian method was the simplest and most efficient way
to accomplish this. Dickens in the text of chapter 38 sets an

example for his illustrator, and it is pointless to object that Phiz
has not captured *all* the qualities of Dickens' portrayal of Vholes
in one etching.

   The Vholes–Carstone illustration is not typical of the plates in
the second half of the novel; of the last seventeen illustrations,
ten are dark plates, and these are foreshadowed by two plates
done with ordinary techniques in the first half. "The Lord Chancellor copies from memory" is linked to "Consecrated ground"
(ch. 16) not only by its darkness but by the pointing hands of
Krook and Jo, and the presence in the first of Esther and in the
second of Lady Dedlock, each with her face mostly or fully hidden. Krook points at the letter "J" which he has just written,
referring to Esther's connection with Jarndyce, while Jo points at
the grave of Lady Dedlock's lover—in total ignorance, but the
episode will involve him unwittingly in Tulkinghorn's pursuit of
Lady Dedlock's secret. As J. Hillis Miller has remarked, Dickens
clearly intended a connection between the pointing "Allegory"
in Mr. Tulkinghorn's chambers—which will eventually point to
his corpse when Lady Dedlock is the prime suspect for his
murder—and Jo's pointing hand, for in the number plan he
wrote, "Jo—*shadowing forth of Lady Dedlock at the churchyard.*/ Pointing hand of allegory—consecrated ground / 'Is it
Blessed?' "[20] "Allegory" is introduced in Part III, chapter 10, but
its pointing hand is not mentioned until Part XIII, ch. 42, just
after Hortense has threatened Mr. Tulkinghorn, although in its
first appearance it is "staring down at his intrusion as if it meant
to swoop upon him" (p. 92). This distant "shadowing forth"
shows how consciously Dickens planned what might be called
the emblematic structure of the novel; in this particular case,
while he has certainly prepared the reader for "Allegory" playing a significant role, the connection between one "pointing" in
chapter 16 and another in chapter 42 is perhaps too distant to be
effective, particularly when the *visual* parallel is not completed
until Part XV, chapter 48.
   Esther and her mother see one another for the first time at a
distance in the part following the graveyard episode, and here, in
"The little church in the park" (ch. 18), Browne interprets the
social role of the Dedlocks and its relation to the *Bleak House*
world by means of several of his customary techniques. The

overall scene recalls the Norfolk parish church, and the London church in which David is married in *David Copperfield;* not only is the cycle of life represented but so are various attitudes toward the hymn singing, from participation to boredom. The congregation is also divided between the lower gentry or middle class in the main pews, the servants from the manor in a pew behind the great one, the tenants standing in the aisle, and the party from Mr. Boythorn's cottage in his pew at some distance from the pulpit, while the Dedlocks seem to rule the entire scene from above in the great pew. But this dominance is undercut by a set of incidental details: in what may be a coincidental—but nonetheless effective—parallel to the third plate ("The Lord Chancellor copies from memory") in which, following the text, a pair of large, broken scales is shown, here an emblematically unbalanced pair of scales of justice is seen over the head of a life-size memorial effigy of a judge in robes and wig who bends over a law book; propped behind his robes a tome labeled "Vol. 30" hints at the law's interminability. This effigy is behind the Dedlocks' pew, implying a connection between the injustice of the Chancery world and the aristocratic "dandyism" of the Dedlock world.

But another possible reason to have this figure intrude on the space of the complacent and isolated Dedlocks is to imply that even as impervious in their magnificence as they seem, the Dedlocks will be judged, either in this life or the Hereafter. For such would seem to be the message of two inscriptions: "Easier for a camel" (above the Dedlocks' heads) indicates that their wealth may thwart chances for salvation, and "All shall be changed" (directly opposite them) suggests that the social arrangements visible in the congregation and assumed by Sir Leicester to be permanent will be altered. A memorial inscription, "Patient Grissle," above the Boythorn pew, makes one think of Esther, as the long-suffering woman who will eventually be righted, though here of course it is not a husband but a mother who has caused her suffering; Browne may have had in mind only Esther's patient endurance, without thinking through all of the implications. Lady Dedlock herself is perhaps alluded to in the rather fuzzy but still legible carving on the pulpit of Eve and the Tree of the Knowledge of Good and Evil, recalling her temptation and fall in early life. Above the whole scene, however, is a shield with "Semper Virens," reminding one of the possibilities of forgiveness and eternal life. Taken together, the details strengthen the fundamental point of the scene: the first encounter, alive with possibilities of revelation and change, of Esther with her mother.

Esther's next encounter with her mother, in the illustrations, is in the second half of the novel, and although the etching is rendered in the ordinary mode it can be said to initiate the long series of dark plates. "Lady Dedlock in the Wood" (ch. 35) and "The Ghost's Walk" (ch. 36) are linked, occurring in the same chapter and forming a continuum in Esther's experience—the revelation of her mother's identity leading to her feeling of terror at the Ghost's Walk and at the idea that it is she "who was to bring calamity upon the stately house" (ch. 36, p. 362). The contrast of tone and mood between the two plates is notable. The first is structured by means of the tree under which Esther sits, which divides the space into three sections with one figure (Lady Dedlock, Esther, and Charley) in each. Phiz has been careful to dress Esther and her mother so that they appear very much alike, and Esther's face is hidden. It is here that the motif of the hidden face becomes most evident; this episode follows Esther's recovery from smallpox and in the illustrations her scarred face will remain hidden throughout. The text implies that Esther's illness is a kind of symbolic retribution for Lady Dedlock's crime of sexual waywardness, for Esther divests herself of her lifelong guilt feelings only after the illness and the encounter with her mother. Simultaneously, Lady Dedlock takes on a new and greater guilt, which can only be resolved through her death. From the point of this confrontation onward not only is Esther's face always hidden in the etchings, but her mother's is as well, silently implying a parallel between the two women, between Esther's scarring and Lady Dedlock's guilt. (Phiz apparently had no text to read, since an early but quite finished drawing [Elkins] shows Lady Dedlock walking toward her from the distance; Dickens probably provided inadequate directions and then realized upon seeing the drawing that it would have to be redone.)

Browne's reserving of the dark plate technique until the novel is more than halfway done proves to be an effective strategy, since it groups the dark plates together and restricts their special force (with one partial exception) to depicting the tragedy of Lady Dedlock. Like five others of the ten dark plates in this novel, "The Ghost's Walk" has no human figures (two others have only tiny and barely discernible ones); this is not typical of Browne's dark plates either for Dickens or for other novelists, and the effect here is to accentuate the novel's emphasis upon external, nonhuman or dehumanized forces as the dominant agents in man's life in society—Chancery, Parliament, Telescopic Philanthropy, Law, Disease. Without the special technique, "The Ghost's Walk" might not even be a very good illustration: lacking the varied dark tones that give the sky itself an ominous effect, the large proportion of empty space would unbalance the composition. The "grotesque lions" (ch. 36, p. 361) are, as details in a drawing, puerile, but the contrast of darkness with the white highlights saves them from being ridiculous.

The theme and tone of "The Ghost's Walk" are picked up in the next part, in "Sunset in the long Drawing-room at Chesney Wold" (ch. 40; Illus. 96 and 97), which makes graphically more explicit the doom hanging over Lady Dedlock. At first glance the plate seems to have been executed by a totally different method than its companion in Part XIII, the Hogarthian confrontation of Richard Carstone and Mr. Vholes, for the dark plate technique gives it a powerful quality of depth, and the lack of human figures contrasts with the caricatural content and emblematic devices of the preceding plate. As John Harvey has pointed out, the shadow upon Lady Dedlock's portrait, stressed in the text (ch. 40, p. 398), is in the illustration so subtly combined with the other shadows that the viewer only gradually recognizes its presence and menace.[21] So strong are the effects of tone, perspective, composition, and the feeling that nonhuman forces are in control, that one is liable to overlook the fact that this illustration conveys its thematic emphases by means of methods as emblematic as those of its companion plate. Dickens provides in his text the central emblematic conception by dwelling upon the threatening shadow that encroaches upon the portrait of Lady Dedlock, and this in turn becomes the subject of the plate. But Phiz has added a central emblem, a large statue which gives the plate a focus distinct from the portrait and the shadow, and which complements them. It depicts a woman seated with a winged infant leaning upon her knee and looking up at her. In general terms this probably embodies the idea of motherly love, but its likely source in Thorwaldsen's sculpture of Venus and Cupid makes it possible to be more specific: in Thorwaldsen's piece, Venus is consoling Cupid for the bee sting he has just received, and the application at this stage of the novel would be not only to Esther's parentage, but to Lady Dedlock's failure to mother her, and to prevent her suffering as a young child.

The idea of nurture and protection is carried out further in the small ceramic of the Good Samaritan, while the ornamental doves represented as drinking from the bowl nearby may reflect further the theme of nonerotic love (Thorwaldsen's group of Venus and Cupid also includes two doves, and I suspect that in his statue, and here, they are meant to de-eroticize the god and goddess of sensual love). The fan on the floor and the nosegay and shawl on the chair may indicate the recent presence of Lady Dedlock, but the guitar with its broken string must be emblematic, signifying loss as in *David Copperfield*. All of these emblems quietly introduce thematic emphases which would be maudlin if included in the text; since the drawing room is realistically done, and nothing in it seems out of keeping with the general style of decoration, only gradually do these emphases enter our consciousness. One other touch may be equally important: a bedroom is discernible at the very rear of the design. It is not clear whose room this is, but would it be too farfetched to associate it with the marriage bed and thus with the Dedlocks' disgrace? In the context of the second plate to the next monthly part it may take on an even more sinister meaning, as I shall suggest.[22]

"Tom all alone's" (ch. 46; Illus. 98), perhaps the best known of all the dark plates, is what I have in mind. Although we lack Dickens' instructions, there is evidence pointing to its owing a good deal in conception to Hogarth's *Gin Lane*, probably by way of the novelist's own knowledge of that engraving. Comparing *Gin Lane* to Cruikshank's temperance works in the Hogarthian tradition, Dickens had in 1848 suggested its relevance to his own time: the engraving emphasizes the causes of drunkenness and crime in the way it "forces on the attention of the spectator a most neglected, wretched neighborhood ... an unwholesome, indecent, abject condition of life." Dickens quotes Lamb to the effect that "the very houses seem absolutely reeling," but that this as much implies "the prominent causes of intoxication among the neglected orders of society, as any of its effects." The church whose steeple is seen in the distance "is very prominent and handsome, but coldly surveys these things, in progress underneath the shadow of its tower . . . and is passive in the picture. We take all this to have a meaning, and to the best of our knowledge it has not grown obsolete in a century."[23] Some three years later (in a speech to the Metropolitan Sanitary Association), Dickens spoke of the certainty "that the air from Gin Lane will be carried, when the wind is Easterly, into May Fair."[24] Both the East Wind and the theme of the inevitable infection of all classes consequent upon the neglect of the lowest are of course central to *Bleak House*, which he was to begin a month later. And explicit mention of this theme turns up in the passage the plate is designed to illustrate: "There is not a drop of Tom's blood-but propagates infection and contagion somewhere" (ch. 46, p. 443).

When we look at Browne's version of "Tom" in this context, the connections with Hogarth seem inescapable. Here again, but even more prominently, we have a church tower passively overlooking a scene of degradation; here too, the buildings are in danger of collapsing and are held up by wooden supports. But whereas in Hogarth's picture human beings are central, in "Tom all alone's" they are absent; while Hogarth's composition gives a sense of chaos, Browne makes his composition as symmetrical as possible, so that the contrast between the visual repose afforded by the wooden supports in the middle of the picture and what we know to be their function is full of irony and tension. Most startling of all, Browne has framed the upper edge of the plate with a horizontal brace between two houses so that the very sky seems to be held up by this untrustworthy support, a brilliant way of underlining the relation between the condition of Tom-All-Alone's and the rest of society. In this regard the plate is reminiscent of the *Bleak House* cover, in which all of society is in danger of being brought down by the weight of Chancery. Through the arch at the rear we can see into the churchyard which, like *Gin Lane*, includes the pawnbroker's three balls, symbol of decline into poverty; presumably Esther's father has been buried in that filthy place. But what is most fascinating about this plate—and surely not accidental—is that the churchyard holds the same relative position in the composition as the bedroom in the "Sunset" plate. Hence a subtle connection is made between the liaison of Esther's parents, the Dedlock marriage bed, and the churchyard where Captain Hawdon lies and where Lady Dedlock will die.

Not only are these two plates linked, but connections are also made backwards to "Consecrated ground" and forwards to "The Morning," with the same churchyard visible through the gate at which the corpse of Lady Dedlock lies. But the earliest plate showing the churchyard also forms links with another dark plate, "A new meaning in the Roman" (ch. 48). I have already questioned the visual effectiveness of the connection between two such distant illustrations (one appearing in chapter 16 and the other in chapter 48) but the fact is that the *pointing* of Jo is more vividly brought out in the illustration than in the text. An additional difficulty in tracing the process of Dickens' thought about these parallels and his transmission of them to Browne is suggested by the evidence of a shift in Dickens' mental picture of the Roman "Allegory." Initially, the figure painted on the ceiling is described as "sprawling" (ch. 10, p. 92), and Browne's first version (Illus. 99) incongruously combines pointing with sprawling; evidently Dickens had Browne correct this excessively comic conception. The final version (Illus. 100), with its imposing male figure pointing at the scene below, manages to make "Allegory" every bit as silly as the text suggests, by juxtaposing three figures who flee in terror with three or four (in 29B and 29A respectively) jolly cherubs strewing flowers and blowing trumpets in the direction of the frightened figures. The dark plate technique is used tellingly, with a contrast between extremely dark shadows—the details nonetheless visible in them—and beams of sunlight coming in the window. As in other dark plates the only human figures are effigies. Phiz has also included the decanter of wine and a glass, to remind us of the buttoned-up Tulkinghorn's only real pleasure in life.

The immediate consequence of the murder, Lady Dedlock's increasing sense of guilt, as though she *had* committed that crime, and her preparation for flight, are depicted and summed up emblematically in "Shadow" (ch. 53; Illus. 101), which is paired with another plate whose caption, "Light" (ch. 51), seems intended to suggest a link. Although Richard Carstone's decline in the toils of Chancery, the subject of "Light," and Lady Dedlock's impending flight do belong to separate strands of the plot, within Dickens' scheme they are in fact thematically related. Both individuals are seen as victims of their society's inhumane codes and institutions, yet both share some of the responsibility for their plight. The irony of the seemingly antithetical captions is that the plates are not really in contrast: "Light" refers only to Esther's sudden realization that Ada and Richard are married, and that Ada is devoting herself to him wholly in his decline; and the halo of light surrounding the couple sets off more starkly the hopelessness of Richard's condition. Visually, the illustration is linked to its companion through the figure of Esther, nearly central in the composition and with a hidden face, like Lady Dedlock in "Shadow." The latter caption refers back to the symbolic shadow encroaching upon her portrait, and here the shadows are closing in, so that only a portion of Lady Dedlock's figure remains in light.

The primary subject of "Shadow" is, ostensibly, Lady Dedlock's impression that she is sought for the murder of Tulkinghorn, for she is looking at the reward poster. But three emblematic details broaden the range of reference. Thorwaldsen's "Night," repeated from the stairway plate of *Dombey,* shows a motherly angel carrying aloft an infant, recalling Lady Dedlock's failure to be a mother to Esther and her consequent guilt and self-torment. The "murderous statuary" of the text is specified by Phiz as a sculpture of what appears to be Abraham and Isaac at the point when Abraham is about to sacrifice his son but is stayed by the voice of the Angel of the Lord. Such a detail appears in the form of a print on the wall in *A Harlot's Progress,* III, where, Ronald Paulson suggests, it may allude to the contrast between God's and man's justice.[25] This contrast is certainly relevant here, and the possible allusion as well to Hogarth's fallen Moll is not entirely beside the point. But in addition, the idea of death being prevented by God relates to the fact that Lady Dedlock's child, whom she had thought dead, also has been spared. The third emblem is a clock above Lady Dedlock's head, in its particular position perhaps indicating that her time has run out; it is decorated below with an ominous mermaid, a detail which has some connection with the possible reference to Hogarth's "lost" woman. We may recall Thackeray's use of the mermaid as a simile for Becky Sharp—the creature's slimy tail submerged in the murky depths having to substitute for any detailed discussion of what Becky was actually doing in those disreputable days on the Continent after Rawdon had left her.[26] The implication for Lady Dedlock would be that her hidden, sexually sinful past is about to be revealed.[27]

The next step in Lady Dedlock's flight is represented by an extraordinary dark plate, "The lonely figure" (ch. 56). If ever Hablot Browne succeeded in expressing the essence of a text it is here, in his depiction of

> the waste, where the brick-kilns are burning with a pale blue flare; where the straw roofs of the wretched huts in which the bricks are made, are being scattered by the wind; where the clay and water are hard frozen, and the mill in which the gaunt blind horse goes round all day looks like an instrument of human torture;—traversing this deserted blighted spot, there is a lonely figure with the sad world to itself, pelted by the snow and driven by the wind, and cast out, it would seem, from all companionship. (p. 544)

The possibilities of the dark plate are evident, first of all, in the way the snowflakes have been done, through the stopping-out of tiny bits so that above the relatively even tone of the ruled lines they appear to be in front of the subject, between the viewer and the rest of the etching. Although the "pale blue flare" cannot be captured, Browne has given the kilns on the horizon hovering, ominous shapes, rather like Mexican pyramids. The image of the mill as a torture device is achieved by placing the shaft, with its straps for the horse, so that it points directly at the fleeing figure of Lady Dedlock. A detail not in the text, but which Browne is said to have made a special visit to a lime pit to get right, is the device for crushing lime, a contraption of huge spiked wheels, attached to a frame to be pulled by a horse.[28] It is placed at the top of a rise above Lady Dedlock and appears to threaten to descend and crush her. Even the three piles of bricks in the right foreground look like strange predatory animals, while the precarious board bridges across the pits suggest the danger of the path that the lonely figure is taking.

The first pair of dark plates within a single part, "The Night" (ch. 57) and "The Morning" (ch. 59), have captions which remind us of "Light" and "Shadow," but Browne apparently was confused about which was which, since on the paired proofs in the

Dexter Collection the penciled captions are reversed, and there is a note from Browne, "Which is 'Night' of these subjects?" Such confusion is understandable in view of the darkness of both subjects, and it suggests that Dickens did not always take Browne fully into his confidence by explaining the sequence of the plates and what they represent. Both are effectively in keeping with the dark tone of the novel. The narrative is indefinite about exactly where Bucket spots the brickmaker's wife disguised as Esther's mother, except that they first drive through a riverside neighborhood and then see the woman as they cross a bridge. The etching shows Westminster Abbey in the background, at an angle which suggests that this is where Millbank turns into Lambeth Bridge. The Abbey here has much the same connotations as does the parish church in "Tom all alone's," implying the church's isolation from human suffering.

"The Morning" is still darker in tone, and the more heavily bitten of the two steels (36A) is rather muddy, even in an exceptionally good impression. But the other steel is better: though startlingly dark, in a good impression the gravestones are possible to make out with a *putto* visible on one stone, a skull on another (as in "Consecrated ground"). Although these could not literally be the ones in the earlier illustration, an iconographic connection is made. This dark plate does center on a human figure, but it is still comparable to those which lack such figures because Lady Dedlock's corpse has been reduced almost to a thing by Browne's treatment of it as part of a pattern of light and shade—although her hand can be seen reaching through the bars of the graveyard gate, an important thematic emphasis. Browne has reached a stage in his own art where he seems to find it more and more fascinating to experiment with the possibilities of form, tone, pattern, and structure, and this could contribute to the deemphasis of human figures; yet although many of the dark plates for other novels demonstrate similar aesthetic concerns, they never again, within a single work, appear so devoid of recognizable human figures.

The four plates for the final, double number were executed as usual according to the novelist's directions; a letter survives which indicates that instructions for Part XVIII, and those for

Part XIX–XX, six in all, were dispatched to Phiz from Boulogne within a few days of one another, which implies that Dickens had this group, at least, planned out in advance as a kind of sequence.[29] It is thus conceivable that the dark plate technique and the dehumanized subject matter were specified by him. Only one illustration in the double part pertains directly to any action in that part: "Magnanimous conduct of Mr. Guppy" (ch. 64), which is handled economically and with somewhat more life than the other conventionally comic plates. "The Mausoleum at Chesney Wold" (ch. 46) corresponds to a passage which remarks that although some of "her old friends, principally to be found among the peachy-cheeked charmers with skeleton throats," said that "the ashes of the Dedlocks . . . rose against the profanation of their company" by the presence of Lady Dedlock, in fact "the dead-and-gone Dedlocks . . . have never been known to object." But the etching conveys nothing of this irony, being an atmospheric dark plate of a rather static kind, which includes the trees which "arch darkly overhead," but omits the owl "heard at night making the woods ring" (ch. 46, p. 519). Its rather grim aspect does not fit very well with the hopefulness of the novel's conclusion, although it may have been Dickens' intention to have it represent reconciliation and peace. That Phiz found the subject excessively sober is indicated by the working drawing (Elkins), in the margin of which he has sketched three mocking devils, one thumbing his nose with both hands, one laughing directly at the mausoleum, and the third peeking around the border of the drawing with a smirk on his face. How Dickens felt if he in fact saw this drawing we cannot know, but his doubts about Browne, expressed at least as long before as Mrs. Pipchin, would not have been lessened by it.

The frontispiece and title page, although published originally with the two plates just discussed, were planned with their ultimate position at the opening of the bound edition in mind. The frontispiece shows the manor of Chesney Wold in the distance, evidently at such time as "the waters are out in Lincolnshire" (ch. 2, p. 6), for the foreground shows—with fine dark plate technique—murky, marshy ground, while the trees are blown about in the wind and the sky is full of dark clouds. The manor itself almost bears the aspect of a haunted house; there is no specific indication that this haziness is meant to convey an explicit idea like the fading of the nobility, but the effect of the etching—for me, anyway—is one of ambiguous unpleasantness: loneliness, sterility, the lack of human connection are all suggested. The charcoal working drawing (Illus. 102) is itself quite different in tone from either steel, having been done with free, broad lines, but it is equally effective in its spooky way.

As a complement to the manor, the small title page vignette shows the opposite end of society—urban humanity in its lowest aspect. The subject is taken from chapter 16 (pp. 156–58), the first description of Jo the crossing-sweeper, and the comparison between the conditions of boy and dog in which the narrator argues that the "brute" is in most respects "far above the human" (p.158). In the background, to add a touch of urban squalor, Phiz has drawn tiny figures of two ragged women quarrelling, with a shabby man watching idly. In the context of the novel, the contrast between these two etchings emphasizes the indifference of the powerful classes toward the powerless, but also conveys the feeling that the former, especially the nobility, are to be associated with death, the lower classes with life. The original appearance of these plates with those of the Dedlock mausoleum (in the double part) surely strengthens the point.

We may now frame some replies to Mrs. Leavis' general complaints about the *Bleak House* illustrations. True, Browne does not capture the sense of fog and mud so important in the text; but the dark plates create an atmosphere complementary to that of the text, especially in the literally dark and dehumanized plates depicting "Tom all alone's," "A new meaning in the Roman," "Shadow," "The lonely figure," "The Night," "The Morning," and the mausoleum and manor of Chesney Wold. In such illustrations, oppression, confusion, and the power of dehumanized institutions are evoked as effectively as in the symbolic fog of the text. Dickens truly has achieved new heights through the use of new techniques in *Bleak House*, but his reliance on "Hogarthian" devices has by no means vanished, and they actually appear in certain sections more heavily and emphatically than before. Thus Browne's use of emblematic devices is, again, complementary, and sometimes conveys meanings which might be maudlin or too glaring if included in the text itself. This complementary process operates one way in the Turveydrop and

Chadband plates, which introduce a complexity of satiric allusion that would be difficult to achieve verbally; while it works
another way in the drawing-room plate, which combines tonal
subtlety with an emblematic statement of themes not made
explicit in the text.

One need not attribute the apparent laxness of some of the
more conventional plates to Browne's deterioration as an artist;
rather, his interests seem to have shifted, so that much of the time
the mere portrayal of characters does not engage his energy and
he is more concerned with the arrangement of structures, light,
and dark in seemingly abstract patterns. In the context of Victorian illustration as a whole, "The Morning," whatever its technical shortcomings, is a much more daring and experimental step
than one expects from an illustrator whose role is usually thought
of as subordinate to his author's, and subject to his author's will.
The contemporary dismay at these etchings gives us a hint as to
just how radical a departure it was, and Phiz's willingness to
continue such experimentation into the last years of the decade
may be evidence of the extent to which he desired to break
through the limitations normally imposed on illustrators, as
Dickens in his way was breaking through the limits of novelistic
realism.[30]

A cursory run-through of the etchings for *Little Dorrit* gives
the impression that Browne's excellence in the dark plates is
maintained on a level equal to *Bleak House,* and that many of the
regular plates are more carefully rendered than a high proportion
of those in the earlier novel. On the other hand, definite lapses of
technique are in evidence in some of the conventional plates,
and seven of the eight dark plates occur in the first half of the
novel; not one of the eight includes a single emblematic detail,
consistent with a general reduction in Browne's use of such conceptual techniques. (Such a reduction, already discernible in
Bleak House, becomes rapid for Phiz in the latter half of the
1850s, to the extent that by the end of the decade emblematic
details have virtually disappeared from his work.) As a group, the
Little Dorrit illustrations seem less necessary than those for
Bleak House, and yet some enhance the novel, making its "dark"
feeling visible, and underlining some of its themes by means of
familiar iconographic techniques.

Like *Bleak House, Little Dorrit* depends for a great part of its effectiveness upon Dickens' translation of his social vision into symbolic vision: Mrs. Clennam's paralysis, the parasitic Barnacles, Mr. Merdle's banality of evil, and perhaps above all, the motif of the prison. The successes and failures of collaboration depend partly on Dickens' assignment of subject, and partly on Browne's execution of each subject. Like all the monthly serial novels from *Nicholas Nickleby* onward, this one begins with a cover design intended to embody the novel's main themes; and like *Martin Chuzzlewit, Dombey and Son,* and perhaps more arguably, *David Copperfield* and *Bleak House, Little Dorrit* ends in the monthly parts and thus opens in the bound edition with a complementary pair of etchings that serve both as foreshadowing and retrospective devices. The cover design (Illus. 103) is more unified than *Bleak House*'s, and quite a bit less specific as to individual characters. John Butt and Kathleen Tillotson discuss this cover in some detail,[31] but Browne's original drawing was not available to them, and it reveals differences with the final plate which shed some light on the points they discuss.[32] First, Butt and Tillotson speculate on whether the original design carries the originally intended title, "Nobody's Fault"; they remark that this would have an ironic effect in connection with the political and social details that are depicted. In fact the drawing bears the published title, executed almost precisely as in the cut, with letters of stone and chain. In the center, Amy Dorrit stands at the outer gate of Marshalsea Prison, just having emerged from within; Butt and Tillotson comment that she stands "in a shaft of sunlight," but do not note that this sunlight—which here, as in the etched title page, lends a sanctified air to Amy—comes from *within* the prison, and that in a sense Amy goes into a world much darker than the prison. When it is repeated on the title page, this image is in turn complemented by the novel's frontispiece.

The "political cartoon" (as Butt and Tillotson call it) across the top, showing the blind and halt leading a dozing Britannia with a retinue of fools and toadies, is largely the same in the drawing, but one important detail differs in the extension of this motif down the sides of the design, while others are developed more clearly in the actual woodcut. The crumbling castle tower is in the drawing, as is the man sitting precariously on top of it, a newspaper in his lap and a cloth over his eyes, oblivious of the deterioration of the building. But while in the cut the church tower is clearly ruined, with a raven (or jackdaw?) atop it, the ruin is less evident in the drawing, and on the tower we have a fat, bewigged man asleep on an enormous cushion; this looks like something out of the *Bleak House* cover, since the cushion is probably meant to be the woolsack, and the man a high member of the legal profession. I suspect that Dickens told Browne to remove him, as his place on the church is inappropriate. The black bird in the cut would seem to signify the general decay of Victorian society and the prevalence of death, or, if it is a jackdaw, the thievery of institutions; yet I cannot find it any more appropriate to the church. The child playing leapfrog with the gravestones, a concept we have earlier traced back to Browne's frontispiece for *Godfrey Malvern*, here underlines the theme of indifference and irresponsibility. One other alteration likely to have been at Dickens' insistence is the representation of Mrs. Clennam in her wheelchair, with Flintwinch standing alongside. In the drawing we see instead, from the rear, a woman in a bath chair, pushed by a man. Dickens probably wished to have a more particular representation of Arthur's mother, as she and Jeremiah have a malevolent appearance in the cut and stand out as the only other definite characters, apart from Amy.

Little Dorrit's cover is effective in conveying certain themes—decay, indifference, irresponsibility of government, and confusion—as well as foreshadowing major tonalities of the novel, such as the dark prison, Little Dorrit as central figure, and Mrs. Clennam and Flintwinch as evil genii presiding over the ramifications of the plot. Along with the *Bleak House* cover it is the most socially conscious of the designs, and presents its ideas more directly than its predecessor. Dickens must have supplied a good deal of direction for this wrapper, given that the date of the following letter (19 October 1855) is approximately six weeks before the publication date of Part I:

> Will you give my address to B. and E. without loss of time, and tell them that although I have communicated at full explanatory length with Browne, I have heard *nothing of or from him.* Will you add that I am uneasy and wish they would communicate with Mr. Young, his partner, at once. Also that I beg them to be so good as send Browne my present address.[33]

Similar evidence of concern with illustrations is to be found in a note to Browne regarding the last two illustrations for a novel, possibly *Little Dorrit* (it is undated): "I hope the Frontispiece and Vignette will come out thoroughly well from the plate, and make a handsome opening to the book."[34] In this novel they do, the title page echoing the central motif of the wrapper. The implication that the world outside the prison is darker than that within is borne out by the frontispiece (Illus. 104), in which the figure of Amy is a virtual mirror image of that on the title; but here she is entering the Merdle mansion with Fanny, and from what we have learned of both Mrs. Merdle and her views on "Society," as well as Mr. Merdle, his crimes, and his suicide, this world is indeed more sinister than that of the prison. Yet in line with Dickens' text, Phiz has portrayed Amy in such a way that she conveys the sense of an innocence so strong as to be impervious to the corruptions of either the Marshalsea or Society; this is less true of her figure in the cover design, where her character has not yet been established and she looks as if she is bowed down with resignation.

Phiz continues his role as emblematizer of the novelist's intentions in the chain-and-brick lettering of the title (Illus. 105), and in an amusing touch in the frontispiece. The portly man at the right, behind the footman, is the Merdle chief butler, whom Dickens describes as doing nothing (like the government), and yet who is the terror of Merdle's life. He holds his hands so as to appear to be occupied, but he is no more useful than is the neo-classical statue behind him, which parodies his gestures in pouring an imaginary substance out of an imitation pitcher into an imitation bowl. The butler, in other words, functions as a piece of mobile sculpture for the conspicuously consuming Merdles—he is there for show and performs no real work, which is consistent with both the sham financial empire of Merdle the swindler, and the theme of How Not To Do It.

To return from the effect of the illustrations in the bound volume to that of the monthly installments: tonalities of the cover design are immediately picked up in "The Birds in the Cage" (Bk. 1, ch. 1),[35] particularly in the way the grill of the prison cell door recalls the castle portcullis and the prison theme picks up the cover's central detail. As a dark plate it differs from any of those in *Bleak House* which feature caricaturally drawn figures, but especially in the darker of the duplicate steels it recalls *Bleak House* in the way Phiz creates almost solidly black tones and yet manages to make details emerge from them. In a good impression of the darker steel (1B), the body of Rigaud and the bricks just barely come out of the blackness, as though one's eyes must become used to the dark. A contrast to the central panel of the wrapper is suggested in the way the sunshine comes weakly into a darkened cell from the outer world, while with Amy Dorrit a kind of symbolic sunshine emerges from within the prison itself, despite its internal corruption.

The prison theme is, I think, extended in the companion plate, "Under the Microscope" (Bk 1, ch. 2; Illus. 106). Both illustrations show the constricting interior of a room, both contain a larger, stronger individual dominating (at least temporarily) a weaker one who hates the bondage, and in both the dominant figure stands while the other sits or crouches on the floor. Rigaud and Miss Wade are both embittered and feel justified in taking revenge upon society, while John Baptist and Tattycoram are both lower-class outcasts who seek to escape bondage (though of course Tattycoram's escape from what she feels to be the Meagles' bondage into another form of it with Miss Wade is a more complex situation).

Browne's execution of this plate shows no signs of faltering, and it might be considered a technical advance on certain *Bleak House* etchings. All details are carefully done, including the women's faces, which are modeled by line and dot; the room is given depth by shading, and even the folds in drapery are meticulously rendered. That one extant drawing (Illus. 107) differs significantly from the etching is further evidence of painstaking care: Miss Wade's posture is different, but more importantly, Tattycoram's head is bent upward, she gazes back at Miss Wade, and her right arm, instead of clutching the bedcover, is extended toward the older woman in a gesture of resistance. It is a more melodramatic depiction of the incident and perhaps less in accord with the text, which describes the girl as "drawing the coverlet with her, half to hide her shamed head and wet hair in it, and half, as it seemed to embrace it . . ." (Bk. 1, ch. 2, p. 20). Yet it is not merely a preliminary sketch, since in addition to having been carefully executed it bears the initials of Dickens, indicating his approval. Whether at Dickens' request or his own reconsideration of the subject, Phiz redid it in a sketchy pencil drawing (Suzannet) and a seemingly unhurried etching. Yet he was no less busy than usual, working simultaneously on Lever's *The Martins of Cro'Martin* and several minor works.

In Part II, the visual representation of the prison theme continues in dark and oppressive rooms, and the illustrations provide an example of the effective pairing of a normal with a dark plate. "Mr. Flintwinch mediates as a friend of the Family" (Bk 1, ch. 5; Illus. 108), again, is elaborately etched, with all three faces modeled and the background fully filled in. Mr. Flintwinch's face is the most striking, done with a modified caricature technique which conveys the man's grotesqueness without that impossibility of face one sometimes got in Browne's early work. An emblematic detail appears, done with extreme care in the working drawing as well as the etching, which may at first seem out of place in the mode Browne establishes in these first few illustrations, where tone and composition seem to matter more than minor detail. It is a picture over Flintwinch's head, identifiable as the central portion of John Martin's painting and mezzotint, *Joshua Commanding the Sun to stand still on Gibeon,* probably the most familiar image of this episode in the first half of the century, especially in woodcut illustrations of the Bible.[36] The presence of such a picture in the room of Mrs. Clennam, an extreme self-justifying Calvinist, is plausible. In Dickens' words, Mrs. Clennam has "a general impression" that threatening to disown her son "was in some sort a religious proceeding" (Bk 1, ch. 5, p. 37). Jeremiah's first name also fits well with his function as mediator, speaking for the lordly Mrs. Clennam to the sinful Arthur. In the detail, Joshua's hand is raised in the same way as Flintwinch's, and there is a visual pun: the (supposed) man of God causes the "son" to stand still, to cease his rebellion.[37]

"The Room with the Portrait" (Bk 1, ch. 5) is a pendant to the episode in the preceding plate, as Arthur goes to his late father's room and sees the portrait of the dead man "with the eyes intently looking at his son as they had looked when life departed from them," and which "seemed to urge him awfully to the task he had attempted" (Bk 1, ch. 5, p. 40). The darker of the duplicate

plates goes rather far in the direction of obscurity, and many
readers may prefer the lighter one with more distinct details, yet
the darkness of Arthur's face in the murkier plate strikes me as
more effectively expressing the fact that Arthur himself is becoming engulfed in a darkness of mind and spirit. The illustration as
a whole is a successful follow-up to its companion, representing
the unremitting darkness Arthur has found in the bosom of his
family, and his sense of helplessness against it. It also again
suggests the novel's central image, the prison—literally the
enclosed space and psychologically the identity from which one
cannot escape as Mr. Dorrit never escapes his prisoner role, and
as Clennam feels trapped in the joyless Puritan acquisitiveness
of his family.

A number of plates throughout the novel depict constricting
rooms, some actually in the prison, but Browne's greatest use of
visual imagination in underlining this aspect of the novel is in
certain dark plates as well as certain conventional ones dealing
with the fortunes of the Dorrit family. The dark plates are all
impressive in their use of light and shade, and in the depth of
perspective thus created. While "The Birds in the Cage" depends on emergence of detail from darkness, the scene of John
Baptist's flight from Rigaud, "Making off" (Bk 1, ch. 11), uses an
elaborate pattern of light and dark, from the haze-covered rising
sun on the horizon over the town and the faint glimmer of the
puddles along the muddy road, to the ominous lines of trees
which seem to march toward the vanishing point and into utter
darkness. The figure of John Baptist, who flees from the oppressive association with Rigaud now that they are out of prison,
recalls Lady Dedlock in "The lonely figure," or the woman on
the bridge in "The Night."

Paradoxically, in the next monthly part Amy Dorrit and Maggy,
two more outcasts from society, are imprisoned in the street *outside* the prison, in another dark plate, "Little Dorrit's Party" (Bk.
1, ch. 4). In the darker steel, the prison is the very center of
darkness, its gate looming over Amy and Maggy. Amy's face is
shaded in this steel so that only a part of her dress provides the
center of light opposed to the darkness. The church too, as in
"Tom all alone's," looms indifferent and only slightly less dark
than the Marshalsea. Amy's white clothing and Maggy's bonnet
link their figures visually to the stars which (as in the text) offer

little comfort or hope. Although it may be objected that in the text the church becomes a place of refuge and consolation, in fact it is not the church in any religious sense, but only the "sexton, or the beadle, or the verger, or whatever he was," who offers them a place of shelter, and then only because Amy is one of the "curiosities" of the parish, as Child of the Marshalsea. A Hogarthian touch (corresponding to its use in "Tom all alone's") is evident in the placement of a pawnbroker's three balls on a structure adjoining the prison, in such a way that this emblem appears to be on the church itself as a kind of inverted cross.

"Little Dorrit's Party" is really Phiz's only chance (apart from the cover and the final pair of etchings) to make direct social and thematic comment, but another dark plate, "Visitors at the Works" (Bk 1, ch. 23), imparts a certain Kafkaesque quality to the novel. Ostensibly it is a comic plate (the only fully comic dark plate in Browne's work for Dickens), but the invasion of Doyce and Clennam's workshop by Flora Finching and the retributive figure of Mr. F's Aunt, whose umbrella points threateningly at Arthur, is more grotesque than it is comic, and the dark plate mode gives the machinery which dominates the entire right half of the etching a more ominous air than anything suggested in the text, where Doyce's inventions are said to have great potential for good. It is as though, given no other chance to depict the destructive institutions which form such an important part of the novel's satire, Phiz made use of the mad little woman in combination with the machinery to convey the feeling of dehumanization which Dickens achieves most notably through the Barnacles. If only Phiz had been given Barnacles or, in *Bleak House*, Boodle, Coodle, and Doodle as subjects. . . .

But his more conventional etching techniques do allow Browne to do justice to the prison identity of the Dorrit family in at least three illustrations. The technique of parallel and contrast between plates is evident, even in the captions alone, in "The Brothers" (Bk. 1, ch. 19; Illus. 109) and "Miss Dorrit and Little Dorrit" (Bk. 1, ch. 20; Illus. 110). In the first, a well-fed, supercilious man strolls patronizingly in the Marshalsea yard with "his brother Frederick of the dim eye, palsied hand, bent form, and groping mind," as though it were indeed a "College-yard," the man in the dressing gown and the disreputable characters near the pump were not there, and the woman at the gate with her small child were not taking leave of "a new Collegian" (Bk. 1, ch. 19, p. 163). This horizontal etching takes full advantage of its available space, the figures in the background being serviceable and no more—though creating no feeling of slackness on the artist's part. It is perhaps my fancy, but the smoke which William is blowing out over his brother's head resembles a speech-balloon (a device going back to earlier graphic satire), implying that this puff on a cigar represents an utterance of the conde-scending, self-assumed superiority of the prisoner brother.

In the companion plate the sisters, like the brothers, hold the center of the scene, and Fanny, like her father, extends one hand in a gesture of patronage towards Amy. Thus the Marshalsea taint in Fanny and the similarity of Amy's and Frederick's positions in the family—as the ones who uncomplainingly work to support the rest and are patronized and manipulated in return—are made visually present in the illustrations. In the original drawing for "Miss Dorrit and Little Dorrit" (Suzannet) the stage-prop throne on which Amy sits is on a raised platform, and thus the extent to which Fanny looms above her sister is less pronounced; Amy looks up at Fanny, a less precise expression of her attitude than the neutral but implicitly long-suffering face she has in the etch-ing.

The denouement of the first book, wherein the Dorrits come into their fortune, is depicted in "The Marshalsea becomes an Orphan" (Bk. 1, ch. 36; Illus. 111), an illustration which might be considered unnecessary for Dickens at this stage of his develop-ment, since the relevant paragraph contains all that is required and much that cannot be conveyed in an etching. If not all the psychological varieties of "Collegian" described in the text are present, still Browne's illustration brings before the reader's eyes the crowded scene, centering on the Dorrit family with the contrasting brothers, the haughty Fanny, dissolute Tip, the fol-lower, Maggy, as well as the sorrowing John Chivery. Altogether there are thirty-seven distinct figures, all rendered without artis-tic awkwardness. What is brought out is the squalidness of this particular triumph, the pitifulness of Mr. Dorrit's condescension, and the permanent degradation of his own state and that of two of his children. The drawing technique is characteristic of Browne's style in the late 1850s and early 1860s at its best, with a concern for composition, a pleasant handling of faces, and something of a sparseness of background details. In some of these plates, however, there is a tendency toward excessively rigid symmetry, as in the very next one in this novel, "The Travellers" (Bk. 2, ch. 1).

Browne returns to Mr. Dorrit later to depict his ultimate fate, and the earlier illustrative mode chosen for the plate seems appropriate, though it is unusual for this novel. "The Night" (Bk. 2, ch. 19) is the kind of subject which tended to stimulate Browne's emblematic imagination. No doubt the idea of showing just Mr. Dorrit's arm and hand, and having the illustration center on his loving and devoted brother Frederick, formed part of Dickens' instructions, though in this regard it does not follow the text precisely, since the latter speaks repeatedly of two figures; yet the notion is consistent with the last two sentences in the chapter, especially the description of "the arms easily and peacefully resting on the coverlet, the face bowed down so that the lips touched the hand over which with its last breath it had bent" (Bk. II, ch. 19, p. 492). On the wall are paintings of a king and a ruined castle, the first probably representing the condition of power and eminence Dorrit has so recently imagined himself to occupy, the second the collapse of his castle in the air. A third emblematic detail is a statue of a seminude woman, probably Psyche, with her head turned to look at the butterfly on her shoulder. The butterfly as soul is a traditional emblem, and here as in the plate dealing with Dora Copperfield's death the reference is to the impending departure of the dying person's soul.

Before turning to Phiz's treatment of aspects of evil in the novel, I must remark upon two dark plates which are different from anything else Browne did for Dickens. Both "The Ferry" (Bk. 1, ch. 17) and "Floating away" (Bk. 1, ch. 28) have to do with Arthur's unrequited love for "Pet" Meagles, and neither is strictly necessary for the novel; but they are worth mentioning because of their anomalous place both in Dickens illustrations and in mid-Victorian novel illustration. In the first, Browne fills out a text which gives us only a cursory description of the scene with an extremely delicate and beautiful landscape, "dark" only in a technical sense. Unlike the "Sixties" illustration of novels via the wood engraving (Millais, Marcus Stone, et al), which concentrates on character, these two plates recall the line-engraved or mezzotint illustration of the annuals of the 1820s and 1830s, which usually have only a vague relation to the texts they accompany. In both instances, it is as though Phiz has created a fine etching of a largely natural scene simply because he felt like doing so. Similar dark plates pervade Phiz's work for the novels of Ainsworth, Lever, and Augustus Mayhew during a period of a few years after the appearance of *Little Dorrit;* often, they are what remains of interest in those books, while in Dickens' novel they are, though not out of place, curiously different from all the rest of the illustrations.

Apart from Mrs. Clennam, who is given a rather domestic treatment in the two plates in which she appears, the main embodiments of evil in the novel whom Browne is permitted to draw are Mr. Merdle and Rigaud-Blandois; these two men derive from different literary traditions, and what Browne is and is not able to do with them reveals a good deal about his abilities, opportunities and functions at this stage in both his and Dickens' careers. In the text, Merdle is a special kind of grotesque with largely symbolic qualities. He is always "taking himself into custody" (a hint of the criminal nature of his business); he is tyrannized over by the chief butler, suggesting his *nouveau riche* status as a financial manipulator who has risen to power almost overnight; and his relation to his wife is consistent with the limiting of his identity to the world of finance, for she is purchased as a "bosom" upon which to hang jewels. Even his name, suggesting *merde*, emblematically conveys the idea of a low, filthy substance, brought into unseemly contact with the highest of the land. Yet Dickens at the same time manages to evoke a degree of pity for Merdle as someone who is basically out of sympathy with the shallow society world in which he has risen so high, someone who doesn't know what to do with his success and would be more comfortable as a private man. He is not a monster like such earlier characters who epitomize the cash-nexus values of Dickens' society—Pecksniff, Dombey, Heep, or Bounderby.

Accordingly, the novelist's treatment of the "patriotic" conference for bringing Merdle and Lord Decimus Barnacle together to arrange a rich bit of patronage is very much in the traditions of political caricature, if not literary allegory. Bar, Bishop, Physician, and Chorus are representative types rather than individuals, and this is consistent with all of the Barnacle imagery. Yet, except for the Bishop's collar, there is no way of distinguishing the types in Browne's illustration, "The Patriotic Conference" (Bk. 2, ch. 12; Illus. 112). If we read ahead to page 427, we find that the three men shown behind Merdle and Lord Decimus are the "Chorus," while Bishop's companion is Physician, but in earlier Dickens novels one would not have to consult the text this closely in order to understand an illustration (whereas in "Sixties" illustrations the picture usually relies heavily on the text). Phiz's men are realized as individuals, not as types. One of his problems here is that Dickens has virtually dispensed with physical description beyond Merdle's habit of taking himself into custody. Yet were Phiz to label the characters with obvious symbols of their professions, the result would seem primitive, and jar with the rest of his work in this novel.

In this instance, it is difficult to dispute the argument that Dickens no longer needs an illustrator: illustrations do not work for this particular episode because Dickens chose to make use of a highly stylized, nonrealistic technique. His private imagination is still visual, however, as can be inferred from his instruction to Browne, "Don't have Lord Decimus's hand put out, because that looks condescending; and I want him to be upright, stiff, unmixable with mere mortality"[38]—an instruction Browne followed as best he could. And similarly, in "Mr. Merdle a borrower" (Bk. 2, ch. 24), the financier is remarkable for little but his awkward, bearish, shambling appearance and the blankness of his face, consistent with our sense of him as a nonentity; yet Browne, now eschewing caricature, could not match the effectiveness of the text, nor could he add anything to it through traditional iconography.

Rigaud-Blandois is a somewhat different matter. Dickens' character seems to derive from the folk-fairytale and its later artistic versions (such as Hoffmann's) and thus in the text he gives the impression of representing a more general, nontopical form of evil than does Merdle. Yet to this reader, at any rate,

Rigaud is most successful as an artistic creation when he appears most clearly as a diminution of the devil-type, whose demonism is shown as merely a pose convenient to his philosophy of personal power and absolute self-interest. In most of Phiz's portrayals this complexity cannot emerge, and Rigaud is little more than a weakly drawn demon. But in two effective plates Phiz does complement and enhance Dickens' conception of the character. His first appearance in England as Blandois is illustrated in "Mr. Flintwinch has a mild attack of irritability" (Bk. 1, ch. 30). He has just emerged from the shadows, to give poor fearful Affery a terrible start; in this plate, Jeremiah is shaking his wife for her reaction while Blandois looks on. A preliminary drawing (Suzannet) indicates that this was almost certainly intended first as a dark plate: it is drawn in charcoal with the kind of heavy tone that Browne rarely if ever employed for anything else; and rather than the close-up of the final version, it is a distant view of the same scene, with the figures very small but in similar positions. Perhaps the emphasis (though the sketch is too small and rough for this to be certain) was to be on the old Clennam house, which burgeons larger and larger in the novel until it comes forth as a symbol of the decay of society—reminiscent of the collapse of buildings in Tom-All-Alone's. It is suggested that the next crash will likely "be a good one."[39]

It is possible that Dickens originally intended the opening of Part IX to concentrate more upon the house, and gave Browne directions to this end, but upon having written the chapter found that the characters were more important, and correspondingly gave new directions. In the final version, the demonic aspect of Blandois is played up, both in his black cloak and in the gleam of his eyes and teeth, while the grotesque figures decorating the doorway look down upon the three characters with sinister anticipation. This illustration, even in its final form, could have been a dark plate, for it is literally dark enough; but the particular vein Dickens exploits seems better served by heavy manual shading than by the smoothness of a mechanical tint. The final version complements Dickens' text in the way it sets off against Blandois' gleaming eyes, upcurving moustache, and black cloak the rather horribly comic grotesqueness of Affery and Flintwinch—in other words, it is in a mixed vein which Phiz rarely brings off successfully in *Little Dorrit*.

I have already discussed in some detail the frontispiece and title page to *Little Dorrit* as they stand in the bound volume; but they appeared to the earliest readers in a different context, both visually and textually. Although Browne went on to do a cover and sixteen etchings for *A Tale of Two Cities,* the four plates in *Little Dorrit,* Part XIX, represent for me the illustrator's last major effort for Dickens, since those for the novel of the French Revolution are notably deficient in vitality. In juxtaposition with its original companions, even the weakest of these four final *Dorrit* plates is effective. The first of the four, "Damocles" (Bk. 2, ch. 30; Illus. 113), is the last of the dark plates in any Dickens novel, and one of the strongest. The caption (presumably by Dickens) has an obvious irony: while Blandois thinks of himself as holding the Damoclean sword of blackmail over Jeremiah Flintwinch and Mrs. Clennam, in fact a Damoclean sword (in the form of the collapsing building in whose window he nonchalantly perches) is about to descend upon *him.*

It is of special interest that Phiz includes such indications of the imminent collapse as the stone falling from the eaves and the mangy cat apparently fleeing the house, because the text contains no direct suggestion of what is about to happen (it is left until near the end of the next chapter)—although there has been much previous fuss by Affery about the strange noises in the house. It is thus one of those cases where the novelist left an important fact to be dealt with in the illustration, which thereafter will become an integral part of the novel. Here, the artist has also added details which link the scene and the Clennam house with themes in *Bleak House:* the crude supports holding up the house remind one of "Tom all alone's," and hint at a connection between the middle-class acquisitive work-ethic of Mrs. Clennam and the disease-ridden slum which is "in" Chancery.

In looking at the monthly installment, one turns from this etching to "The Third Volume of the Registers" (Bk. 2, ch. 34), an otherwise rather uninteresting depiction of Amy and Arthur's wedding, which takes on a kind of dramatic interest via the contrast with the implied doom of Blandois, the most archetypally evil character in the book. And that the frontispiece and etched title page follow lends it additional significance: at the novel's conclusion, instead of retreating to a pastoral seclusion as do

protagonists in early Dickens novels, Amy and Arthur go "down
into the roaring streets" (Bk. II, ch. 34, p. 625), and we are reminded by these two visually parallel etchings of the similarities
between the prison world and society. As I have mentioned early
in my discussion of *Little Dorrit*, Dickens evidently conceived of
these two plates as opening the bound volume, and so that must
be considered their primary function; but they did first appear
together with the Damocles and wedding illustrations, and as
such provide us with a final example of how Browne was able to
work in several different modes, fulfilling dramatic and sequential, as well as more general, symbolic functions as Dickens'
illustrator and interpreter.

THE ILLUSTRATIONS

All items are by Hablot Knight Browne unless otherwise noted. Where no credit line is given, items are from the author's collection.

BL: Reproduced by courtesy of the British Library.
BM: Reproduced by courtesy of the Trustees of British Museum.
Elkins: Reproduced by courtesy of the Free Library of Philadelphia.
     From the Elkins Collection, Rare Book Department.

1. John Leech, etching for W. H. Maxwell, *Brian O'Linn*, 1846.

2. Etching for Anthony Trollope, *Can You Forgive Her?*, Vol. I, 1864.

3. E. Taylor, wood engraving for Anthony Trollope, *Can You Forgive Her?*, Vol. II, 1865.

4. Wood engraving for Charles Dickens, *Sunday Under Three Heads*, 1836.

5. "Traddles and I, in conference with the Misses Spenlow," etching for *David Copperfield,* 1850.

6. "I make the acquaintance of Miss Mowcher," etching for *David Copperfield*, 1850.

7. "I make the acquaintance of Miss Mowcher," working drawing (Elkins).

8. "The Picture Gallery—Sir Andrew puzzled," etching for
Charles Lever, *Roland Cashel*, 1849.

9. Moritz Retzsch, "The Decision of the Flower," engraving for *Twenty-Six Outlines Illustrative of Goethe's Tragedy of Faust,* 1820.

10. "The Goblin and the Sexton" (illustration for *Pickwick Papers*, 1836), preliminary drawing (courtesy of the Pierpont Morgan Library).

11. "The Goblin and the Sexton," second drawing (courtesy of the Pierpont Morgan Library).

12. "The Goblin and the Sexton," working drawing for the etching (courtesy of the Pierpont Morgan Library).

13. "First appearance of Mr. Samuel Weller," etching for
Pickwick Papers, 1836.

14. "Mrs. Bardell faints in Mr. Pickwick's arms," new etching for
second edition of *Pickwick Papers*, 1838.

15. George Cruikshank, "The Unwelcome Intruders," etching for
A. Moore, *Annals of Gallantry*, 1814 (BM).

16. "Mr. Pickwick in the Pound," etching for *Pickwick Papers*, 1836.

17. "Mr. Pickwick in the Pound," working drawing (courtesy of
the Pierpont Morgan Library).

18. "Christmas Eve at Mr. Wardle's," ?first state of etching for
Pickwick Papers, 1836.

19. "Christmas Eve at Mr. Wardle's," ?second state of etching.

20. "Christmas Eve at Mr. Wardle's," preliminary drawing for ?second state of etching (courtesy of the Pierpont Morgan Library).

21. "The first interview with Mr. Serjeant Snubbin," etching for *Pickwick Papers*, 1837.

22. "The Discovery of Jingle in the Fleet," etching for *Pickwick Papers*, 1837.

23. William Hogarth, *The Rake's Progress*, Plate VII (1735), etched by T. Smith for John Major's edition of Trusler's *Hogarth Moralized*, 1831.

24. "Mrs. Bardell encounters Mr. Pickwick in the prison," etching for *Pickwick Papers*, 1837.

Christmas and His Children

25. Robert Seymour, etched frontispiece for Thomas K. Hervey,
The Book of Christmas, 1836.

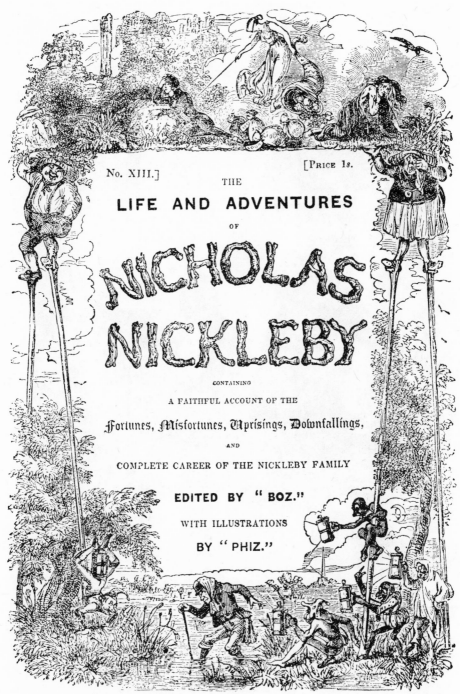

27. Cover for monthly parts of *Nicholas Nickleby*, wood engraving, 1838.

26. Etched frontispiece for *Pickwick Papers*, 1837.

28. "Mr. Ralph Nickleby's first visit to his poor relations," etching for *Nicholas Nickleby*, 1838.

29. "Nicholas astonishes Mr. Squeers and family," etching for *Nicholas Nickleby*, 1838.

30. "Mr. Crow well plucked," etching for Charles Lever, *Charles O'Malley*, 1840.

31. "A sudden recognition, unexpected on both sides," etching for
Nicholas Nickleby, 1839.

32. "The last brawl between Sir Mulbery and his pupil," etching
for *Nicholas Nickleby*, 1839.

33. William Hogarth, *A Midnight Modern Conversation* (1733), etched by T. E. Nicholson for John Major's edition of Trusler's *Hogarth Moralized*, 1831.

34. The Marchioness playing cards, wood engraving for *The Old Curiosity Shop*, 1840.

35. "The Marchioness," engraving by Hablot K. Browne and Robert Young, 1848.

36. Quilp leering at the Brasses, wood engraving for *The Old Curiosity Shop*, 1840.

37. Mr. Chester and Edward, wood engraving for *Barnaby Rudge*, 1841.

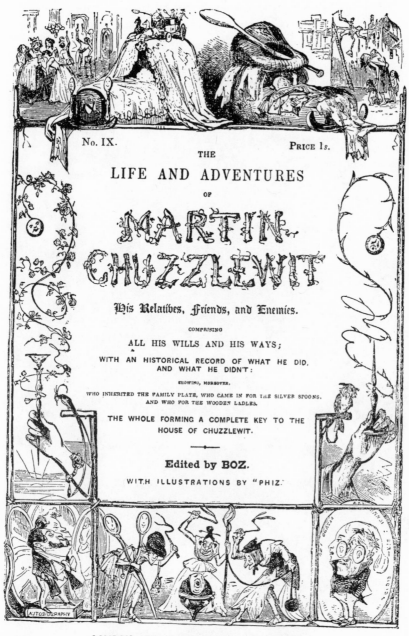

No. IX.   PRICE 1s.

THE

LIFE AND ADVENTURES

OF

MARTIN CHUZZLEWIT

His Relatives, Friends, and Enemies.

COMPRISING

ALL HIS WILLS AND HIS WAYS;

WITH AN HISTORICAL RECORD OF WHAT HE DID,
AND WHAT HE DIDN'T:

SHOWING, MOREOVER,

WHO INHERITED THE FAMILY PLATE, WHO CAME IN FOR THE SILVER SPOONS,
AND WHO FOR THE WOODEN LADLES.

THE WHOLE FORMING A COMPLETE KEY TO THE
HOUSE OF CHUZZLEWIT.

Edited by BOZ.

WITH ILLUSTRATIONS BY "PHIZ."

LONDON: CHAPMAN & HALL, 186, STRAND.

September 1843

38. Cover for monthly parts of *Martin Chuzzlewit*, wood engraving, 1843.

39. Etched frontispiece for *Martin Chuzzlewit*, 1844.

40. "Mr. Pecksniff renounces the deceiver," etching for *Martin Chuzzlewit*, 1843.

41. "Mr. Pecksniff renounces the deceiver," working drawing (BM).

42. "Pleasant little family party at Mr. Pecksniff's," etching for *Martin Chuzzlewit*, 1843.

autograph inscriptions by Charles Dickens

43. "Pleasant little family party at Mr. Pecksniff's," working drawing (BM).

44. "The thriving City of Eden, as it appeared on paper," etching for *Martin Chuzzlewit*, 1843.

45. "The thriving City of Eden as it appeared on paper," working drawing (courtesy of The Huntington Library, San Marino, California).

46. "Mr. Jonas Chuzzlewit entertains his cousins," etching for *Martin Chuzzlewit*, 1843.

47. "Mr. Jonas Chuzzlewit entertains his cousins," working drawing (BM).

48. "The Board," etching for *Martin Chuzzlewit*, 1843.

49. "Easy Shaving," etching for *Martin Chuzzlewit*, 1843.

50. "Mr. Moddle is led to the contemplation of his destiny," etching for *Martin Chuzzlewit*, 1844.

51. Early alternative design to "Mr. Moddle is led to the contemplation of his destiny," drawing (The Beinecke Rare Book and Manuscript Library, Yale University).

52. Early drawing for "Mr. Moddle is led to the contemplation of his destiny" (The Beinecke Rare Book and Manuscript Library, Yale University).

53. "The Nuptials of Miss Pecksniff receive a temporary check," etching for *Martin Chuzzlewit*, 1844.

54. "The Nuptials of Miss Pecksniff receive a temporary check,"
working drawing (BM).

55. Etched title page for *Martin Chuzzlewit*, 1844.

56. Title page for *Martin Chuzzlewit*, preliminary drawing (BM).

57. Title page for *Martin Chuzzlewit*, working drawing (by courtesy of the Trustees of the Dickens House).

58. William Hogarth, *A Harlot's Progress*, Plate I (1734), etched by W. H. Watt for John Major's edition of Trusler's *Hogarth Moralized* (1831).

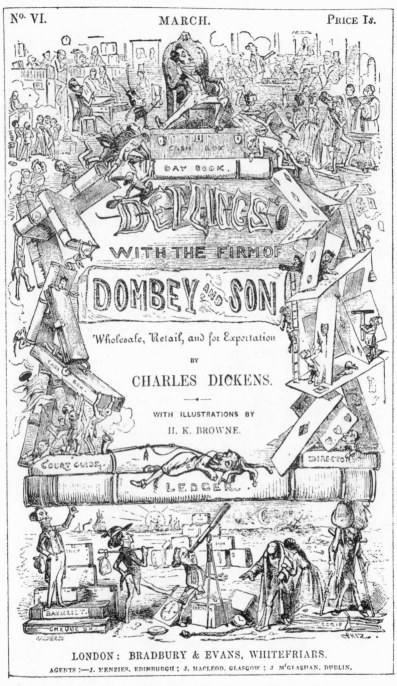

No. VI.   MARCH.   Price 1s.

DEALINGS
WITH THE FIRM OF
DOMBEY AND SON
Wholesale, Retail, and for Exportation

BY

CHARLES DICKENS.

WITH ILLUSTRATIONS BY
H. K. BROWNE.

DAY BOOK.

COURT GUIDE.   LEDGER.   DIRECTORY

LONDON: BRADBURY & EVANS, WHITEFRIARS.
AGENTS:—J. MENZIES, EDINBURGH; J. MACLEOD, GLASGOW; J. M'GLASHAN, DUBLIN.

59. Cover for monthly parts of *Dombey and Son*, wood engraving, 1846.

60. "Paul and Mrs. Pipchin," etching for *Dombey and Son*, 1846.

61. "Paul and Mrs. Pipchin," working drawing (Elkins).

62. "Major Bagstock is delighted to have that opportunity," etching for *Dombey and Son*, 1847.

63. "Major Bagstock is delighted to have that opportunity," working drawing (Elkins).

64. "Mr. Dombey introduces his daughter Florence," etching for
Dombey and Son, 1847.

65. Portrait of Mrs. Skewton, etching from a series of eight separately published etchings, 1848.

66. "Coming home from Church," etching for *Dombey and Son,* 1847.

67. "The Midshipman is boarded by the enemy," etching for *Dombey and Son*, 1847.

68. "The Midshipman is boarded by the enemy," working drawing (Elkins).

69. "Abstraction and recognition," etching for *Dombey and Son*,
1848.

70. "Florence and Edith on the staircase," etching for *Dombey and Son*, 1848.

71. "Mr. Carker in his hour of triumph," etching for *Dombey and Son*, 1848.

72. "Mr. Carker in his hour of triumph," working drawing (El-kins).

73. "Another wedding", etching for *Dombey and Son*, 1848.

74. Etched frontispiece for *Dombey and Son*, 1848.

75. "Our Pew at Church," etching for *David Copperfield*, 1849.

76. "Our Pew at Church," working drawing (Elkins).

77. "I make myself known to my Aunt," etching for *David Copperfield*, 1849.

78. "I make myself known to my Aunt," preliminary drawing No. 1 (Elkins).

79. "I make myself known to my Aunt," preliminary drawing No.
3 (Elkins).

80. "I am married," etching for *David Copperfield*, 1850.

81. "Martha," etching for *David Copperfield*, 1850.

82. "The River," dark plate etching for *David Copperfield*, 1850.

83. "The River," working drawing (Elkins).

84. "Mr. Peggotty's dream comes true," etching for *David Copperfield*, 1850.

85. "A stranger calls to see me," etching for *David Copperfield*, 1850.

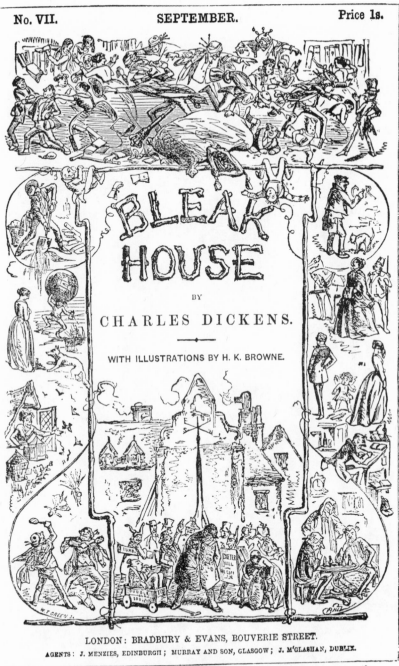

No. VII.   SEPTEMBER.   Price 1s.

BLEAK HOUSE

BY

CHARLES DICKENS.

WITH ILLUSTRATIONS BY H. K. BROWNE.

LONDON: BRADBURY & EVANS, BOUVERIE STREET.

AGENTS: J. MENZIES, EDINBURGH; MURRAY AND SON, GLASGOW; J. M'GLASHAN, DUBLIN.

☞ The Author of this Work notifies that it is his intention to reserve the right of translating it.

86. Cover for monthly parts of *Bleak House*, wood engraving, 1852.

87. Etched frontispiece for Albert Smith, *The Pottleton Legacy*, 1849.

88. "The Dancing School," etching for *Bleak House*, 1852.

89. George Cruikshank, engraved portrait of King George IV, 1820 (BM).

90. "A model of 'parental deportment'", etching for *Bleak House*, 1852.

91. George Cruikshank, wood engraving of George IV as Prince of
Wales, from William Hone, *The Queen's Matrimonial Ladder*,
1820 (*BM Cat* 13791).

92. "Mr. Chadband 'improving' a tough subject," etching for *Bleak House*, 1852.

93. "Attorney and Client: fortitude and impatience," etching for
Bleak House, 1853.

94. "Attorney and Client: fortitude and impatience," first drawing (BM).

95. "Attorney and Client: fortitude and impatience," working drawing (Elkins).

96. "Sunset in the long drawing-room at Chesney Wold," ?preliminary drawing (not reversed) for *Bleak House*, 1853 (The Beinecke Rare Book and Manuscript Library, Yale University).

97. "Sunset in the long drawing-room at Chesney Wold," working drawing, reverse of etching (Elkins).

98. "Tom all alone's," dark plate etching for *Bleak House*, 1853.

99. "A new meaning in the Roman," working drawing, detail (El-kins).

100. "A new meaning in the Roman," dark plate etching for *Bleak House*, 1853, detail.

101. "Shadow," dark plate etching for *Bleak House*, 1853.

102. Frontispiece for *Bleak House*, 1853, working drawing (El-kins).

No. IX. AUGUST. Price 1s.

LITTLE DORRIT

BY
CHARLES DICKENS.

WITH

ILLUSTRATIONS BY H. K. BROWNE.

LONDON. BRADBURY & EVANS, BOUVERIE STREET.

AGENTS: J. MENZIES, EDINBURGH; MURRAY AND SON, GLASGOW; J. M'GLASHAN. DUBLIN.

☞ The Author reserves the right of Translation.

103. Cover for monthly parts of *Little Dorrit*, wood engraving, 1855.

104. Etched frontispiece for *Little Dorrit*, 1857.

LITTLE DORRIT,

BY

CHARLES DICKENS.

105. Etched title page for *Little Dorrit*, 1857.

106. "Under the microscope," etching for *Little Dorrit*, 1855.

107. "Under the microscope," preliminary drawing (BM).

108. "Mr. Flintwinch mediates as a friend of the family," etching for *Little Dorrit*, 1856.

109. "The Brothers," etching for *Little Dorrit*, 1856.

110. "Miss Dorrit and Little Dorrit," etching for *Little Dorrit*, 1856.

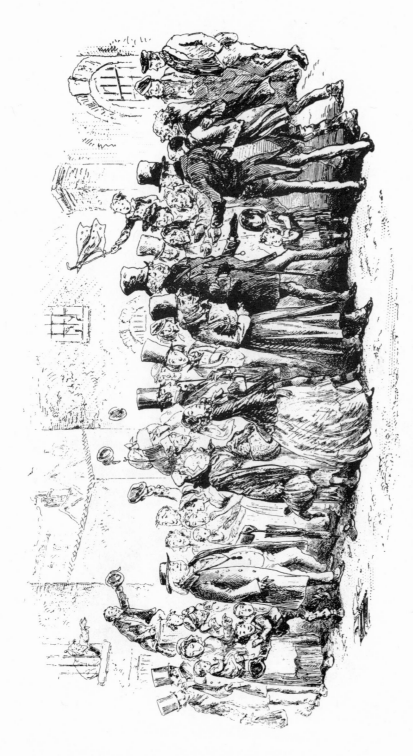

111. "The Marshalsea becomes an Orphan", etching for *Little Dorrit*, 1857.

112. "The Patriotic Conference," etching for *Little Dorrit*, 1857.

113. "Damocles," dark plate etching for *Little Dorrit*, 1857.

114. "The Abstemious young Lady," etching for "Quiz," *Sketches of Young Ladies*, 1837.

115. "Out-door Relief," etching for James Grant, *Sketches in London*, 1838.

116. "The Supper at Father Malachi's," etching for Charles Lever, *Harry Lorrequer*, 1838.

117. "The Prosperity going down," etching for W. J. Neale, *Paul Periwinkle*, 1840.

118. "The Sunk Fence," etching for Charles Lever, *Charles O'Malley*, 1840.

119. "Gregory Gruff's Honeymoon," etching for Thomas Miller,
Godfrey Malvern, 1843.

120. "The Ruined house in the Vauxhall Road," etching for W. Harrison Ainsworth, *Auriol*, 1844.

121. "A Prairie—evening ride," dark plate etching for Charles Lever, *Roland Cashel*, 1849.

122. "A meeting under the Greenwood Tree," dark plate etching for Charles Lever, *Roland Cashel*, 1849.

123. "Night," hand-colored etching for Browne's *Home Sketches*, 1851 (BM).

124. "Old Mat's last resting-place," etching for Charles Lever, *The Martins of Cro' Martin*, 1856.

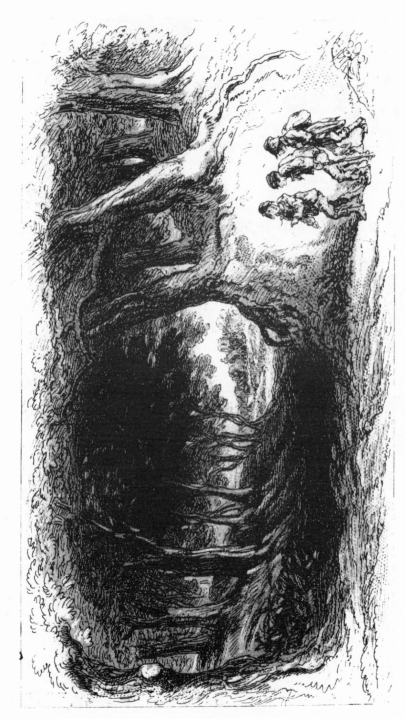

125. "The Tramps," dark plate etching for Augustus Mayhew, *Paved With Gold*, 1858.

126. Dark plate etched title page for George Halse, *Agatha*, 1860.

CHAPTER SEVEN

Phiz the Illustrator:
An Overview
and a Summing Up

Hablot Knight Browne illustrated ten novels by Dickens in whole or in part, but he illustrated with etchings some sixteen for Charles Lever (as well as contributing wood engravings to several others by that author), and between June 1836, when he began work as a replacement for Robert Seymour's replacement, Buss, on *Pickwick*, and his death in 1882—a span twice the length of his association with Dickens—he produced an enormous amount of other work: illustrations for serial novels and those in volume form, for periodicals and "yellowbacks," for children's books, and for a few of his own published collections of designs on assorted subjects, as well as a goodly number of unpublished drawings in pencil, pen, and watercolor, and some paintings, both in watercolor and oil. A complete survey of his career would involve a large study in itself, and here I shall only attempt to provide a perspective on Browne's work for Dickens and his contributions as an artist by means of a selection of typical examples at various stages of his career. An appended checklist of his work during the Dickens period provides at least an enumerative overview.

Although Browne's initials appear on some of the engravings in the first two volumes (1835–38) of Winkles's *Cathedrals of England*, for all practical purposes the young Browne made his debut as the rather crude designer of three cuts for *Sunday*

Under Three Heads, which foreshadow to some extent his subsequent collaborations with its pseudonymous author, "Timothy
Sparks." His really significant debut, of course, was with Part IV
of *The Posthumous Papers of the Pickwick Club*. At the time,
Browne was already developing something of his own style even
though his work clearly shows the influence of Seymour. For the
first year it does not seem that he received much work, aside from
three cuts for Chapman and Hall's *Library of Fiction* (1836), the
main interest of which lies in a visual prototype of Tony Weller.[1]
The first important non-Dickensian job done by "Phiz"—whose
pseudonym doubtless determined that of the author, "Quiz"—is
Edward Caswall's *Sketches of Young Ladies* (1837), again published by Chapman and Hall. The eighty-page text, which de-
lineates "two dozen classes of young ladies" (p. 78), is small
beer, but the six etchings are delightful, executed with great care
somewhat in the style of Seymour, but with far more elan.
Perhaps best is "The Abstemious Young Lady" (Illus. 114),
which combines a group of rather Seymourean faces and figures,
carefully modeled, with several emblematic details both larger
and jollier than Phiz usually employed for Dickens: a pair of fat
stuffed ducks, an equally fat ceramic Chinaman, two feasting
satyrs, and a framed picture of a tankard of beer with some dead
game, all commenting upon the secret nursery feasts of the
young lady who plays the fraudulent role of a self-starving, "interesting" beauty in public.

Weak though Quiz's satire is, Dickens felt it was enough to
hang a rebuttal on, and so the next year produced *Sketches of
Young Gentlemen*, followed by *Sketches of Young Couples* in
1840. John Harvey has said of the illustrator's contribution to
these three titles that in them can be observed the "gradual
relaxation" which "foretells the later slackness of Browne's
work."[2] Browne's work certainly did change between 1837 and
1840, but one may attribute the change to more positive factors: a
gradual breaking away from Seymour's influence and the development of a distinct style. If one were to show the illustrations of
the first *Sketches* (signatures omitted) to someone who knew
Phiz's later work only, such a person might be hard put to identify the artist; but the style of the third *Sketches* is unmistakable.
The *Young Gentlemen* may be inferior to the *Ladies*, but I think

"relaxation" is a virtue of the etchings for *Young Couples*, which are more like drawings, with a loosening up of line and a pervading impression that the artist is his own man. Most of the awkwardness of the earliest figures is gone, the characters are less grotesque, and a pleasant humor is achieved in such a plate as "The Couple who coddle themselves."

After *Pickwick*, the first major project for Phiz was James Grant's *Sketches in London* (1838), apparently an imitation of *Sketches by Boz*. Most of Browne's eighteen plates are small and lacking in any clear signs of invention, but a few are of some interest. In particular, both plates for chapter 7, "Workhouses," may owe something to Cruikshank, for the hollow cheeks of the paupers in "A Workhouse dinner" recall "Oliver asks for more," and "Out-door relief" (Illus. 115) resembles "The Beadle" in *Sketches by Boz*, although Phiz's beadle looks more malevolent than Cruikshank's, or even than the great Mr. Bumble himself. The wretched, starving adults and children are more shocking than anything allowed into *Sketches by Boz*. The design is well laid out, but a comparison with "Oliver asks for more" indicates something of Phiz's limitations: the faces of Cruikshank's workhouse children achieve a response in the viewer seemingly beyond Phiz's powers to evoke. The author, unlike so many of those for whom Browne worked, took pains to comment upon his twenty-three year old collaborator in a preface:

> With regard to the Illustrations by "Phiz," which embellish the volume, the Author can speak more unreservedly than he could do of the letter-press. They are among the happiest achievements of the genius of one who, though yet but young in years, is unquestionably, in this particular style of engraving, the first artist of the day.

(The confusion of etching with engraving is usual during this period, and later.)

As I have suggested in an earlier chapter, during the period of *Nicholas Nickleby* (1838–39) Browne seemed to have been casting about for his own proper style, and sometimes fell below the level of quality already attained in *Pickwick*. Probably the most important work of this time for demonstrating both Phiz's strengths and his stylistic uncertainties is Lever's *Harry Lorrequer*. The plates for *Lorrequer* are, like the novel, boisterous, exaggerated, and seemingly done in a fair hurry. The hero resembles Nicholas Nickleby (as Lever complained),[3] and nowhere more so than in "The Supper at Father Malachi's" (Illus. 116), where he gives the impression of a normal man who accidentally happens to be present at a gathering of grotesques invented by a follower of Gillray and Rowlandson. The illustrations are generally uneven, though a plate like "Mr. O'Leary charges a Mob" displays a good control of composition in the way Browne has enclosed violent action within a balanced visual structure. The plates in this novel are also notable for the absence of emblematic details, a possible consequence of the hurry with which Phiz had to work owing to Lever's dilatoriness with copy, and his own simultaneous work on *Nickleby*, for which triplicate and even quadruplicate steels were sometimes required.

The illustrations for Neale's *Paul Periwinkle*, another serial novel (with forty plates, to *Lorrequer's* twenty-two) begun late in 1839, are much in the vein of Lever's work, with the addition of a good deal of bloodshed; but there is more attention to backgrounds and details, and considerably more firmness of line. One of the later plates, "The Prosperity going down" (Illus. 117), can actually induce giddiness, while in others Phiz's skills in architecture and landscape design are evident. He introduces rather sardonic emblematic details into two of the plates. "Mr. Bamboozle's delicate disclosure & dismissal" has to do with the revelation that Nora—one of the main female characters—is pregnant; above her swooning form there is a painting of the goddess Diana, symbol of chastity. And in "The Haunted Bed," upon which lies a woman who has recently been raped by several barbarous Irish Catholic seamen, Browne decorated the headboard with an amoretti-framed carving of a Roman soldier and a naked woman in amorous dalliance, possibly an allusion to the rape of Lucrece. In both cases Phiz went counter to the spirit of the novel, and perhaps should be given credit for viewing the melodramatic tripe he illustrated with such ironic detachment.

Eighteen-forty was an extremely busy year for Browne (see checklist, p. 318), and some of his work is understandably perfunctory; yet there is evidence of artistic growth. A comparison of *Harry Lorrequer* and *Charles O'Malley* is especially revealing because of the similarity of the two novels' subject matter. The very first plate in the latter, "The Sunk Fence" (Illus. 118), showing the hero being thrown off his horse during a fox hunt, is far beyond what Browne appeared capable of two years earlier in its handling of perspective, landscape, degrees of biting-in to provide depth, and management of detail and figures in action. Much of the comic Irish physiognomy is still caricatural—more so than most of his work for Dickens at any time—but his line is surer, and there are few examples of really monstrous grotesquerie in the characters' faces.

From 1841 to 1850, Browne kept up a terrific pace; the number of etchings for the decade (and my list may be incomplete) is 567, and there are 250 designs for wood engravings, which amounts to an average production of about 1 etching per week (not counting the many duplicates done for the Dickens novels), or a design for either etching or engraving every four and one-half days. This rate was continued for some years thereafter, and in the process Browne developed into a skillful and distinctive illustrator, whose work not only complemented the novels of the one true genius with whom he was associated, but bolstered up many literary performances that would have been less interesting— and in some cases entirely negligible—without his illustrations. Up through *The O'Donoghue* (1845), Charles Lever's novels remained within the limits of comic and/or sensational accounts of military and amorous exploits of Irishmen; yet Browne's style in collaboration with Lever continued to change, as it did with the more versatile and inspiring Dickens. In a potboiler called *Chronicles of Crime* (1840–41) he used heavy crosshatching as a way of creating texture for the etching, a technique more typical of John Leech. By the time of Lever's *Jack Hinton* (1841–42), he had largely abandoned this method, and instead alternated plates containing much open space (their incidental shading achieved by combined roulette and irregular crosshatching), with others more heavily shaded, but again with irregular and multidirectional lines. The general effect is much freer and less confined than that of Leech's etchings of the period—Leech's real talent having been for wood engravings.

The Career of Puffer Hopkins (1842) is, so far as I know, the

only work illustrated by "H. K. Browne, Esq. (Phiz)" specifically
for an American publisher, and in its preface the author points up
one of the central problems of illustration from a novelist's
standpoint:

> It will be perceived that a portion of the text is illustrated by H.
> K. Browne, Esq. (PHIZ,) of London. In justice to the artist, it
> should be added, that the great distance, at which he labored,
> from the author, has caused him to depart, in some particulars,
> from the conception it was the author's purpose to embody. As
> they are the first and only designs procured from that gentleman
> for America, the author ventures to add, that he regards them,
> with this reservation, as eminently ingenious and spirited.

I have read carefully the passages depicted in Phiz's three etchings, and can find no apparent respect in which they differ from
the text—indeed, Phiz has been scrupulously careful to get in all
the incidental details mentioned by the author. Thus the divergence seems to have been entirely from the author's mental
conception—a problem which, as we know, was felt keenly by
Dickens at times, but which can hardly be blamed on the illustrator.

Thomas Miller's *Godfrey Malvern* (1842–43), in itself a novel
of a good deal more interest than many of the minor works Phiz
illustrated, in some respects was a turning point in Phiz's career,
and bears more extensive examination than most of his other
non-Dickensian work. Miller himself was a country-man who
(like his hero Godfrey, whose writing career resembles Miller's
in some respects) came to London and achieved a modest but
continuing success as a bookseller, poet, novelist, and essayist of
country life. Where Lever was at this stage little more than a
remarkably prolific picaresque novelist, Miller in *Godfrey Malvern* attempted a serious picture of a young man struggling to
become a writer in London, torn between a beautiful but passive
wife, and an intelligent but unstable young woman with whom
he has a passionate and tragic love affair. Miller's tendency
toward long passages of moralizing and digression is not re-
deemed by any Dickensian genius for comic or metaphorical
improvisation; yet the novel as a whole gives the impression of
total sincerity and a good deal of intelligence. The sketches of
the London world of hack writers and editors are lively, and a

few comic characters are more than mere mechanical Jonsonian humors.

How much Miller influenced his collaborator is difficult to say, but this is the first full-length work illustrated by Phiz in which emblematic details are used extensively, and for that reason alone it is significant in his career, predating *Martin Chuzzlewit* by about a year. (I have already mentioned that the image of a child playing horsey with a tombstone on the *David Copperfield* cover first occurs in the text and frontispiece of *Godfrey Malvern*.) Miller's narrative bent is certainly of the emblematic kind, describing moral and psychological situations in terms of traditional symbols, or creating physical details which sum up situations or character.

The emblematic details in the etchings are special enough in Browne's work to merit some discussion. The hero's difficult position and the obstacles to his success are symbolized in "Godfrey's Interview with the Publisher" by a print captioned "Distressed Author," based on Hogarth's *The Distressed Poet;* by a bust of Milton, looking rather unhappy and languishing behind jumbled volumes (perhaps a reference to mute inglorious Miltons); by a manuscript on the floor entitled "The Handbook of Brain-Suck," referring to the endemic plagiarism of Grub Street; by another manuscript, "A Tragedy"; and by a phrenological head half hidden behind some papers, perhaps intended to represent the stifling of Godfrey's natural talents. In one sequence, the vicissitudes of Godfrey's marriage to Emma and his affair with Maria are developed in emblematic details as well as literal depictions. Thus, "Emma waiting for her Husband" includes a picture, "The Truant," and an open book, "Don Juan." The etching entitled "Love and Remorse.—Godfrey and Maria" has a print of Ariadne just deserted by Theseus—a detail which turns up, in different form, in *Dombey and Son*—and further, on the piano a songsheet, "The Light of Other Days," clearly alludes to Emma. Between these two details is a version of a statuette Phiz used in various contexts, a pair of lovers embracing—likely meant for Cupid and Psyche. A contrast is clearly intended in the caption of another plate, "Guilt and Innocence—Godfrey and Emma," in which Godfrey's state of mind is summed up in a picture labeled "The Penitent." These harrowing relationships are concluded in yet another plate with a parallel title, "Love and Death.—the end of Maria," where an angel is shown (in a picture) carrying a baby to heaven, just as Maria has wished in her dying words.

Emblematic details used with irony are prominent in the suite of illustrations dealing with the comic subplot of Gregory Gruff's unfortunate courtship and marriage to the Widow Clarkson. A large and rather comical "Samson and Delilah" (Delilah with an enormous pair of shears) comments warningly on the intentions of Mrs. Clarkson as she has Gregory examine a lump on her neck ("Gregory Gruff and the Widow"), while Phiz's ubiquitous peacock feathers and a stuffed wild bird under glass are slightly more subtle omens. A print of a handsome, half-clad woman, entitled "Snake in the Grass," implies that both the attraction and the treachery have gone a step farther in "Gregory taking his Gruel." In "Gregory Gruff's Honeymoon" (Illus. 119), which depicts the aftermath of a crockery-throwing altercation, a large picture entitled "The Flitch of Bacon"—referring to the story of a prize awarded to a couple who didn't quarrel all year (and based on a well-known Stothard engraving)—contrasts ironically with another of a cockfight; the final commentary is offered by the figurine of a fallen cupid. One is reminded of Gillray's before-and-after pair, *Harmony before Matrimony,* and *Matrimonial Harmonics,* the second of which includes a similarly deceased cupid.[4]

Some of the emblems described above are trivial, and few if any achieve the subtlety of comment of Phiz's emblems for Dickens, but they are part of the sudden flowering of a technique which remained a dominant feature of Browne's illustrations for more than a decade. The stylistic developments in *Godfrey Malvern* are less obvious because Phiz is halfway between the lively, sometimes flowing and compositionally brilliant style of *Charles O'Malley,* which nonetheless uses a crude kind of caricature, and the more individualized method of portraying characters in *Martin Chuzzlewit,* a method that entails a more carefully worked out relation between text and illustration, and much more formal control. The *Godfrey Malvern* plates may seem static in comparison with earlier work for Lever, and unfinished compared with those of *Martin Chuzzlewit,* but they represent a genuine advance, both in use of emblematic details and in the versatility of their manner and tone.

William Ainsworth's *Auriol* (1844–45), which followed *Martin Chuzzlewit*, shows still more of Browne's versatility. It is one of the few supernatural tales he illustrated during his prime, and the plates differ from nearly all his other work. None of them makes use of the dark plate method, but a number surely would have been executed that way a few years later, for they are unusually dark and texturally filled out, with a close and careful crosshatching reminiscent of George Cruikshank's work for such Ainsworth novels as *Jack Sheppard, The Tower of London,* and *The Miser's Daughter.* Indeed, the author may have wished for a continuation of the style of his earlier illustrator, or Browne on his own may consciously have emulated his predecessor. Doubtless the subjects as well have something to do with the technique, since there are many dark Renaissance interiors and sinister characters and situations. Most impressive is Browne's handling of small dark and light shapes—building materials, iron objects, sections of interior architecture—to create striking compositions. Perhaps the best of all, and the one which foreshadows Phiz's handling of shading and form in his dark plates, is "The Ruined house in the Vauxhall Road" (Illus. 120), where the stones, ornaments and contents of the house form a phantasmagorical surrounding for the light-bathed figure of Auriol, being lifted out of the ruins; not least effective are the ominous faces of broken stone ornaments, which appear to be glowering at the novel's protagonist.

The dark plate technique, first used in 1847, is applied to *all* of the plates in Lever's *Roland Cashel* (1848–49), which is thus unique among the full-length novels that Browne illustrated. In some of the etchings the only function of the technique is to produce an even tint, softening the general tone; in others, the grayish background helps to set off the foreground subject (for example, "Bravo Toro!"); and in several, a basically dark tone plays against grays of varying shades and white highlights. Perhaps the most noteworthy of these latter is "A Prairie— Evening Ride" (Illus. 121), a horizontal plate in which a horde of stampeding bison emerge from gray skies and form an almost

abstract pattern of black bodies and white eyes around the protagonist on his struggling white horse. Browne displays his compositional abilities in "A meeting under the Greenwood tree"
(Illus. 122), where trunks and foliage form a design around the
human figures. The artist varied the texture with great effectiveness by using several kinds of roulette. In some of the interior
scenes, the mechanical tint adds a degree of depth unchar-
acteristic of most such subjects among Phiz's work, and at least
some reviewers were impressed: Chapman and Hall's catalogue
for November 1849 quotes the *Edinburgh News* on the topic of
Roland Cashel to the effect that "the illustrations by Phiz are the
finest we have ever seen anywhere, combining, in a new and
noble style, line with etching, thus producing all the mellowness
of mezzotint in the happiest manner." The dark plate is, indeed, a
kind of shortcut to mezzotint effects, whereby the laborious pre-
treatment of the steel with a "rocker" is bypassed. The inclusion
of such a quotation in advertising suggests that the publishers
were well aware of the part played by Browne's illustrations in
the sale of Lever's novels.

By the 1850s, the pace had slackened somewhat for Browne,
but he still seems to have been fully employed. There are some
short periods when work was evidently slack, but the number of
etchings in serial novels amounts to 400, and there are 33 other
etchings plus numerous cuts; in addition, Browne did 21 title
page designs for the Library Edition of Dickens in 1858–59,
which look to me like steel engravings, though they may be etchings. Although it seems that Browne was a poor businessman
(possibly owing to innate shyness), the publication early in the
decade of two books under his own name and made up solely of
his etchings suggests a degree of ambition and self-confidence.
Home Sketches, the first of these, is a small quarto volume of
"Sixteen Domestic Sketches of Childhood," machine-tinted (i.e.,
like dark plates) and hand-colored etchings. The subjects and
style are dated and sentimental by modern standards, but within
the context of Browne's work they have special interest. He evidently devoted more time and care to them than to all but the
most finished of his work for novelists. Although, as Harvey has
pointed out, one etching seems to derive from *David Copperfield*, most of them are original to this volume, and rather in the

style of the many watercolor drawings of women and children Browne produced during the 1850s and 1860s.[5]

The dark plate technique is used in this volume mainly to soften the tone. The faces and bodies of the figures have an untypical three-dimensionality, and Browne represents female and infant faces in a stylized fashion, full and rounded, in fact nearly circular (the painters Daniel Maclise and C. R. Leslie may have had some influence in this regard). Emblematic details prevail throughout, and in ways which make them more prominently part of the subject than is usual in the novel illustrations. In "Night" (Illus. 123), the wall space behind the two women who hover protectively over a sleeping child is taken up by pictures of a setting sun; of two angels standing over a pair of sleeping children; of a jovial will-o'-the-wisp near a swamp, which here apparently represents dreams rather than the pursuit of riches; and of a woman with a lantern, leading a small girl through a swamp, with a prone body between them—suggesting something about the relation between sleep and death (perhaps an allusion to the most popular bedtime prayer). Other details of this type include a wall painting of St. Cecilia in "The Musician," a book open to an ostrich and a picture of a stilt-walker in "The Pedestrian" (the main subject of which is a baby's first steps), and in "The Bath," a large picture of Neptune in a chariot, a fisherman, cherubs in shell boats, and a Noah's Ark toy. The concluding plate, "Good Night," shows a ship sailing on calm water through the window of a child's room, a reminder of the type of detail used by Phiz repeatedly in his work for many novelists, but especially in *Dombey and Son*, where Dickens' use of similar imagery points up the affinities of author and illustrator.

Browne appears to have felt that his talents, outside of what he could do as an employee of writers, lay in the realm of sentimental–humorous pictures of mothers and children. The 1853 sketchbook now in the Victoria and Albert Museum contains forty-eight charcoal and chalk drawings almost entirely on such subjects, but a number are concerned with death, such as Number 24, "Please M'um y're wanted!" in which a skeleton calls to a young woman who is looking in a mirror, or the one immediately preceding, where the skeleton is what the woman sees in the mirror. It is my guess that the sketchbook consists of

trial subjects for possible future ventures on the order of *Home Sketches* and *Illustrations of the Five Senses* (the other independently published collection of Phiz's etchings). Harvey has rather overstated the case in remarking that motifs from *Dombey* are found throughout, for, not to put too fine a point on it, the main images are the traditional and hackneyed motifs that Browne often used when working on his own—and in some of his book illustrations as well.

Up through Lever's *The Dodd Family Abroad* (1852–54), Browne's use of emblematic details in illustrations remains fairly steady, but from 1855 on their number dwindles, and although *Little Dorrit* has a few, Lever's *The Martins of Cro'Martin* (1854–56) has none at all. Browne's etched line becomes darker and bolder, but it has not lost its sensitivity, and there are a number of plates for this novel which are scenically splendid (Illus. 124). They reveal Browne's new interest in composition, and in the arrangement of light and dark shapes almost for its own aesthetic, as distinct from conceptual, value. But what I think must be considered the last three major sets of illustrations are those for Mayhew's *Paved With Gold* (1857–58), Lever's *Davenport Dunn* (1857–59), and the completion of the suspended *Mervyn Clitheroe* (1851–52; concluded 1858). Dark plates abound in all three, and a certain coarsening of technique is not yet evident.

I shall limit my discussion to Augustus Mayhew's *Paved With Gold, or, The Reality of the London Streets: An Unfashionable Novel*, a fictionalized version of brother Henry Mayhew's researches and moral viewpoint. Augustus' preface "humbly" boasts of the "extreme truthfulness with which this book has been written," and remarks that parts of it were undertaken at Henry's suggestion. The subjects for some of the plates are of a kind that Phiz had not undertaken (unless we count "Tom all alone's") since *Sketches in London* or *Chronicles of Crime*, and a glance back at, for example, "Out-door Relief" from the former book will reveal how far the artist has come. Of the twenty-eight plates in *Paved With Gold*, only nine (including the allegorical title page) are not dark plates, and the latter contain some of the best and most technically daring among all of Browne's work. Admittedly, the treatment of faces is uneven and at its worst

perfunctory, though at its best, as in "Baby 'Phil' in the Work-house," up to Browne's highest level. In this etching, more than half a dozen women's faces are carefully distinguished as to physiognomy and expression, and the infants are neither gen-eralized nor idealized. This etching is a "dark" plate, but its tones are mostly light, and carefully stopped-out into several different grades, to show the varieties of wall coloring and differ-ing lights and shadows.

We also have some of the very darkest of dark plates, such as "The Meeting at Stonehenge," which is a marvel of threatening sky and looming stones, with the very small light of the homeless boys' fire in the center foreground. In "The family of Nathaniel Crosier, Esqr. aroused by an alarm of Thieves," darkness is al-most too much of a good thing, though I credit Phiz for the extent to which he has succeeded in conveying the effect of objects seen in an all but pitch-dark night. Probably the most visually beautiful plate is "The Tramps" (Illus. 125), which shows the three boys walking through the wooded grounds outside an aris-tocrat's estate; the trees are reminiscent of "Making off" in *Little Dorrit*. The title page has a different kind of interest: its major theme is the pursuit and worship of money, and this is expressed in two allegorical motifs (both represented as the faces of coins): Pluto as the king receiving homage, and a bunch of ragged chil-dren playing with piles of money bags. A third motif, referring to another aspect of the novel, depicts the circus as embodied in demonic harlequin figures sitting on posts, a stage with dancers, and a Punch show with a gallows as its most identifiable prop, suggesting the danger that hovers over several of the novel's principal characters.

There is little or nothing in Browne's final work for Dickens, *A Tale of Two Cities* (1859), that comes near to matching his own best work in either *Little Dorrit* or *Paved With Gold*. The cover design is inferior to many Phiz did for Dickens and other novelists, there are no dark plates or emblematic details among the sixteen etchings, and only a few scenes of revolution in their energetic depiction of the mob add very much to this last collab-oration with Dickens. On the basis of his work for Lever in *Davenport Dunn* (completed shortly before *A Tale of Two Cities*) and *One of Them* (which appeared the following year), it is difficult to understand why this decline in quality took place. Extant drawings for *Davenport Dunn* (Huntington Library) make it clear that Browne was still working as assiduously as ever at his illustrations, as we find for several of the etchings two or even three drawings in various degrees of finish and with differing major details; further, most of the plates have an incisive line, a greater attention to detail, and a depiction of human figures which is charged with life and energy. In addition, Browne executed for Lever's novel fourteen good dark plates. *One of Them* is closer in style to *A Tale of Two Cities,* and it is perhaps a notch or two below Browne's previous work for Lever, but on the whole the etchings are still more interesting than those for Dickens' novel. There is room for endless conjecture here, and perhaps the most plausible answer is that Dickens himself had by this time lost much of his earlier interest in illustration, and hence gave Browne less interesting subjects and relatively little guidance. Perhaps another factor was that *A Tale of Two Cities* was written for weekly part publication (in *All the Year Round*), and it is thus unusually compressed in its bulk and schematic in its plan and development. This is not meant as a critical judgment of the novel, but it is conceivable that Browne simply found it less inspiring than Dickens' other books. Whatever the case, this collaboration was not a very happy ending to the twenty-four year relationship of Dickens and Phiz, nor of Phiz's career during the 1850s.

With the beginning of the next decade Browne, though still respected (if the frequent and prominent use of his name on the title pages of works to which he contributed a few among many illustrations is any gauge), and still receiving many commissions, was clearly, though gradually, deteriorating as an artist. An increasing proportion of what he did can be considered hackwork, as can be seen in some cuts he designed for boys' books before 1860. It would be a very large task to compile a bibliography of his work from 1860 on, because so much of it is ephemeral and difficult to date. For example, from early in the decade Phiz illustrated a series of undated yellowbacks issued in six-penny or penny parts, sometimes with colored printing by Edmund Evans, including such titles as *Grimm's Goblins* (issued in forty-two parts with a colored wood engraving in each, but possibly not published *in toto* in bound volumes); *Ruth, the Murdered Child; The Battle and the Breeze; Life and Adventures of Peter Wilkins;* and *The Confessions of a Page.* This last carries "Illustrated by Phiz" on the title page of each part, but his contributions are infrequent after the first. The others are sometimes illustrated wholly by Phiz, sometimes only partly, but his designs are consistently rudimentary and indifferent, although in *Fortunes of the House of Pennyl* he makes an interesting use of something like the dark plate technique in a wood engraving.

One of the more interesting items of the early 1860s was a projected collaboration with Browne's friend (and in later years, patron), George Halse. Thomson describes it as originating in the "artist's original idea" to publish "between fifty and sixty quarto drawings" under the title "'The Adventures of Pott,' with a rhyming commentary by himself," but Halse, seeing the work, chose forty of the drawings and wrote a narrative poem to fit them.[6] The drawings were apparently chopped up and ultimately destroyed when bits of them were used for the volume that emerged, but photographs of the drawings (now in the Victoria and Albert Museum) suggest that in some ways they are the most ambitious venture ever undertaken by Phiz. The series of comic–fantastic adventures is the artist's invention, and each large sheet (with a few exceptions) includes a clockwise sequence of tiny figures around the perimeter (much like a circular comic strip without words), and a larger subject related to the same episode in the center. The work is delightful, and had the time been ripe or had Phiz managed the right connections with a publisher, he could perhaps have been a successful mid-Victorian comic strip man. But the actual result, a volume called *Sir Guy de Guy,* gives practically no sense of the original, and certainly no hint that it was to have been a series of comic drawings "illustrated" in the Combe–Rowlandson manner by verses, rather than a narrative poem illustrated by occasional mediocre cuts. The most successful illustration Browne did for Halse was the dark-plate title page for *Agatha* (1864), in which some of the power of his earlier allegorical creations is retained (Illus. 126).

Assignments continued, though in diminishing numbers. Unhappily, in the middle of the decade Browne was humiliated by the appearance of *Our Mutual Friend* with illustrations by Marcus Stone; he was also relieved of his commission for Trollope's

Can You Forgive Her? halfway through. The etchings for the
Trollope novel are indeed quite poor, the several dark plates
being no more than ordinary designs with a uniform tint that
does little to enhance them. During the late 'sixties Browne also
produced *Racing and Chasing,* and *Sketches of the Seaside & the
Country,* published by the Graphotyping Company. Both contain competent quarto pictures in the vein of John Leech, but
somehow lacking Leech's incisiveness and humor. It seems
likely that Browne garnered no substantial economic rewards
from these and similar ventures.

Whether his humiliations and financial difficulties were factors
or not, we know that in 1867 an illness left Phiz partially
paralyzed for the remaining fifteen years of his life, and made
work exceedingly difficult; in view of the handicap—loss of the
use of the right thumb was the worst affliction from an artist's
viewpoint—it is astounding how much he produced and got
published, but none of the work is really of interest to anyone but
a collector or enthusiast, and some of it is pitiable, perhaps none
so much as *All About Kisses,* "by Damocles / with one hundred
illustrations by Hablott K. Brown (Phiz)," which the British Library dates as 1875. It would be heartless to say more about this
book than that the cuts are more pathetic than the misspelling of
the artist's name on the title page. The name, however, did apparently mean something to publishers for some years, as
Browne executed designs for the periodical *Judy* from 1869 to
near the end, a number of toy books, and two or three collections
of humorous drawings, as well as wood engravings for reissues of
Ainsworth and Lever, and illustrations for the Household Edition of *Pickwick* which, however, hardly bear scrutiny.[7]

In his biography, Browne's son Edgar passes over the last fifteen years of his father's life rather quickly, but Thomson
suggests that the artist was in a bad way financially, especially
during his later years. He seems to have done no etching after his
illness, and the assignments for woodcut designs, although coming in at least until 1878, were probably not enough for him to
live on comfortably. An annuity from the Royal Academy a few
years before his death was no doubt helpful, and at times he also
earned added income from the redrawing of his Dickens illustrations for private patrons. The most extensive assignment was a

complete set of watercolor drawings done between 1866 and 1869 for F. W. Cosens (who also gave the elderly George Cruikshank similar assignments), but there were others, such as drawings for an unknown patron from *The Old Curiosity Shop* and *Barnaby Rudge* (now in the Gimbel Collection); and in 1878 he apparently sold the *Little Dorrit* drawings to another collector, substituting three new drawings for missing ones.[8] There may have been others, but it is evident that Browne had few saleable drawings apart from *Dorrit*, as an 1880 letter finds him informing one William Wilson, "I regret to say I have no 'Dickens'—but will mention yr. name and give your address to my friends,"[9] which suggests that he had earlier in life been overly generous in giving away such valuable material, as he had been overly modest in destroying a large batch of his own drawings and letters from authors in 1859.

It is probably in part owing to his long decline, as well as to Browne's lack of association with any important literary artist during the last two decades of his career, and to the ephemerality of many of the works he illustrated throughout his career, that his reputation remained generally low for so many years. The letter to William Wilson underlines the fact that Browne's importance lies in his association with Dickens, the novelist's attitude toward him remained very much that of an employer to a hired hand. Dickens may never have fully appreciated the contribution of his primary illustrator to the effectiveness of his novels, but we now have the knowledge to evaluate that contribution for ourselves. Even if the circumstances surrounding the creation of a new kind of verbal–visual novel in *Pickwick Papers* are in some sense accidental, the importance of the role of Phiz's illustrations is not. Dickens was from the beginning a novelist much of whose artistic force depended upon modes of symbol formation which were visual, allusive, or both, and who repeatedly created implicit or explicit parallels in the structure of his novels. In the *Pickwick Papers* and *Nicholas Nickleby* the parallelism tends to remain local—as in the attorney's office and the pound—while the allusiveness lacks the intensity it reaches in his later novels. In these early novels, Browne's illustrations help to make explicit certain themes and implications, through both traditional symbolism and visual parallels. But as Dickens' art develops so does Browne's. The allegories of the monthly cover and frontispiece and the tacit allusion to Hogarth in the etched title page of *Martin Chuzzlewit* are more complex visual interpretations than anything Browne had done earlier, as both the structure and texture of this novel are new achievements for Dickens. In *Dombey and Son* and *David Copperfield* Browne reaches his highest concentration of allusive, emblematic interpretation, as well as continuing to emphasize meanings implicit in these novels' structures, through visual parallels among the illustrations.

We should take seriously Mrs. Leavis' remark that Dickens no longer needed an illustrator for *Bleak House:* the increase in complexity and frequency of metaphoric and allusive language in the novel is immense. But at this point Browne reduces the level of his own emblematic commentary, and makes a new and striking use of the dark plate, underlining the novelist's vision of a depersonalized world. The same technique is used by Browne to good effect in *Little Dorrit*, whose social vision is a development of that in *Bleak House*.

From *Pickwick* through *Little Dorrit*, then, Browne's illustrations are essential: in a variety of ways, they complete Dickens' artistic achievement. We must therefore take Hablot Browne seriously as an artist, understanding that the importance of his art lies ultimately in the way he fulfilled his role as a subordinate—but not wholly subservient—collaborator with and interpreter of Dickens. Although Dickens had other illustrators, none fulfilled this role so extensively or so well. One is hard put to think of a comparable achievement by any other British artist of the nineteenth century.

APPENDIX

A Checklist of the Work of Hablot Knight Browne, 1836–1859

I have divided Browne's career during the time of his collaboration with Dickens into three periods; and although there is unavoidable overlap given the facts of serial publication, the periods make sense in terms of stylistic development and certain milestones in the life or career. These lists make no claim to completeness or total accuracy, though they should be a considerable advance in both respects on Thomson's list; they are intended only as general guides to Phiz's career. With a few exceptions, I list no work that I have not actually seen myself, and those exceptions are marked with an asterisk.

PERIOD 1: 1836–1841.

1836

The Library of Fiction (monthly periodical), Vol. I. 3 cuts.
"Timothy Sparks" (Charles Dickens), *Sunday Under Three Heads.* 3 cuts and engraved wrapper.

1836–1837

Charles Dickens, *The Posthumous Papers of the Pickwick Club.* Monthly parts. 36 etchings (from Part IV onward, plus 2 replacement etchings for Part III).

1837

"Quiz" (Edward Caswall), *Sketches of Young Ladies.* 6 etchings and engraved wrapper.
Richard Johns, "The Little Bit of Tape," *Bentley's Miscellany,* Vol. I. 1 etching.
Advertising circular for *Bentley's Miscellany.* 1 cut.

1837–1838

James Grant, *Sketches in London.* Monthly parts. 18 etchings (out of 24—first 6 not by Browne).

1838

Charles Dickens, *Posthumous Papers of the Pickwick Club,* 2nd edition. 12 fully redesigned etchings, plus 6 duplicates of Seymour's originals.
Charles Dickens, *Sketches of Young Gentlemen.* 6 etchings.
*Richard Falconer, *Voyages.* 2 etchings.
Morals from the Churchyard. 8 cuts.
Stephen Oliver, *The Old English Squire.* 6 etchings.
R. S. Surtees, *Jorrocks' Jaunts and Jollities* (first bound edition). 12 etchings.

317

1838–1839

Charles Dickens, *Nicholas Nickleby*. Monthly parts. 39 etchings and engraved wrapper.

Charles Lever, *The Confessions of Harry Lorrequer*. Monthly parts. 22 etchings and engraved wrapper.

1839

"Joseph Fume" (W. A. Chatto), A *Paper:—of Tobacco*. 6 etchings.

"Captain Barabbas Whitefeather" (Douglas Jerrold), *The Hand-Book of Swindling*. 4 etchings.

New Sporting Magazine, November. 1 cut.

J. P. Robertson, *Solomon Seesaw*. 7 etchings.

1839–1841

W. J. Neale, *Paul Periwinkle, or, The Press Gang*. Monthly parts. 40 etchings and *engraved wrapper (?).

1840

Charles Dickens, *Sketches of Young Couples*. 6 etchings.

"The Diurnal Revolutions of Davie Diddlecroft," *The London Magazine, Charivari, and Courrier des Dames*. 3 etchings.

Henry Fielding, *Jonathan Wild*. 4 etchings.

Theodore Hook, *Precepts and Practice*. 10 etchings.

Theodore Hook, "Fathers and Sons," *New Monthly Magazine*. 3 etchings.

A Legend of Cloth Fair, and Other Tales. 6 etchings.

Review of *The Newgate Annual*, in *New Monthly Magazine*. 1 etching.

G. W. M. Reynolds, *Robert Macaire in England*. 18 etchings.

1840–1841

Charles Dickens, *Master Humphrey's Clock* (including *The Old Curiosity Shop* and *Barnaby Rudge*). Weekly numbers. 155 cuts, including 22 initials and 2 frontispieces.

Charles Lever, *Charles O'Malley*. Monthly parts. 22 etchings and engraved wrapper.

"Camden Pelham," *The Chronicles of Crime*. Monthly parts. 52 etchings.

Mrs. F. Trollope, *The Adventures of Charles Chesterfield*, in *New Monthly Magazine*. 12 etchings.

1841

Charles Dickens (ed.), *The Pic Nic Papers*. 6 etchings.

Joseph Thomas Hewlett, *Peter Priggins*. 12 etchings.

John Poole, "Phineas Quiddy; or, Sheer Industry," in *New Monthly Magazine*. 3 etchings.

PERIOD 2: 1841–1850.

1841–1842

Charles Lever, *Jack Hinton, The Guardsman* (Part I of *Our Mess*).

Monthly parts. 26 etchings, 9 cuts, engraved wrapper.

G. P. R. James *The Commissioner.* Monthly parts. 28 etchings.

1842

Cornelius Mathews, *The Career of Puffer Hopkins.* 3 etchings.

W. H. Maxwell, *Rambling Recollections of a Soldier of Fortune.* 3 cuts.

"The Physiology of London Evening Parties," *Punch,* Vol. 2. 4 cuts.

Punch, Vol. 2. Engraved cover.

"Punch's Valentines," *Punch,* Vol. 2. 2 full-page cuts.

"A Review of the Book of the Season," *Punch,* Vol. 3. 4 cuts.

Sir Walter Scott, *Waverley* (Abbotsford Edition). 2 cuts.

Sir Walter Scott, *Guy Mannering* (Abbotsford Edition). 2 cuts.

1842–1843

Thomas Miller, *Godfrey Malvern.* Monthly parts. 26 etchings and engraved wrapper.

1843

William Carleton, *Traits and Stories of the Irish Peasantry.* 9 etchings.

1843–1844

Charles Dickens, *Martin Chuzzlewit.* Monthly parts. 40 etchings and engraved wrapper.

Charles Lever, *Tom Burke of "Ours"* (Part II of *Our Mess*). Monthly parts. 44 etchings (wrapper same as *Jack Hinton*).

1844–1845

W. Harrison Ainsworth, *The Revelations of London,* in *Ainsworth's Magazine.* 15 etchings (republished as *Auriol,* 1845).

1845

Fiddle Faddle's Sentimental Tour. 1 etching.

Charles Lever, *The O'Donoghue.* Monthly parts. 26 etchings and engraved wrapper.

Charles Lever, *St. Patrick's Eve.* 4 etchings and 12 cuts.

Charles Lever, *Tales of the Trains.* Monthly parts. 15 cuts.

George Raymond, *Memoirs of R. W. Elliston, Comedian. New Monthly Magazine.* 2 etchings.

G. Herbert Rodwell, *The Memoirs of an Umbrella.* 68 cuts.

1846

William Carleton, *Tales and Stories of the Irish Peasantry.* 7 etchings (2 repeated from *Traits and Stories . . .*).

"Democritus," *A Medical, Moral, and Christian Dissection of Teetotalism.* 5 etchings and 1 cut.

Charles Rowcroft, *Fanny the Little Milliner.* 4 etchings.

1846–1847

J. Sheridan Le Fanu, *The Fortunes of Colonel Torlogh O'Brien.* Monthly parts. 22 etchings and engraved wrapper.

Charles Lever, *The Knight of Gwynne*. Monthly parts. 40 etchings and engraved wrapper.

1846–1848
Charles Dickens, *Dombey and Son*. Monthly parts. 40 etchings and engraved wrapper. (1 dark plate which does not appear until 1848.)

1847
W. Harrison Ainsworth, *Old St. Paul's*. 2 etchings. (2 dark plates.)
William Carleton, *Valentine M'Clutchy*. 20 etchings.
The Long-Lost Found. Monthly parts (discontinued after three). 6 etchings and engraved wrapper.
R. S. Surtees, *Hawbuck Grange*. 8 etchings (hand-colored).
6 "extra" illustrations (cuts) for *Pickwick Papers*.

1848
W. Blanchard Jerrold, *The Disgrace to the Family*. 12 etchings.
The Brothers Mayhew, *The Image of His Father*. Monthly parts. 12 etchings. (2 dark plates.)
Angus B. Reach, *A Romance of a Mince-Pie*. 28 cuts.
12 "extra" illustrations for *Dombey and Son:* a set of 8 etchings, and a set of 4 steel engravings.
4 "extra" illustrations for *The Old Curiosity Shop:* three steel engravings and 1 etching.

1848–1849
W. Harrison Ainsworth, *Crichton. New Monthly Magazine*. 18 etchings. (8 dark plates.)
Charles Lever, *Roland Cashel*. Monthly parts. 40 etchings and engraved wrapper. (40 dark plates.)
Albert Smith, *The Pottleton Legacy*. Monthly parts. 20 etchings and *engraved wrapper (?). (1 dark plate.)

1849
James Hannay, *Hearts are Trumps*. 28 cuts.
G. P. R. James, *The Fight of the Fiddlers*. 21 cuts.
4 "extra" illustrations to *Barnaby Rudge:* 4 etchings.

1849–1850
Charles Dickens, *David Copperfield*. Monthly parts. 40 etchings and engraved wrapper. (1 dark plate.)

PERIOD 3: 1850–1859.

1850
Edward Bulwer-Lytton, *Godolphin, Last of the Barons, Last Days of Pompeii*. 1 cut in each.

1851

Hablot K. Browne, *Home Sketches*. 16 etchings (issued both colored and plain). (16 dark plates.)

*J. S. Le Fanu, *Ghost Stories and Tales of Mystery*. 4 etchings.

1851–1852

W. Harrison Ainsworth, *Mervyn Clitheroe*. Monthly parts (1–4 only—resumed 1858). 8 etchings and engraved wrapper.

Charles Lever, *The Daltons*. Monthly parts. 48 etchings and engraved wrapper.

F. E. Smedley, *Lewis Arundel*. Monthly parts. 42 etchings and engraved wrapper.

1852

Hablot K. Browne, *Illustrations of the Five Senses*. 5 etchings (issued both colored and plain). (5 dark plates.)

Mrs. J. C. Maitland, *The Doll and Her Friends*. 4 cuts.

1852–1853

Charles Dickens, *Bleak House*. Monthly parts. 40 etchings and engraved wrapper. (10 dark plates.)

1852–1854

Charles Lever, *The Dodd Family Abroad*. Monthly parts. 48 etchings and engraved wrapper.

1853

F. E. Smedley, *Fortunes of the Colville Family*. 2 etchings. (2 dark plates.)

1853–1854

Vizetelly (publisher), *The Illustrated Byron*. Monthly parts. 10 or fewer cuts (most cuts unsigned).

1854

Mrs. Bray, *A Peep at the Pixies*. 6 cuts.

*Lady Campbell, *A Cabin by the Wayside*. 2 cuts.

*C. Le Ross, *Christmas Day*. 4 cuts.

Horace Mayhew, *Letters Left at the Pastrycooks*. 7 cuts.

1854–1855:

F.E. Smedley, *Harry Coverdale's Courtship*. Monthly parts. 30 etchings and engraved wrapper.

1854–1856

Charles Lever, *The Martins of Cro'Martin*. Monthly parts. 40 etchings and engraved wrapper.

1855

A Dozen Pair of Wedding Gloves. 2 cuts.

Illustrated Times. 11 cuts.

1855–1857

Charles Dickens, *Little Dorrit*. Monthly parts. 40 etchings and engraved wrapper. (8 dark plates.)

1856

Illustrated Times. 1 cut.

1857

W. Harrison Ainsworth, *The Spendthrift*. 8 cuts.
Henry Fielding, *Amelia, Joseph Andrews, Tom Jones*. 8 cuts each.
Illustrated Times. 20 cuts.
Charles Lever, *Nuts and Nutcrackers*. 6 etchings, 44 cuts.
Tobias Smollett, *Humphrey Clinker, Peregrine Pickle, Roderick Random*. 8 cuts each.

1857–1858

Augustus Mayhew, *Paved With Gold*. Monthly parts. 28 etchings. (19 dark plates.)

1857–1859

Charles Lever, *Davenport Dunn*. Monthly parts. 44 etchings and engraved wrapper. (18 dark plates.)

1858

W. Harrison Ainsworth, *Mervyn Clitheroe*. Monthly parts (resumed and concluded). 16 etchings. (12 dark plates.)
Mrs. Alfred Gatty, *Legendary Tales*. 4 cuts.
Walter Thornbury, *The Buccaneers*. 6 cuts.

1858–1859

Title pages for the Library Edition of Dickens. 21 engravings (or etchings?).

1859

Robert B. Brough, *Ulf the Minstrel*. 19 cuts (ostensibly all by Browne, but this seems doubtful on stylistic grounds).
Charles Dickens, *A Tale of Two Cities*. Monthly parts. 16 etchings and engraved wrapper.
James Grant, *The Cavaliers of Fortune*. 8 cuts.
Once A Week. 24 cuts.

NOTES

References in the notes or in parentheses in the text to the following published and manuscript sources are given by these abbreviations:

BM Cat   M. Dorothy George, *British Museum Catalogue of Political and Personal Satires*, Vols. VII–XI (London: British Museum, 1942–54).

J   Albert K. Johannsen, *Phiz Illustrations From the Novels of Charles Dickens* (Chicago: University of Chicago Press, 1956).

N   *The Letters of Charles Dickens*, ed. Walter Dexter (London: Nonesuch Press, 1938), 3 vols.

P   *The Pilgrim Edition of the Letters of Charles Dickens*, ed. Madeline House and Graham Storey, Vols. 1–3 (Oxford: Clarendon Press, 1965, 1969, 1974).

BM   Drawings or prints in the Department of Prints and Drawings of the British Museum.

Dexter   Letters and drawings in the John Furber Dexter Collection, now in the British Library.

DH   Drawings in the Suzannet Rooms of Dickens House, of the Dickens Fellowship, London.

Elkins   Drawings in the collection of the late William M. Elkins, now in the Free Library of Philadelphia.

Gimbel   Drawings in the collection of the late Colonel Richard Gimbel, now in the library of Yale University.

Suzannet   Drawings formerly in the collection of the Comte de Suzannet, location now uncertain.

I. DICKENS AND BROWNE:
ILLUSTRATION, COLLABORATION, AND ICONOGRAPHY.

1. A list of some twenty such discrepancies has kindly been made available to me by Mr. Nicolas Bentley, and as Mr. Bentley remarks, there are undoubtedly many more.

2. David Croal Thomson, *Life and Labours of Hablot Knight Browne, "Phiz"* (London: Chapman and Hall, 1884), p. 19.

3. Edgar Browne, *Phiz and Dickens* (London: Nisbet, 1913), p. 3.

4. Reproduced in E. Browne, fac. p. 4.

5. Thomson, p. 21. E. Browne, p. 5.

6. H. and B. Winkles, *Architectural and Picturesque Illustrations of the Cathedral Churches of England and Wales*, 3 vols. (London:

Effingham Wilson and Charles Tilt, 1836–42). These were first issued in monthly parts, from 1835 onwards.

7. Such a complaint is offered by Lauriat Lane, Jr., "Dickens Studies 1958–1968: An Overview," *Studies in the Novel* 1 (1969): 245.

8. Ronald Paulson, *Emblem and Expression: Meaning in English Art of the Eighteenth Century* (London: Thames and Hudson, 1975), p. 46.

9. Ronald Paulson, *Hogarth: His Life, Art, and Times,* 2 vols. (New Haven and London: Yale University Press, 1971), 1: 265.

10. Paulson, *Emblem and Expression,* pp. 38, 43.

11. Ronald Paulson, *Hogarth's Graphic Works,* revised edition, 2 vols. (New Haven and London: Yale University Press, 1970), 1: 145.

12. Paulson, *Emblem and Expression,* pp. 64ff.

13. Ibid., p. 51.

14. See David Kunzle, *The Early Comic Strip* (Berkeley: University of California Press, 1973) for examples of sequential graphic satire.

15. The circumstances have been most fully outlined by John R. Harvey, *Victorian Novelists and Their Illustrators* (London: Sidgwick and Jackson, 1970), p. 164.

16. Gleeson White, *English Illustration "The Sixties": 1855–1870* (London: Constable, 1897); Forrest Reid, *Illustrators of the Sixties* (London: Faber and Gwyer, 1928).

17. Clarke was author of the 1830 work, *Three Courses and a Dessert,* illustrated by George Cruikshank. See Edgar Johnson, *Charles Dickens: His Tragedy and Triumph* (New York: Simon and Schuster, 1952), I, pp. 115–16.

18. Since both *Sunday Under Three Heads* and the fourth part of *Pickwick,* for which Browne was engaged, were published in June 1836, the order of events is not certain.

19. Paulson, *Hogarth's Graphic Works,* I, p. 207.

20. *Sunday Under Three Heads,* in *The Nonesuch Dickens,* 23 vols. (London: Nonesuch Press, 1938), 22: 507.

21. Ibid., p. 516.

22. *The Posthumous Papers of the Pickwick Club* (London: Chapman and Hall, 1837), p. 453. All subsequent references to passages from Dickens' novels will be to the first published editions and will be given in the text.

23. Arthur Waugh, "Charles Dickens and His Illustrators," *Nonesuch Dickensiana* (London: Nonesuch Press, 1937), pp. 33–34.

24. A different method of transfer for etchings is described by John Harvey, *Victorian Novelists and Their Illustrators,* p. 183, which may be correct for George Cruikshank but is demonstrably not the method Browne used.

25. E. Browne, p. 164.

26. My account of the method of transfer is derived from E. Browne, pp. 160–62.

27. Anthony Burton, in his review of Harvey's book, calls it a "proof"—see *Dickensian* 67 (1971): 109.

28. Harvey, p. 150.

29. *Retsch's Series of Twenty-six Outlines Illustrative of Goethe's Tragedy of Faust* (London: Boosey and Sons, 1820), fac. p. 39 (British publisher anglicized spelling of Retzsch's name). It is also worth noting that Mephistopheles is present in this engraving though not standing next to Faust, and that the similarity of feathers is also to be seen here.

30. E. Browne, p. 53.

31. Two extant letters contain such details: one is to Maclise, regarding that artist's single design for *The Old Curiosity Shop;* the other is to Cattermole, about the cut for the death of Nell and the one following. In the first case, Dickens specified "an old broken hour glass," which Maclise ignored; in the second case, he asked Cattermole for holly and ivy around Nell's bed, with which the artist complied, and another hour glass in the church where her grandfather is mourning, which Cattermole put instead in the death-bed scene. See letter to Daniel Maclise of ?6 November 1840, *P*, II, p. 146; and letter to George Cattermole of ?22 December 1840, *P*, II, p. 172.

32. Letter to James M'Glashan, 11 January 1839, in Edmund Downey, *Charles Lever, His Life in His Letters*, 2 vols. (Edinburgh and London: Blackwood, 1906), 1: 109–11.

33. Harvey, pp. 38–42.

34. E. Browne, p. 171.

35. Ibid., p. 167.

36. Thomson, p. 234. (Four etchings means two in duplicate.)

37. Harvey, pp. 187–88.

II. THE BEGINNINGS OF "PHIZ":
PICKWICK, NICKLEBY, AND THE EMERGENCE FROM CARICATURE

1. Harvey, pp. 106–109.

2. Thomas K. Hervey, *The Book of Christmas* (London: William Spooner, 1836).

3. Captions given here for the *Pickwick* illustrations are those added in the 1838 edition, for which these two etchings plus ten others were etched anew with fundamental changes.

4. A. Moore, Ll. D., *The Annals of Gallantry*, 3 vols, (London: M. Jones, 1814), 1, facing p. 121.

5. From Plate 22 on, Browne etched duplicate steels for the first edition; the earlier steels, not etched in duplicate, required re-etching because they were worn. (Two steels etched by Browne for Part III were to replace those done by Buss.)

6. Ronald Paulson, *Hogarth, His Life, Art, and Times,* 1: 459.

7. Robert L. Patten, "Boz, Phiz, and Pickwick in the Pound," *ELH*, 36 (1969), 575–91.

8. Ibid., p. 580.

9. Ibid., p. 582.

10. Ibid.

11. Ibid., p. 589.

12. Ibid., p. 586.

13. Ibid., p. 585.

14. Ibid., p. 580.

15. The variant steels are reproduced in *J*, pp. 40–42.

16. I base my assumption as to which is the first version on the fact of awkwardness corrected, and the subsequent addition of a caption only to the "second" in the 1838 edition. Cf. *J*, p. 40.

17. "Boz, Phiz, and Pickwick in the Pound," 581.

18. This is the Rake's wedding, where the one-eyed bride is paralleled by a one-eyed dog; a similar detail is used by Browne in an illustration of "Fleet weddings," in *Chronicles of Crime* (1840).

19. *P*, 1: 222.

20. An unused version, showing even more riotous behavior, is in the Pierpont Morgan Library, and reproduced in the Victoria Edition of *Pickwick*, 2 vols. (London: Chapman and Hall, 1887), 2: 201.

21. The result is perhaps what Hillis Miller has called "oscillation" between picture and text—cf. J. Hillis Miller, "The Fiction of Realism: *Sketches by Boz, Oliver Twist*, and Cruikshank's Illustrations," in Miller and David Borowitz, *Charles Dickens and George Cruikshank* (Los Angeles: Clark Memorial Library, 1971), p. 46.

22. In the 1837 and 1838 editions, two chapters were numbered 28; I refer here to the second. I have followed throughout the chapter numbering of the first edition.

23. Robert L. Patten, "The Art of *Pickwick*'s Interpolated Tales," *ELH*, 34 (1967), 349–66.

24. Cf. the examples reproduced in Samuel C. Chew, *The Pilgrimage of Life* (New Haven: Yale University Press, 1962).

25. *J.*, p. 77.

26. For a fuller discussion, see my article, "Cruikshank's Peacock Feathers in *Oliver Twist*," *ARIEL*, 4, No. 2 (April, 1973), pp. 49–53.

27. The first use of the roulette by Browne that I have found is in Dickens' *Sketches of Young Gentlemen*, published in February 1838.

28. See Harvey, pp. 183–85, for a discussion of Cruikshank's and Browne's use of the roulette.

29. John Dixon Hunt, "Dickens and the Traditions of Graphic Satire," in Hunt, ed., *Encounters: Essays on Literature and the Visual Arts* (London: Studio Vista, 1971), p. 134.

30. *P*, 1: 513. The drawing is in DH, and is reproduced in F. G. Kitton, *Dickens and His Illustrators* (London: Redway, 1899), fac. p. 64.

31. Taylor Stoehr, *Dickens: The Dreamer's Stance* (Ithaca: Cornell University Press, 1965), p. 276.

32. That Browne was aware that he was having trouble with the pose of Madeline is indicated by the several marginal sketches of her figure in the working drawing. The drawing is in DH, and is reproduced in Michael Slater, ed., *The Catalogue of the Suzannet Charles Dickens Collection* (London and New York: Sotheby Parke Bernet Publications, 1975), p. 47.

III. FROM CARICATURE TO PROGRESS:
MASTER HUMPHREY'S CLOCK AND *MARTIN CHUZZLEWIT*

1. Williams and Maclise also contributed one cut apiece to *The Old Curiosity Shop*.

2. Joan Stevens, "'Woodcuts Dropped into the Text': The Illustrations in *The Old Curiosity Shop* and *Barnaby Rudge*," *Studies in Bibliography*, 20 (1967), pp. 113–34, has dealt extensively with the placement of the cuts at particular points in the text.

3. See David Kunzle, *The Early Comic Strip* (Berkeley: University of California Press, 1973).

4. Textual references are to the first, three volume bound edition of *Master Humphrey's Clock*.

5. J. A. Hammerton, *The Dickens Picture Book: A Record of the Dickens Illustrations* (London: The Educational Book Co., 1910).

6. E. Browne, p. 165.

7. It has always been assumed that at some point fairly early, Cattermole took over the transferring of his own drawings; yet among the tracings in the Gimbel Collection there are ones for Cattermole's designs for *Barnaby Rudge*, all initialed "HKB," indicating that Browne continued to do at least some of this work for Cattermole nearly all the way through *Master Humphrey's Clock*.

8. *P*, 2: 110.

9. Q. D. Leavis, "The Dickens Illustrations: Their Function," in F. R. and Q. D. Leavis, *Dickens the Novelist* (London: Chatto and Windus, 1970), p. 344.

10. For the most recent reprinting of the excised passages in which the Marchioness' parentage is revealed, see the Penguin English Library edition of *The Old Curiosity Shop*, ed. Angus Easson (Harmondsworth: Penguin, 1972), pp. 715–16.

11. *Four Plates / Engraved Under the Superintendence of Hablot K. Browne and Robert Young, / To Illustrate the Cheap Edition of The Old Curiosity Shop* (London: Chapman and Hall, 1848), second plate "The

Marchioness." See also the reproduction of an initial sketch for this engraving in E. Browne, fac. p. 254.

12. Leavis, p. 346.

13. Mark Spilka, "Little Nell Revisited," *Papers of the Michigan Academy of Science, Arts, and Letters,* 45 (1960), 429.

14. The first but not the second point has been made by Gabriel Pearson, "The Old Curiosity Shop," in John Gross and Gabriel Pearson, eds., *Dickens and the Twentieth Century* (London: Routledge and Kegan Paul, 1962), p. 87.

15. One might compare Dickens' later violent reaction to Millais' oil painting, *Christ in the House of His Parents,* whose realism he considered unsuitable for the subject, in "Old Lamps for New Ones" (*Household Words,* 1850), *Collected Papers,* 2 vols. (Nonesuch edition), 1: 291–96.

16. Browne's tracing of Cattermole's first cut in No. 1 (Gimbel), also showing Master Humphrey's room, makes it evident that Christ and the children were originally intended for that cut as well, though barely discernible in the cut itself. The Pilgrim editors describe Cattermole's final cut as including a "recumbent full-breasted nude" (*P,* 2: 382), but although the engraver's rendering is a bit careless, it is in fact clearly the Good Samaritan.

17. The passage occurs in chapter 24 of *Vanity Fair.* See my article, "*Barnaby Rudge* and *Vanity Fair:* A Note on a Possible Influence," *Nineteenth-Century Fiction,* 25 (1970), 353–54.

18. Paulson, *Emblem and Expression,* p. 36.

19. *P,* 2: 218.

20. Quilp's derivation from Shakespeare's Richard III has often been noted. For the connection between Richard and the medieval Vice, see A. P. Rossiter, *Angel With Horns* (London: Longmans, 1961), p. 15.

21. Joseph Gardner, "Pecksniff's Profession: Boz, Phiz, and Pugin," *Dickensian,* 72 (1976), 75–86, makes a number of interesting points about Pecksniff's career as architect, including the observation that "Pecksniff's Pump" is surmounted by a flame. It is thus connected with Pugin's scorned modern town pump, which has been transformed into a gas lamp. It seems to me that Browne also may be suggesting that Pecksniff has a head of "gas"!

22. *J,* 190–91.

23. See the illustration in Asa Briggs, *The Nineteenth Century* (London: Thames and Hudson, 1970), p. 51.

24. Harvey shows a Daumier influence on Browne's Mrs. Gamp—Harvey, pp. 132–34.

25. See John Butt, "Dickens's Instructions for 'Martin Chuzzlewit,' Plate xviii," *Review of English Literature,* 2, No. 3 (July, 1961), pp. 49–50.

26. Cf. a similar emblem in Johann Abricht's *Divine Emblems* (London: Thomas Ward, 1838), p. 47 (etching by Robert Cruikshank). Mario

Praz cites this book as last in a debased emblem tradition—see *Studies in Seventeenth Century Imagery* (Rome: Edizioni di Storia e Letteratura, 1964), pp. 166–68.

27. This drawing was sold as part of the Suzannet collection in 1971.

28. A similar sign including "To those About to Marry" appeared in a comic plate to *Godfrey Malvern* ("An unexpected Meeting").

29. *Punch*, 8 (1845), 1.

30. Angus Wilson, *The World of Charles Dickens* (London: Secker and Warburg, 1970), p. 178.

31. Ibid.

32. Dickens' instructions for the last two text illustrations, the frontispiece, and etched title page are in the Huntington Library, San Marino, California, where they are designated HM 17501. They have been published previously in my article, "*Martin Chuzzlewit*'s Progress by Dickens and Phiz," in *Dickens Studies Annual* 2 (1972), pp. 139, 140, 143, 146, and are reprinted here with the kind permission of the Huntington Library and Mr. Christopher C. Dickens.

33. *Seymour's Humorous Sketches . . . Illustrated in Prose and Verse by Alfred Crowquill* (London: Bohn, 1843), n.p.

34. The drawing is reproduced in Thomson, p. 66.

35. *Hogarth: His Life, Art, and Times*, I, p. 265.

IV. *DOMBEY AND SON:*
ICONOGRAPHY OF SOCIAL AND SEXUAL SATIRE

1. *N*, 1: 787.

2. *N*, 1: 768.

3. Dickens' number plans include the two captions actually used, plus a third, "Mr. Dombey keeps an eye upon Richards," which is partially descriptive of the second plate. See the Clarendon edition of *Dombey and Son*, ed. Alan Horsman (Oxford: Clarendon Press, 1974), p. 835.

4. Leavis, p. 350.

5. The original drawing, with Dombey standing (Dexter), is reproduced in the Clarendon edition, fac. p. 865. For this drawing and several of the other early ones in *Dombey and Son*, Phiz used pen and (blue) ink, but for the working drawings he went over the lines with a blunt point. The effect on the style of the drawings—though not the etchings—is very noticeable, and one might conjecture that Browne was attempting a different kind of line. (It is also possible that he was temporarily out of pencils!)

6. The much-quoted letter to Forster is in *N*, 1: 809.

7. Leavis, pp. 352–53.

8. Forster remarks that Dickens "felt the disappointment more keenly, because the conception of the grim old boarding-house keeper had taken back his thoughts to the miseries of his own child-life, and made her, as her prototype in verity was, a part of the terrible reality"—*The Life of Charles Dickens* (1872–74; repr. London: Dent, 1966), 2: 29.

9. The sketch is reproduced in the Clarendon edition, fac. p. 866.

10. *N*, 1: 824–25.

11. *N*, 1: 17–19.

12. This may be the Dexter sketch, reproduced in the catalogue of the Victoria and Albert Museum Dickens Centenary exhibition (London: Victoria and Albert Museum, 1970), Plate 26, although both Dombey and the Native (who may have been erased) are missing.

13. The working drawing for this plate (Elkins), which Dickens in his second letter told Browne he did not need to see, contains nearly all the details of the etching, but the Native is little more than a blur, having obviously been erased. However, a careful perusal reveals that Browne has, without drawing the lines in, used his blunt point to transfer the final version of the Native to the etching ground.

14. In the companion etching, "Solemn reference is made to Mr. Bunsby" (ch. 23), Florence is almost an exact mirror-image of herself, even linking her arm in someone else's in both plates; in both she also listens to a man speak of Walter's fate at sea.

15. The similarity to Leslie's painting has been noted by T. W. Hill ("Kentley Bromhill"), "Phiz's Illustrations to *Dombey and Son*," *Dickensian*, 39 (1943), 51.

16. One group of eight etchings, and another of four engravings, were published separately after the novel's completion.

17. Harvey, p. 141.

18. In my article, "*Dombey and Son*: Chapter XXXI, Plate 20," *English Language Notes*, 7 (1969), 124–27.

19. "Phiz's Illustrations to *Dombey and Son*," 51.

20. There are two extant drawings for this plate. Both are reversed and in pencil, but the less finished one (Elkins) does not contain the "Medusa" inscription, and Captain Cuttle's hook is on the wrong hand, though there is clear evidence that this drawing was the one used in transferring the design to the steel, including indentation on the misplaced hook. The other drawing (DH) is very finished, with each detail nearly identical to the etching: the "Medusa" is included, and the hook is on the proper hand, although the tiny head of Medusa is not evident. It seems likely that this drawing was used as a guide to the details of the etching, as I have suggested is the case with two of the drawings for *Martin Chuzzlewit*.

21. Browne's "Medusa" conceivably could refer to Gericault's famous painting, *The Raft of the Medusa*, which would at least explain the linking of this title with a sea scene, although the picture looks more

like a ship than a raft. The theme of cannibalism associated with the Medusa's shipwrecked passengers is even relevant to the predatory world of *Dombey and Son*.

22. Allardyce Nicoll, *History of English Drama, 1660–1900*, 6 vols. (London: Cambridge University Press, 1960), 4: 442.

23. Philip Massinger, *The City Madam*, act 1, sc. 1, lines 11-12.

24. Letter to Forster of 21 December 1847—N, 2: 63.

25. Thomson, p. 223; reproduced on p. 221.

26. N, 2: 63.

27. See Mrs. Leavis, p. 356, and John R. Reed, "Emblems in Victorian Literature," *Hartford Studies in Literature*, 2 (1970), 19–39, but especially 28–30.

28. Despite the fact that the pre-tint proofs are in the Dexter Collection upon which they base most of their findings, Thomas Hatton and Arthur R. Cleaver state that the steel was tinted *first*—see *A Bibliography of the Periodical Works of Charles Dickens* (London: Chapman and Hall, 1933), p. 276. Hatton and Cleaver are clearly wrong, and a surviving proof (Dexter) of the thirty-ninth plate of *Nicholas Nickleby* further confirms the point, since its mechanical tint must have been ruled after the rest of the design was etched. Yet the same technical misunderstanding is still subscribed to by Alan Horsman, in the Clarendon edition of *Dombey*, p. 871.

29. For examples of such locomotives in George Cruikshank's work of a few years earlier, see my article, "*Dombey and Son* and the Railway Panic of 1845," *Dickensian*, 67 (1971), 145–48.

V. *DAVID COPPERFIELD:*
PROGRESS OF A CONFUSED SOUL

1. Gwendolyn B. Needham, "The Undisciplined Heart of David Copperfield," *Nineteenth-Century Fiction*, 9 (1954), 81–107; J. Hillis Miller, *Charles Dickens: The World of His Novels* (Cambridge: Harvard University Press, 1958), pp. 156–59; Q. D. Leavis, "Dickens and Tolstoy: The Case for a Serious View of *David Copperfield*," in *Dickens the Novelist*, pp. 34–107.

2. G. K. Chesterton, *Appreciations and Criticisms of the Works of Charles Dickens* (London: Dent, 1911), pp. 132–35; Robert Graves, *The Real David Copperfield* (London: Arthur Barker, 1933); James R. Kincaid, "The Darkness of *David Copperfield*," *Dickens Studies*, 1 (1965), 65–75, and "The Structure of *David Copperfield*," *Dickens Studies*, 2 (1966), 74–95. The latter article provides a complex and convincing reading. Kincaid's thematic systematization of the text is somewhat parallel to my systematization of the illustrations for *David Copperfield*.

3. Mark Spilka, *Dickens and Kafka* (Bloomington: Indiana University Press, 1963), p. 179.

4. Leavis, "Dickens and Tolstoy . . .", p. 50.

5. Harvey makes a similar point about the parallel between Dora and her dog Jip, in "Our Housekeeping"—Harvey, p. 151.

6. *Hogarth: His Life, Art, and Times*, 1: 459.

7. *J*, p. 349.

8. The drawing (Elkins) is reproduced in Kitton, *Dickens and His Illustrators*, fac. p. 84.

VI. *BLEAK HOUSE* AND *LITTLE DORRIT:*
ICONOGRAPHY OF DARKNESS

1. Leavis, pp. 359–60.

2. Leavis, "Bleak House: A Chancery World," in *Dickens the Novelist*, p. 165.

3. Edgar Johnson, *Charles Dickens: His Tragedy and Triumph*, 2 vols. (New York: Simon and Schuster, 1952), 2: 750.

4. J. R. Tye, "Legal Caricature: Cruikshank Analogues to the *Bleak House* Cover," *Dickensian*, 69 (1973), 38–41.

5. Copied in this case by Doyle from Retzsch—"HB," *Political Sketches*, Series 2, No. 509, "Satan Playing at Chess With Man For His Soul," dated 29 September 1837.

6. H. P. Sucksmith, "Dickens at Work on *Bleak House:* A Critical Examination of His Memoranda and Number Plans," *Renaissance and Modern Studies*, 9 (1965), p. 67.

7. Again, the motif first turned up in John Doyle's *Political Sketches*, Series 2, No. 150, "A Will o' the Wisp," dated 22 August 1831. Cruikshank also created versions of the emblem but they post-date Browne's own use on the *Nicholas Nickleby* wrapper.

8. By Professor Irene Tayler, in conversation.

9. I know of no other use of this emblem by Browne, nor have I noted it in Cruikshank or his contemporaries. The animal is identifiable as a fox in this illustration (rather than the "wolf" at the door which Miss Flite speaks of) by its bushy tail.

10. I have not located with certainty the print Esther refers to, but it could be Doyle's "A Political Riddle," *Political Sketches*, Series 1, No. 21, dated 6 June 1829.

11. *Portrait of His Most Gracious Majesty George the Fourth*, dated 1821, engraved by G. Maile.

12. Sucksmith, "Dickens at Work on *Bleak House*," p. 69.

13. The drawing for "A Model of parental deportment" (Elkins) is much like the etching, but it is reversed and lacks the details on the

screen; that for "Mr. Chadband 'improving' a tough subject" (Elkins), also used for transferring the design to the steel, is rather different from the etching: Chadband, instead of standing upright, is somewhat bent over, his right arm raised, but his left pointing at Jo, who faces the opposite way. The change in Chadband's position makes the parallel with Turveydrop much more evident. As usual, we have no way of knowing who originated the change, but since the drawing had been used for transferring it seems plausible that the original had already been approved by Dickens, and Phiz made the changes on his own. The drawing for this plate is reproduced in Kitton, *Dickens and His Illustrators*, fac. p. 92.

14. The pamphlet appears to have been immensely popular. It was perhaps the cleverest and best-illustrated satire of the Regent/King to have been published, and Browne might easily have seen a copy.

15. M. Dorothy George identifies Cruikshank's cut as an "adaptation" of Gillray's etching—see *BM Cat*, X (1952), p. 78.

16. Draper Hill, *Fashionable Contrasts: 100 Caricatures by James Gillray* (London: Phaidon, 1966), p. 163.

17. Trevor Blount, "Sir Leicester Dedlock and 'Deportment' Turveydrop: Some Aspects of Dickens's Use of Parallelism," *Nineteenth-Century Fiction*, 21 (1966), 149–65. Blount also stresses parallels between Turveydrop and Chadband.

18. Leavis, p. 360.

19. This drawing is in the Berg Collection of the New York Public Library, and is reproduced in Lola Szladits, ed., *Charles Dickens, 1812–1870: An Anthology* (New York: New York Public Library and Arno Press, 1970), p. 131.

20. Miller, Introduction to *Bleak House*, Penguin English Library edition (Harmondsworth: Penguin, 1971), pp. 16–17; Sucksmith, "Dickens at Work on *Bleak House*, "p. 70.

21. Harvey, p. 155.

22. Two drawings survive: one, reversed and indented as usual (Elkins), contains all the details, though some are sketchy and the drawing as a whole—in charcoal—is a bit fuzzy; the other (Gimbel) is in pen and wash, not reversed, and almost certainly a preliminary drawing, since it contains neither guitar, nosegay, nor fan. Once again, I hypothesize that left–right orientation was important for Browne in this plate.

23. "Cruikshank's 'The Drunkard's Children' " (*Examiner*, 1848), *Collected Papers* (Nonesuch edition), 1: 158.

24. Speech of 5 October 1851, in *The Speeches of Charles Dickens*, ed. K. J. Fielding (Oxford: Clarendon Press, 1960), p. 128.

25. Paulson, *Emblem and Expression*, p. 36.

26. The relevant passage is in chapter 64 of *Vanity Fair*.

27. The similarity to the mermaid clock in *Sketches of Young Couples* (in the plate, "The old Couple") is not very strong—the latter clock has no threatening aspect, and is primarily a Cupid and Psyche design.

28. Kitton, *Dickens and His Illustrators,* p. 107.

29. E. Browne, pp. 292–93.

30. A contemporary magazine, *Diogenes,* published a parody entitled "A Browne Study," which included a supposed illustration of "Lady Dedlock Lamenting Her Happy Childhood." It suggested that the dark plates were nothing more than a way of avoiding proper draftsmanship—see *Dickensian,* 65 (1969), 144.

31. *Dickens at Work* (London: Methuen, 1957), pp. 224–26.

32. This drawing is part of a set of Browne's drawings for *Little Dorrit,* formerly in the collection of the late Comte de Suzannet; the set was put up for auction with the rest of the Suzannet collection in 1971, but not sold; subsequently it was stored in the Dickens House. I am grateful to Dr. Michael Slater, editor of *The Dickensian,* and Miss Marjorie Pillers, curator of the Dickens House Museum, for the opportunity to examine these drawings in 1972, and to the late Comtesse de Suzannet for permission to photograph several of them. Since then, they have been sold to a collector who will not permit their reproduction.

33. *N,* 2: 698.

34. *N,* 2: 814. I can find no direct evidence that this in fact refers to *Little Dorrit,* but it is printed in the Nonesuch *Letters* with other correspondence of the *Little Dorrit* period.

35. *Little Dorrit* is divided into two "books." I identify the illustrations by book and chapter.

36. See William Feaver, *The Art of John Martin* (Oxford: Clarendon Press, 1975).

37. There is a similar pun in a detail in James Gillray's "L'ASSEMBLE NATIONALE ..." (*BM Cat* 10253), which anticipates the Prince of Wales's becoming Regent; and see chapter V, above, for a related pun in a *David Copperfield* illustration.

38. *N,* 2: 814.

39. The Gimbel Collection contains what seems to be a preliminary sketch of the final version, unreversed, with the background only roughly indicated; the second Suzannet drawing is the working one, reversed as usual, and quite detailed.

VII.   PHIZ THE ILLUSTRATOR: AN OVERVIEW AND A SUMMING UP

1. The wood engraving at page 293 of the sixth number, illustrating Edward Mayhew's "John Smith," shows a sheriff's man named Pate Poinden who resembles Tony Weller down to his striped waistcoat (previously noted by Kitton, *Dickens and His Illustrators,* p. 62).

2. Harvey, p. 112.

3. In letter previously cited, by Lever to James M'Glashan, in Edmund Downey, *Charles Lever, His Life in His Letters*, I, pp. 109–11.

4. *BM Cat* 10472–73.

5. Harvey, 151–52.

6. Thomson, p. 217.

7. Johannsen (*J*, p. xi) seems to have been under the impression that Phiz did all 866 cuts for the Household Edition, but in truth he did only the 57 for *Pickwick*.

8. See Slater, *Catalogue of the Suzannet . . . Collection*, pp. 214–16.

9. In the present author's possession.

INDEX

I: NAMES

II: References to Illustrations for Dickens' Novels in Monthly Parts

Numerals in italics designate by number the illustrations reproduced in this volume.